AS PISTONS FLEW

AS PISTONS FLEW

So Turns the World

Jane A. Gottschall

Library of Congress Number:		00-190662
ISBN #:	Hardcover	0-7388-1276-5
	Softcover	0-7388-1277-3

This book was printed in the United States of America.

To order additional copies of this book, contact:
Xlibris Corporation
1-888-7-XLIBRIS
www.Xlibris.com
Orders@Xlibris.com

CONTENTS

"As Pistons Flew" is dedicated to
the memory of Virginia Roiz Valentine,
whose loyalty, integrity, friendship, and guidance
to all who knew her, will ever be part of
Pan American's history.

And for the many men and women
whom the author feels fortunate
to have shared those wonderful years
with an airline that was "first".

Wings that soared
may now lie shattered
They lived! They lived!
That's all that matters.
JG

PREFACE

In the beginning of airline travel, before the jet age, flight transportation was accomplished with crews who flew propeller planes and "old boat boys" who flew seaplanes. They were trailblazers to the industry. With chuckles of laughter amid nostalgic feelings, piston crewmembers, like campfire cowboys, tell stories of days that will never return again. Enhanced aircraft, adjustments in the airline business, occur almost as often as changes in the computer business. What may be inevitable development is called "progress". And progress makes memories for us all.

One major airline did not hire women as flight attendants until World War II was almost over. This book is a compendium of tales taken from the life of one of those women in piston aircraft days. The places are real, but have altered in time. The characters' names and locations may be diffused, but they existed. The sequence of events may not be completely in order, but they happened. The airline no longer exists, but it once extended around the world.

This writing recalls a life style of people who may never "work an aircraft" again, about whom in the future only similarities may be seen or compared. It is about an age, as that of the pioneers of our American West, hopefully never to be forgotten.

AIRCRAFT DOWN

Chapter 1

"It's a DC-3! It's got to be. Hear it? Hear it?" As if all in the world were listening, when no one was around.

The screen door slammed shut and locked as I ran down the steps of my family home. I had been resting on the porch glider when disturbed by a distant drone that triggered an impulse to rise and take notice. I looked toward what little sky could be seen between oak tree branches, but I saw no aircraft. I only heard an engine hum that had awakened memories and a tight feeling in my heart.

"It had to be a DC-3. I'd know it anywhere," I said to myself. Digging a key out of a fern pot, I unlocked the screen door, lay upon the glider again to drift back in time.

Most airlines called the DC-3 the "old Douglas workhorse", the reliability of which kept the owners in business. Without pressurization or apt sound proofing, it flew low and slow compared to larger planes to come. From its windows one seldom looked upon a flat, hazy, distant surface to the world. Instead, earth's features could be seen—curves of mountains, colors of lakes, cars moving on roads, ocean waves crashing upon shores, and cloud formations as a sea of popcorn and powder puffs. Pilots liked the DC-3 for its proficiency and ease, giving them a "hands on wheel" feel to flying, with instruments used as an aid rather than a control. The DC-3 was so dependable; pilots swore it could land on a postage stamp. I might almost believe it from my own experience.

It happened back in 1945 when I was a new stewardess flying over Guatemala. The DC-3 held a complement of 21 passengers, three cockpit crew, and one cabin attendant. We left Merida, Mexico, in the Yucatan Peninsula, after connecting via the Boeing-307 flown down from New Orleans. The flight was scheduled to Panama, making several stops in Central America. We left New Orleans at night and Merida in the darkness of early morning, as all flights to Panama had to arrive before sunset. No commercial aircraft could fly over Panama at night, to protect the Canal. World War II was not over.

I was on my own as stewardess for the DC-3, an airplane with two engines, and all mine from the cockpit door to the aft galley. Ours was the only plane at the ramp after the Boeing departed to return to New Orleans. Seldom were there more. A crowd of people in a festive mood remained. Their jollity measured up to the exciting fresco paintings on the walls. Mariachi musicians were shaking bead gourds in rhythmic motion, so familiar to Mexico, and elevated the sound at the time of departure.

The DC-3 had no public address system; an electric bell was used for communication from cockpit to cabin. One bell indicated the steward/ess should assure that seat belts were fastened and no cigarettes were lighted. Two bells were for the attendant to be seated. If three bells were sounded it usually meant the steward/ess must come to the cockpit "muy pronto." The latter could mean we left a passenger or cargo on the tarmac or, what was most unwanted, an R-E-M (return due maintenance), which could be anything from a sudden drop in oil pressure to just a panel light bulb needed.

Everything was satisfactory as the co-pilot read the checklist. The engines were put to takeoff power, brakes released, and away we went. Normally it took only a minute or two after leaving the "blocks" before becoming airborne.

After the last breakfast trays were served, a passenger stopped me in the aisle and pointed to the starboard engine, saying, "Why aren't those propellers moving?" I glanced out the window and saw three blades, silent and still. It was the first time I had ever seen a "feathered engine," and there was no cockpit call.

Only months before I had walked into the sales office of Pan American Airways in New Orleans, answering an ad for reservation clerks. With WWII still going on, women were better able to obtain work. The closest I had come to any airplane affiliation was summer employment at Higgins Aircraft, a war plant in Louisiana, which never produced one plane. The factory only existed in case any fully productive plant was bombed. (Nearby, Higgins built the famous P-T boats used so successfully in the war.) I had worked in the blueprint department making good money for a teenager, with the title of Draftsman-2, when all I did was make diagrams legible. The idea of traveling had long appealed to me, since working in my college library and getting lost in the *National Geographic* magazine racks. At least the reservations office of an airline had seemed a closer step. There was great excitement in being associated with Pan American Airways. The airline promoted passenger and freight service abroad, sponsored construction of airports, runways, even overnight accommodations, and assisted the U.S. government in equipment and troop transport for our armed forces even into battle areas. I got the job and felt proud in just being a part of "PanAm".

After envisioning glamorous places against four walls and a Teletype, I hungered to accompany the passengers. Opportunity arose when recruiters came to the office to interview stewardess applicants. (Up until that year [1944], PanAm had only hired men as crew.) Before the recruiters were to leave, I had gathered the courage to announce a final applicant. When asked to show her in, I replied, "She is I." However, there was one qualification about which I had great trepidation—to have a fair speaking knowledge of Spanish, as this was the Latin American Division of the airline. I had studied Spanish in college, could read it fairly well, but to comprehend as spoken was a struggle. Brushing up on my textbooks, I decided to memorize a few expressions and gamble on that I might be asked the same questions that I had overheard. The plan worked. My pronunciation must have sounded fair, though I knew I had not fooled the handsome male recruiter. Later I learned I had been accepted, subject to passing a physical examination.

Going to Miami for six weeks of training was by way of a company ferry flight from New Orleans. All aboard had to be employees, as government regulations prohibited PanAm from carrying any revenue passengers from one U. S. stop to another. PanAm had no domestic flights, but when an airplane was due for primary maintenance check, it was ferried to Miami. This flight on the Boeing-307 was my first on any airliner.

I found living quarters with girls who were already flying. I listened to their talk and envied them, even when they would return and say, "I'm pooped!" Being fitted for uniforms was a highlight—powder blue in color, a skirt with a front kick pleat, a collarless jacket, a long-sleeve, white blouse with pointed lapels. The hat was like a bowl with a stiff front, holding a side wing tip for the company emblem, picturing North and South America on a blue globe. My roommates introduced me to PanAm and military friends with whom we shared good times. When the orchestra at the Coral Gables Country Club played "it might as well be spring", it was the springtime of my life.

On this day, I opened the cockpit door and asked a very calm appearing pilot, "Captain Cornwell, that motor out there on the right side, I mean 'engine', that has stopped—what should I tell the passengers?"

"Oh, there you are. Sorry not to 'beep' you sooner but we've been a little busy up here. It's okay now. We're just going to let that 'motor' rest awhile," he replied. The co-pilot grinned, as both men knew I was new at the job. The captain started to say, "tell the passengers—", but was interrupted when suddenly the port side, and only other engine, began to sputter. Rarely were both engines in trouble at the same time. Quick movements came with the captain's commands, responses from his co-pilot, and the radio operator clicking SOS by Morse code. There was no aircraft-to-ground telephone contact at that time, unless close to an airport.

As I backed out of the cockpit with a "Secure the Cabin" order, I was assured that the plane would land in La Libertad, a small clearing in the Peten jungles of Guatemala, about 15 minutes away. In the cabin I looked up to see 21 faces with the most pathetic expressions. Like anticipating children, they waited for me to speak. I looked toward the passenger who had first alerted me and saw that the starboard engine props were spinning again. "Ah," I said aloud with relief, "it's all right now." Then I heard, "Well, why's the other engine feathered?"

The remark embarrassed me to think how this was MY airplane. It HAD to recover. I walked down the aisle telling everyone that we would land in "La Libertad", as though it was a familiar place. One passenger was a young boy traveling alone; another, a U.S. senator who remained silent. Some passengers asked what was wrong; seasoned flyers pretended not to be disturbed. As I had to insist upon picking up unfinished meal trays and storing loose objects, the problem sounded serious. When we began to lose altitude, affecting pressure in our ears, it became eminently more serious. The fast descent made walking the aisle feel as though heavy weights were carried on each foot. There was no doubt—we were falling! I could barely lift my body after securing low latches, such was the force from a rapid descent.

Fifteen seconds is a short period, unless you are witnessing an earthquake. Fifteen minutes in an aircraft with both engines barking spits and threats, can be an eternity. The pilots had turned the engines on and off alternately to gather as much power as could be mustered. Activating a sick engine can cause its complete demise, like a car's wheel rim when driving on a flat tire; however, the choice is not healthy either. Years later, when asked about this flight, I would say I was too young to be really frightened, and too busy to think of fear. Something about youth makes you believe that death is not today, nor tomorrow; maybe when you are old, but never today. I had yet to see my 21st birthday.

Though no passenger required a sick bag, one aspect came up too quickly—the sight of the approaching Peten jungles. The earth appeared to be coming to us, not our going to it. I saw no clearing. Where was this La Libertad? I pressed my hand to the shoulder of the young boy—but to him it all seemed a thrill. Fear came upon even the courageous when suddenly there was no sound outside, not even the wind. Both engines were extinguished. We were floating down.

Almost as I got seated and called out, "We'll make it, okay," there was the thump of wheels to earth; a landing for any pilot to be proud of and for the DC-3 to prove its worth. The plane lightly bounced over a grassy field, rolled to the end of the area and braked to a halt, abruptly but safely. As pilots will say—any landing you can walk away from is a good landing.

ETERNALLY SPRING

Chapter 2

La Libertad only had a couple of native huts in the area, but it was a navigation point for aircraft flying overhead. We spent four hours there, during which the U.S. Army sent a small plane with mechanics who found that our aircraft needed complete new engines. We awaited for another plane to rescue us.

Though the Army had brought food, they had failed to carry anything with which to eat. I retrieved some Camay soap from my suitcase and waded across the weeds toting our dirty utensils, hoping to borrow a pot and water from a woman I saw using an outdoor fire near a hut. Chigger bugs gave no mercy and gnats let me know I was not welcome. The snags in my stockings made them an expensive loss, as nylons were prohibitive in a rationed wartime. Discomfort was increased by the uniform requirement to wear a long sleeve blouse, high heels, and a girdle. At least two of the three were easily removed. In my best Spanish, I asked the woman for the use of her pot while offering an extra bar of my soap. I learned that though soap was a luxury, clean water was a rarity. At least the water could be boiled. Lunch was eventually served in a hot aircraft, away from what buzzed or crawled. Doors and cockpit windows were opened to create a draught of air. With the meal over, the sound and appearance of our rescue plane was a welcome sight.

To leave the heat of La Libertad somewhat compensated for a natural tension in again being aloft. I sat buckled in my pull-down "jumpseat," attached to the bulkhead, and thought of the events which led to my present occupation—training in Miami, new friends, beach days, the belief that life would be wonderful.

. Stewardess school was a concentrated six weeks of study and acquaintance with everything from First Aid, land or sea survival, life raft familiarity, swimming, life saving, handling of diverse peoples' customs, government documentation, ticketing, geography, aircraft types, routes, airport codes, lessons in Spanish, the airline's history, and even identification of clouds and weather conditions. Little attention was given to meal services because of the simplicity of it. Pre-setup trays, hot meals in crockery dishes out of insulated canisters, was the way then. But we were expected to foresee other passenger needs, and therein lay the emphasis. The girls in my class had come from every corner of the U.S. Those chosen were under the age of 27, and none of them could be married.

Now I strolled again the aisle of my DC-3 in flight. The terrain below gradually changed to rolling green hills and the sight of a stream or two. Guatemala City lay at an altitude of 5,000 feet, in a country called "Land of Eternal Spring" because the climate allowed pleasant cool evenings with moderate warm days. The plane approached the city in the sight of volcanoes to the southwest—Volcan Pacaya, Agua, Acatenango and Fuego, some with tops in a cloudbank. Agua rose from the earth like a peaked, green ice cream cone, and Pacaya like a misshapen camel's back. In descending, pastel colored buildings with tiled roofs gave contrast to the verdant surrounding. Placid Lake Amatitlan nestled south of the city below Pacaya. No city skyscrapers emerged. A metal tower, like the Eifel in Paris, was the city's tallest structure and proud landmark. The airplane flew over the city to a place where a single runway dipped in the middle and rose toward the south end.

When the handle was turned to open the cabin door, I could immediately breathe the unadulterated odor of sweet tree bark and flowers. This scent was so strong that it permeated clothing and could still be detected upon opening my suitcase at home. With fewer cars in 1945, fumes had not yet affected the purity of the atmosphere. La Aurora Airport's terminal building had pink and green trimming, with dark wooden rafters in the interior, Mayan frescoes on the walls, and a huge, wood-carved chandelier. In the arched entrance, a native woman in tribal wear handed a small bouquet of flowers to each passenger.

As the last to leave the aircraft, I removed the crew nameplates from inserts on the cockpit door. Hiram Gomez, our Guatemalan supervisor, came aboard after everyone had disembarked and while government officials made their inspection. As I had once been reprimanded for a messy ship on arrival, I was determined that this would never happen again. Blankets had to be refolded and placed in the hat racks above the seats. They were to be neatly wrapped around the pillows, showing the airline emblem. Hiram excused me from this duty, owning that he knew of my La Libertad landing. He also advised me of a two-day layover in Guatemala, because our aircraft had caused delays throughout Central America. News of a longer stay drew a big smile from me. I was enamored with the country.

After the pilots gave their reports on the flight, and farewells were exchanged with the passengers, the baggage was loaded in the crew car. Guatemala City was a foreign base with cockpit crews living there. Company transportation was provided before and after a flight for everyone. Traffic was light and only oxen-driven carts caused slowdowns. We drove under the tall metal tower, which earlier had welcomed us from the air.

The Palace Hotel, located a block from the main street, Sixth Avenue, was only a couple of stories high, as were most of the buildings in a country with a history of earthquakes. The lobby held a ceiling skylight, and tree-sized palms. Plant laden patios existed throughout the hotel, which abutted the sidewalk, enclosing and hiding the decor within. At the front desk I was given a key attached to a large aluminum disk marking the hotel name and room number. I also received quetzales, Guatemalan dollars one to one with U.S., which the airline provided as per diem—an amount determined by the hours of layover. (The Quetzal is the national bird with its multicolored picture on the bills.) A twist of my key opened a door to show three single beds in one room, one bath, and two steps up to another room. One girl stretched out with a pillow over her head, obviously trying to sleep. Another sat in bed with a tray of food just delivered by Room Service. Everywhere were suitcases and scattered purchases of local goods.

After greeting Marge, a check stewardess, who was briefing Patty, a new stewardess, on what to see, buy, and avoid, I attached myself to one of the beds. In my fatigue my head succumbed to the pillow and I only heard a background murmur; however, first I hung my skirt from a top dresser drawer to loosen the wrinkles. Dry-cleaning service abroad meant a washed suit that could never be worn again. I carried my own fluid to get the spots out. At home, a cleaned uniform was not always ready in time, so while wearing one, the other was in the wartime dry cleaners. I left a wake-up call for 6 p.m., a few hours away. Five minutes later the door opened and in walked another blue uniform. "Any old beds left?" the new voice asked. When shown one covered with purchases, she exclaimed, "Isn't anyone leaving soon?"

"Not now. Everything's delayed since one of us stopped to get chiggers in the jungles," Marge laughingly advised, as she pointed to me.

It was Frannie. Sleep was impossible with Frannie around. She pulled at my sheet with a "Getup, old gal, let's hear all about it."

"Not now, Frannie. Please, when I wake up," I admonished, with one eye open. Just at that moment the telephone rang. With suitcases cluttered about the floor, someone crossed over my bed to get the phone. This disturbance really roused me, so I headed for the shower. It took a few minutes to rearrange nylon stockings hung to dry.

Frannie asked me about my landing in La Libertad, but before I could say anything, she remarked, "Did you know they're closing the New Orleans base? It'll just be a layover station. Now if you transfer to Miami you're to stay at our place. We have an extra cot on the sleeping porch, and one roomie is getting married so then you can . . ."

"Frannie, thanks, but right now let me bathe and get five minutes of sleep. Roger's taking me to the U.S. Embassy party tonight." On a previous trip, Roger, a pilot living in Guatemala asked if I would like to go to the U. S. Embassy that evening. I had almost forgotten it was the 4th of July. (It was the custom for every U.S. Embassy to have a celebration party to which all Americans were invited.) Roger lived with other single pilots in a house called the "Casa de Lobos." Mayans worked for them as cook, gardener, and housekeeper, taking proud care of the home they served. In the driveway was a 1930s Model A Ford and several chrome-laden motorcycles. I wondered upon which I would ride when Roger came that evening.

Frannie could not stay quiet but my shower water drowned out everything. When I walked out of the bathroom scantily covered, I jumped at the sight of Room Service delivering a food tray.

"Frannie, why didn't you tell me there was a man in the room?"

"Oh, it's just Jose. Besides, he doesn't even speak English." At that moment the phone rang again and there was another knock on the door.

"Grand Central!" Marge chimed. Calling to the door, "No more beds left in here." Into the phone, "Carol isn't around. No, but she did say something about a Rio trip. Sure, I'll tell her you called."

Frannie, responding to being asked if she were going to the Embassy party that night, replied, "I might show up with Carson."

"Carson Quinlan! Frannie, you're not going with that roué?"

"Now, girls, I can handle him, and his fancy cream-colored convertible too. What a car! He had it shipped all the way from Kentucky to Puerto Barrios. Despite his conceit, you have to admit he's damn good looking, and pretty good on the dance floor too. Besides, if Carson gets too frisky I'll complain to the Ambassador, whom I shall meet personally this evening. I wonder if the Ambassador can tango?"

Frannie waved her hands in the air and did a rumba turn on the little floor space remaining. For the moment there was utter silence, which there had not been in hours, until we all started laughing together.

EMBASSY PARTY

Chapter 3

By six o'clock that evening, a cyclone of activity hit the stewardess quarters at the Palace Hotel, with each one wanting to shower at once. Somehow we all dressed in time. In the lobby were Roger, Sparks and his wife, Emily with Harry, another Casa de Lobos pilot. We finally left and Sparks drove his old Studebaker toward "Embassy Row" on the Avenida de Reforma. We passed the pink Post Office building of Moorish architecture, with its arched walkway high above the street, and the Escuela Politecnica, the West Point of Guatemala, surrounded by a high wall with portico similar to an old fort.

At the U.S. Embassy people had gathered in the garden. No invitations or passports were required. U.S. Marines stood at attention upon entering. The Ambassador's home was of pale-colored stucco, a one-story, Spanish style that encompassed several patios with Bougainvillea vines climbing the walls. Servants wearing colorful native costumes walked about offering beverages. A marimba band, musicians dressed indigenous to the area, played music of mixed popularity. Tables of bounteously decorated platters of food were located throughout. We mingled with our airline and other American friends living in Guatemala, as the night brought on a pleasant coolness. I met the Senator who was our passenger earlier that day. "Hello," he approached me, "I've told Ambassador Kyle all about you and our La Libertad stop. He's anxious to meet you." The Senator took my hand to his arm and led me away.

Greeting guests, and standing tall in his immaculate white suit, was U.S. Ambassador Kyle. The Senator introduced me to the handsome, elder gentleman. His bearing was so regal, his manner so gracious, I wanted to curtsy but extended my hand. Ambassador Kyle insisted upon hearing about my La Libertad flight, as we walked to a bench under a ceiba tree. He showed interest in the reaction of my passengers. Men in various uniforms, with gold braid and ribbons adorning their chests, encircled us. I had no idea what countries they represented. They waited to address Ambassador Kyle, who did not seem anxious for me to leave. It was an impressive meeting for me.

When the Studebaker was directed back to the center of town, twenty-four hours had passed since I had left New Orleans. This was my first experience of wanting sleep so badly until my body went beyond craving the need and I was wide-awake again.

"Let's stop at the Casablanca," Sparks offered. It was a popular nightclub located near the Palace Hotel, and quite dark inside. The combo was playing "Besame Mucho" and Roger immediately whirled me to the dance floor. "Order us a couple of daiquiris," he called, as the others stumbled to a table in the darkness. Harry and Emily also sought the dance floor, saying, "Make it margaritas for us, Sparks." The night was early for the young. Music and dancing made the World War seem so far away. However, I knew I was fading and had to insist on retiring to the hotel after hearing "Noche," a popular song at the time. It was the slow, sweet music and lovely lyrics of the age. Seldom did any evening date not comprise the pleasures of dancing, and Roger was an excellent partner. Thus ended a most memorable day.

No sooner was I in bed when the door flew open and in walked Frannie, crying "Are you awake? You've got to be. Listen, I found him. A dream. I met the most wonderful guy. He's gorgeous. Has the damnedest dimples and a grin to make the devil smile. A fog horn for a voice, but I love it."

"Frannie, who are you raving about? I thought you left here with Carson."

"Oh, forget Carson, that s.o.b. chased a different butterfly in every patio. What a bore. No, I met this beautiful Marine that stood near the Ambassador most of the night; that is, until I rescued him. He wore all those lovely things on his chest. Clyde Thortonberry is his name. MAJOR Clyde Thortonberry, I want you to know.—Frances Thortonberry. Sounds pretty good, huh? I'm going to marry that soldier."

"He proposed?"

"No, but he will. He's going to be in Miami soon and I promised to bake him a real pecan pie. What a darling. He's everything I want."

"Congratulations, Frannie, but I wish that door would open with Major Thortonberry on a big white tank to take you away so we could get some sleep."

"Great idea," spoke a voice from the back room. "Amen." called another. Frannie finally stumbled into bed, mumbling something about—, but no one really heard her.

ANTIGUA

Chapter 4

Early the following morning the phone rang several times before Frannie reached over to silence it. Her extended hand made an unsuccessful grab for the receiver, so the phone fell to the floor, rousing all the girls.

"This is Hiram. Hello. Who's there?"

"It's the paper boy," yelled Frannie, picking up the phone, "guess he wants to tell us which wagon we take out of here—Buenos dias, Senor Gomez, como esta?"

Hiram had called to advise us of schedule changes. I was not to return to New Orleans until the next day. Who went where was figured on plot boards holding "snail trail" graphs, updated via wires from Miami that kept the Master Plan. Once again there was activity in the stewardess quarters. As each one left for the airport there were the usual "see you later" comments. Parting was as casual as going for a walk. With my extra time in Guatemala, Roger and I decided to see the old city of Antigua, located about 25 miles southwest of Guatemala City. Emily and Harry were going with us and our transportation was to be the Model A Ford.

En route to Antigua we stopped at the village of Mixco where much of the dyes and threads were made for the weaving of cloth. In a factory of weavers, just seeing the women who do this work, dressed in their own prints of wearing apparel, was a colorful picture. We purchased tea towels, dining sets, and I ordered two shirts for my father and a tablecloth for my mother (which took years to wear out). We were told to use cold water for washing the dyed cloth—the first time with a little vinegar to "hold" the color.

Women from the same village wore identical patterns in a wrap around skirt called a "huipil." Many men wore pantaloon trousers and shirts of matching prints, also defining their home area. Footwear, if not sandals, was the same with which they were born. After years of walking barefoot, pounding the earth, their feet spread to flatten. Were they dressed in any other style, their features would not belie their Mayan origins, as distinct as the Conquistadors sighted them hundreds of years before.

Driving in the old Ford was slow; birds could have reached our destination in minutes. The winding road climbed higher, bordering steep cliffs. At every turn, Harry blew the horn, as did drivers coming from the opposite direction. Traffic was light but horn warning was a necessity for whatever might be coming around a bend, like oxen-driven carts. Mayan men walked with racks of wares upon their backs, bracketed in a ladder far above their height. Approaching them from the rear, shelves of pottery or woodwork had two human legs moving down the road. The women held platters on their heads with textile materials or fruit.

We came upon an inn, a copy of a chalet in the Alps, which revealed that customers and tourists were sparse in 1945. The inn was owned by German-born people who, Roger explained, had settled in this country and bought land for their *finca*, a name for the coffee plantations in Central America. During WWII their land was confiscated, though it was well known that these Germans, who claimed citizenship, had operated their fincas most efficiently.

At first Antigua, the old capital before Guatemala City, seemed like any small place in Central America with cobblestone streets, until reaching the central square. Covered archways extended over the sidewalk; one held the colonnaded, Spanish Renaissance architecture of the Palacio de los Capitanes. An earthquake and the eruption of Volcan Agua in 1773 devastated Antigua. The destruction from that catastrophic event was left as found, especially the church of San Francisco and the mission of Santa Clara. The city was rebuilt as part of these ruins, without disturbing the grandeur of their remains. The ruins of the San Francisco Cathedral elevated above all. It must have been a magnificent edifice, judging from what survived. The central courtyard alone revealed the enormity of space it had occupied. We saw the catacombs and the remains of the Santa Clara Monastery, taking pictures of ourselves amid the ruins. Looking up at Volcan Agua, towering so close in its attractive green mantle, so majestic in its perfect cone shape, it was hard to imagine it as ever being destructive.

Later we came upon an open doorway to a patio filled with native women working handlooms. Beside them were piles of cloth in Guatemalan patterns. The flower garden in the patio also drew our attention. A woman with an American accent, seated in a wicker chair, invited us in further. It was her home, open to the public once a week to allow local people an opportunity to work and sell their handicrafts. The woman who greeted us was a native of Louisiana. Coming to Antigua years before, she was attracted to the area and purchased this dwelling as a retreat. Now she was contributing a means to help the Mayan women, whose land had so impressed her.

Once again it was time to head back to Guatemala City, blowing our horn at every turn in the road. The only hindrance to the drive was a small dog that chased us, trying to nip at the tires like he had never seen a Ford before. Maybe he never had, or perhaps he showed resentment toward a big black monster in his peaceful countryside.

A new stewardess group had arrived at our quarters. After a good night's sleep, I was ready to return home in the morning. I had my first celebrity passenger, Mayor de Lessups Morrison, of New Orleans. He was much admired and a pleasure to meet. What a loss to the city when later he and his young son were both killed in a small, private plane crash.

HOME AND OUT AGAIN

Chapter 5

Unable to land ahead of schedule on the return flight, the pilots chose to circle and view the Chichenitza Mayan ruins in the Yucatan Peninsular, not far from Merida. The DC-3 flew low enough to see stone sculptures, steps to the pyramid, even hieroglyphics. Jungles did not surround Chichenitza, as the Tikal or Uxmal ruins in Guatemala. The latter were difficult to find even from the air, as the jungle crawled over every structure. Had it not been for pre-war archaeologists clearing away part of those ruins, they might have been completely hidden. With little excavating during WWII, the jungles once more became greedy; however, Chichenitza was in an open area with less foliage.

At Merida the DC-3 turned back to Guatemala while I continued on the Boeing aircraft for New Orleans. This Boeing-307, called a "Stratoliner," was one of three owned by Pan American—the Comet, the Rainbow, and the Flying Cloud. Most PanAm planes were named after famous sailing vessels of the past century, with the adjunct of "Clipper."

The B-307 was the first pressurized aircraft for passengers. The interior had nine single, reclinable seats on the port side and four private compartments to starboard. Each compartment had a draw curtain for privacy, its own collapsible dining table, and could be made into sleeper berths. Like the DC-3, the B-307 "three pointed", standing on wheels under the wings and sloping to a small tail wheel in the rear. With both planes, when on the ground, one walked "uphill" to go forward. The B-307 also carried a radio operator and flight engineer. The cockpit had twelve circular windows giving wide visibility, and bunks that were more often used to hold pilot briefcases with flight manuals and ever changing revisions. (The pulley tote-cart had not been "invented" yet; so much was carried by hand.) PanAm's three Boeing-307s were ultimately to be sold. The Rainbow would be destroyed and the Comet I would meet unexpectedly years later. The Flying Cloud, after being tossed from one owner to another, would be found in a decrepit condition; fortunately, the National Air and Space Museum purchased it. Boeing Aircraft would offer to restore it and PAA employees would give their money and time to restore it as it looked when a PanAm aircraft. (As of this writing, the Flying Cloud is moored in the original hangar where it took birth in 1939.)

New Orleans' Shushan Airport was on filled land over Lake Pontchartrain. It was not close to where I lived but I seldom had to use a cab. The Company station wagon driver would take me home and he would drive for any of us who needed transportation on departing too. It was a small crew base with only Flight 701, destined to Balboa in Panama, which departed at 11 p.m., and Flight 703, a Merida shuttle which left at 11 a.m. The Boeing was only taken as far as Merida, while the passengers and one stewardess went on to Guatemala in the DC-3. Our superintendent, Mr. de la Pena, was so fatherly that when one of us suddenly could not take a trip, he would hop on the aircraft and work it himself. This was before the existence of any Union contract for Flight Service. We were not paid by the hour, but when the co-pilot called "Block time—four-zero-two—," I would note this in my personal flight log.

Marge had checked me out on my first trip in March of 1945. With cheerful disposition, she guided me through the duties, emphasized the enjoyable, and joked about annoyances or difficulties. She epitomized the necessary attitude for a good flight attendant. In Guatemala City, Marge's fiance, a local resident, met her at the airport. Eric and Marge introduced me to the city. In an outdoor park we mounted wooden stairs to a stand from which one looked down on a huge relief map of Guatemala's mountains, volcanoes and valleys. Later, we toured the pale-green "National Palace", Guatemala's elegant government building on the Plaza de Espana. Upon entering, a wide marble staircase leads the visitor to a magnificent crystal chandelier overhead. Afterwards, we walked to the cathedral on the Plaza, dark and cool inside. The women all knelt with shawls over their heads. Without hats, Marge and I covered our tops with handkerchiefs, held by bobby pins.

Another day, Eric drove Marge, Roger and me to beautiful Lake Amatitlan, south of the city near Volcan Pacaya, whose camel hump crater from the air appears as though cut out with a giant ice cream scooper. Lake Amatitlan had cottages and affluent homes near the water's edge. We had skiffs to row on the lake and paddled around until I warned Roger he was headed into rocks. Eric lifted a pebble and threw it further away. It did not sink. It was porous lava rock, light as a feather floating on the water, spewing from an eruption that occurred centuries ago. After knifing our initials in a tree like a group of playful youngsters, clouds gathered around Pacaya and we drove back to the Palace Hotel.

While in the stewardess quarters, Hiram called on the phone with sad news. The father of one of our managers had died, and the burial was to be that afternoon. Hiram urged that it would be respectful if we attend the funeral. Frannie, who had just arrived, shrieked, "A funeral! K-rist!"

"Frannie," I asked, "When's the last time you spoke one sentence without swearing?" Frannie was from one of the Carolinas. Cursing seemed so incongruous to the soft quality of her drawl. I never met anyone who could escape with profanity better than she did. Thinking about my question, she replied, "I've never said—please fasten your Seat Belts and put out your G.D. cigarettes."

We did attend the funeral, and were perhaps the only ones in colored apparel. I shall ever remember that day, walking down the middle of a dusty, unpaved street to the cemetery. Behind the horse drawn hearse walked mourners all in black, men in dark suits, women with coal black shawls, followed by two stewards in PAA Navy darks and three stewardesses in their powder blue uniforms. We paid our respects but did have a few daiquiris later.

ERUPTIONS AND HURRICANES

Chapter 6

Once I had the mishap of leaving the mail sacks lying on the tarmac in Merida, which I should have had transferred to the DC-3. It was a night when all the ground workers were busy unloading a crated Diesel engine from one plane to the other. I looked for the loaders to carry the sacks but everyone was busy with the crated engine that appeared difficult to get through the cargo door. I was distracted as well as amused by what went on. Much verbal activity ensued, with everyone giving advice on loading the oversized crate, consuming a long time before anyone tried to do anything. It was no excuse for me, the U.S. Mail sacks were my responsibility and I left them in Merida. I was later called to explain my negligence. Years later, when I studied my Personnel Jacket, I found a letter of reprimand for my mail oversight, but nothing about my La Libertad trip. Oh well, on one I made it safely.

Toward the end of July 1945, Volcan Fuego began to show temper and spew lava from its peak. Flying northbound, our captain decided to visit Fuego with our DC-3. The only objection the co-pilot had to the idea was his eagerness to meet his stewardess bride who was waiting for him in Merida. The two had married on a trip together, but she had to obtain a passport to live with her husband in Guatemala. (At that time, marriage obliged a stewardess to retire from the job.) Crewmembers carried "Seaman's Passports"; unless living overseas. A few years later we all had to have regular passports.

Fuego could be seen soon after takeoff from Guatemala. We flew to the side where the smoke taken by the wind did not obliterate our view; so close that the hot lava could clearly be seen rolling down the side. The passengers were ecstatic. The skipper was an original, "seat of the pants", Alaska pilot, familiar with mountainous terrain. In his late forties, he was senior for a pilot in those days, but well regarded. When the cockpit window was opened for better photography, heat and an odor of sulfuric fumes could be detected. Air currents rocked the airplane as we flew away, but turbulence was common to aircraft flying low, especially over land. We had to fly around huge "Seabees" that looked like pink cotton candy with the sun on them. The DC-3 seldom reached 15,000 feet.

Flying over the Gulf could be fairly smooth "sailing" in the pressurized Boeing-307, able to reach loftier heights. It always amazed me how the Boeing could fly above rain and storms, to break out of dark clouds into clear atmosphere with sunshine and rainbows. However, on one flight from New Orleans I learned about the power that a hurricane can administer. We had a delay before departure, as meteorologists and pilots discussed a storm in the Gulf of Mexico. Hurricanes were not as frequent as in later years, nor were their spiraling easy to predict. On this flight, the bell sounded for boarding.

To explain the bell, departures on the Boeing from New Orleans were done somewhat in a military way. A small, tower bell with a knocker was attached to the outside of the terminal building. Whenever PanAm departed, the bell tolled and the crew in full uniform marched double file to the aircraft, more or less in step, and in order of rank. Those who came to watch airport activity were impressed.

Even on this rainy departure everything seemed normal. "Hap" Erwin, a member of my class, was anxious to be in Guatemala and see her particular interest from the "Casa de Lobos". I was the turnaround stewardess who would fly back to New Orleans from Merida. We served a hot meal and were settling ourselves to eat when interrupted by turbulence. The Fasten Seat Belt sign lighted and passengers were checked. We would hold one hand to the edge of the port side overhead rack as we walked down the aisle during rough weather.

Suddenly the airplane lurched and Hap flew into a starboard compartment, landing on a passenger's lap. Turbulence increased and the big Boeing, which we thought to be impregnable, was moving like a raft through rough water rapids. Galley latches came undone, with food and plates flying out, making a frightening racket as well as a mess. The radio operator came back to check on us but had to grab a seat for safety when he could neither walk nor crawl. One passenger unbuckled his safety belt and tried to go to the lavatory. "Stay belted," we cried. The tossing went on with many getting sick. Objects that we believed were secure came loose and flew about. A woman screamed and yelled that we were all going to die. She was answered by another passenger saying, "Aw, shut up!"

We had skirted the hurricane and had gone beyond the "point of no return", which is the term used when past midway in flight. We eventually landed safely in Merida with some wobbly legs that left the aircraft. Hap went on to Guatemala in the DC-3, while those of us waiting to return to New Orleans on the Boeing, stayed in Mexico. Compania Cubana and Compania Mexicana were unable to continue their flights. Aircraft scurried to whatever safe place they could find as the hurricane progressed with fervor. Hotel rooms were at a premium. Crews had to sleep on the aircraft. A member of the local staff offered his home to three stewardesses, which was my good fortune.

This PanAm employee showed us gracious hospitality and provided an insight into a living style of an old Mexican city. We were offered nourishment with enticing local dishes and, while the son entertained with guitar music, the daughter taught us some Mexican dances. We slept in mosquito-shrouded hammocks on their patio, which on a hot night with no air-conditioning was a most enjoyable treat. A PanAm family had given us their best accommodations.

On a later trip, the same day an atomic bomb was being dropped over Japan, I reached my 21st birthday in Guatemala. (News of the bomb did not surface until later.) On arrival I went directly to bed thinking, "What a way to spend my 21st." I was unable to sleep; not an unusual reaction when one is really tired and the body engines are still running. The door flew open and in walked Patty Tibbets crying, "There's a revolution brewing. We all have to leave here for a safer place." As Guatemala had experienced troubles before, it gave an uneasy feeling, but not a shocking one. (On a previous insurrection, one of the girls had taken a sleeping pill and could not be roused effectively. She was willingly rolled under her bed until it all blew over.)

"Why now?" I replied, "I'm too tired for this." I dressed and went out to the lobby with Patty. "We're all gathered back here, "she said, as we headed for the music room. There, with Hap at the piano playing "Happy Birthday," were Hap's pilot, Bob Henry, Roger, Harry, Ginger Ruiz from Brownsville, and several others. Patty came back carrying a birthday cake made in the hotel kitchen. Whatever anyone could hum, Hap could play on the piano, and a few she made up with her own lyrics. What a talent! She had arranged the party in her usual delight for any celebration.

On a corner chair in the room sat a cage holding a paraquito. I was told that Harry had found Patty and the bird in La Tienda Grande and took both of them back to the hotel on his motorcycle. Now an American pilot on a motorcycle with a girl holding a birdcage was a rare sight perhaps, but more difficult because slacks were rarely worn by American women abroad in those days. I asked what were the plans for the bird.

"It's for you," said Patty. "I can't take it to Texas."

"Patty, thanks, but if Texas won't allow it, what makes you think Louisiana will? I believe they're both still part of the same country."

The Department of Agriculture would have quarantined and refused the bird if it got beyond the mouth of the Mississippi River—if it had survived the DDT spray which every aircraft was required to have before arrival. Of course as soon as the U.S. ordered spraying aircraft with DDT, other countries had the same requirement. I guess it was a matter of—"if you don't want our bugs, we don't want yours." Even after we had sprayed, local officials might come aboard and spray again. The spray could be so severe; it left clouds in the cabin. If DDT was discontinued after its deadly effect upon birds' eggs and animals, I wonder what it did to the lungs of humans? Perhaps the insects had the last laugh.

As for Patty's paraquito, it was placed on a rack in the stewardess quarters of Room 109, given the name of "Clipper" with instructions on it's care (por favor). How long that lasted, I do not know, for I never saw it again.

MEXICO

Chapter 7

By the summer of 1945, New Orleans base flying expanded to include a shuttle to Mexico City from Guatemala, with just a few hours to spend in the big city. Just before my first trip, a CMA aircraft had flown into Popocatepelt, a snow covered mountain in Mexico. All contact was lost after the plane left Puebla. Fatal crashes of any airline draw particular empathy from crewmembers. Their possible causes were discussed in Emergency classes, required bi-annual training.

We left Guatemala and flew over Lake Atitlan to the Pacific coast; then northerly up the beach where ocean breakers showed clearly to the right of the aircraft. Inland, beyond Tehuantepec, the plane gained altitude, as the terrain became mountainous. We viewed Mt. Orizaba, another snow topped, 20,000 ft. mountain. The crew used their oxygen bottles over a 15,000 ft pass into the valley where lay Mexico City at 7,000 feet. I did not realize how thin air affected me until I picked up trays and started breathing heavily. Through the pass, the mountain was so close I thought surely the plane would scrape the top, had the wheels been down.

In the few hours spent in Mexico's capital, the crew rented a taxi to take a quick view of Chapultepec and the Xochomilco Gardens. Our biggest problem was holding on while the driver sped through traffic. Cab drivers, when carrying uniformed pilots, are often inclined to think their fare want to speed. As the co-pilot said, "Taxi drivers scare the hell out of me. Let's get back in the air."

On return, when landing at Guatemala City, it was 4 a.m. By

5 p.m. the same day I was back on flight to Merida, which should have left at 11.25 p.m. The reason for the early departure was because a "temporal" was expected, and if the aircraft did not leave early, it might have been many hours before it could. A "temporal" was a severe fog condition which closed the field. I remember one night being at the airport when a temporal came suddenly before one of our planes could land. In Flight Operations I listened to conversation between the pilot and ground control. The latter reported, "All field lights on." The pilot answered, "Can't see a thing. I'll make another pass." A second attempt, and you could hear the plane pull up. "Still can't see you. I'll try again," the pilot said, without any panic in his voice. Ground control responded, "Better take it to San Jose. Doesn't look like this stuff will clear soon." The pilot replied, "I'm low on fuel." San Jose was the city on the west coast of Guatemala, where the U.S. was allowed a military base. Volcanoes and mountains lay between, with no place to land. Tapachula was twice as far away.

Suddenly the pilot called back, "I see some runway lights—yes, just barely, but believe I can make it." And he did land safely. It was Carson Quinlan, the roué with the Don Juan reputation. On my next trip we played tennis together. I praised his pilot ability, but tennis was as far as I would encourage him.

When the nights were clear, Volcan Fuego showed a bright red glow in the sky. Its activity had lessened, but the crater had expanded since it first erupted. Periodically, a little geyser of sparks fired skyward, as from a welder's torch; then puffs of smoke and rocks increased the lava flow.

On my second shuttle to Mexico City, inclement weather obliged us to go to Vera Cruz, along with other planes forced to land. We waited for hours at the airport. One of my passengers was the national radio announcer, Ben Grauer, an interesting gentleman with great patience during the delay. Eventually everyone was sent to hotels. Crews were placed in the Hotel Villa del Mar. Our captain chose to sleep on the aircraft, vowing that by the time we got to a hotel, the fog would lift. Crews referred to airport/

hotel/airport rides as "suitcase drill". It was not an era of motels on airport perimeters. My accommodation was one of the cabin facilities on the hotel grounds with no lock to the door, no telephone, and a dark area without any outside lights. I could not sleep. Two hours later there was a pounding on the door—"Pick-up in 40 minutes!" By the time we returned to Guatemala, it had been a 24-hour shuttle.

Thus it was that the life style necessitated dealing with irregularity of sleeping and eating habits, including sometimes doing without one or both. Accommodations could be negligible if not questionable, but more often all that could be found for passengers and crews in the 1940s. Nothing was ever definite and planning ahead was done with tongue in cheek.

I had a full day in Guatemala before flying home. I met Harry and Bob from the "Casa de Lobos" who had promised to show me their new horse at the stables. I had my riding jodhpurs with me, awaiting the promise. This was the day. After taking turns in the corral, Bob suggested we all ride outside the gate. Grand idea, except we were short one horse. That problem was solved when another owner offered to let me ride his mare. She was a beauty, but seemed a little testy as I put my left foot in the stirrup. My right foot was not secure before she bolted, jerked away the reins and broke into a gallop down a dirt road. Struggling to retrieve the reins, I grasped the horse's neck to keep from falling and tried everything I ever learned to halt that animal. We came to a paved road and I prayed no one would be driving by. The horse skidded across the asphalt towards a barbed wire fence. I was no jumper, and neither apparently was the horse, but at the last second she swerved. My left leg scraped the barbed wire, tearing my pants and cutting into my thigh. I grabbed the fence and pulled away, as the horse disappeared. There was no great damage outside of a ruined pair of jodhpurs. I learned that the animal had once been owned by a woman who was cruel to it and the horse had accepted no female rider ever since.

At the "Casa" I was painted with iodine and Harry let me use a pair of his trousers. I wondered which was worse—to walk in the hotel with ripped pants, or Harry's oversized ones. It was Thursday, the one night of the week the Palace Hotel had a marimba band that drew people all dressed for a party.

"Wait here, I'll remove your pants." I said to Harry as I picked up the key to my room. A stranger walking by only heard the last half of my sentence and gave me a look I laugh now to remember.

KEY EPISODES

Chapter 8

By the fall of 1945, Miami crews were not only usurping our flying into Guatemala via Merida as well as Panama, but rumors again circulated on closing New Orleans as a crew base. The DC-4s (C-54s which had been used by PAA to carry troops and supplies during WWII) were to replace the Boeing-307, (and eventually the little DC-3).

Men in WWII service were slowly leaving the armed forces and parties were taking place all over the Vieux Carre of New Orleans. Hap and her roommate, Dottie Mack, were living in an apartment in this old section of the city, with buildings noted by high ceilings, French windows and iron grill balconies. The "French Quarter", popularized by its history, was also an area for restaurants, boutiques, night clubs, antique shops, and well known bars like Lafitte's Cabin and the Old Absinthe House.

One farewell party ended when only half started. A naval officer friend of Dottie's had reserved rooms for his "good-by Navy blow" above a famous restaurant on Royal St., to which I attended. Just when all seemed to be going well, a waiter arrived and precluded the party by advising of a fire in the building. We began to smell smoke and our host beseeched us not to rush out and jam the exit.

Hap sat at the piano giving forth her talent as the guests picked up their wraps and walked casually down the stairs. If she had not been playing music to which everyone was singing, there might have been panic. Hap was one of the last ones to leave. "That calm control was your stew training coming out," we later teased her. Of course, we all had "a few".

One late night over the Gulf of Mexico, I was serving the pilots coffee when out the front window we saw green and red blinking lights on the horizon, seemingly dead ahead. "Why the S.O.B.'s in southbound altitude," exclaimed the co-pilot. Northbound and southbound aircraft are assigned different altitudes, as with eastbound and westbound planes, which universally averts the possibility of an airborne collision. The use of odd and even number altitude for direction has been an international language to all pilots. In this case, it was a military plane, which we safely passed to port. The cockpit language got a little bizarre, so I returned to my galley.

Later at Guatemala City, the sun gave light but the earth held a solid embankment of clouds. It was a white shroud with only the peaks of volcanoes poking above. The pilots chose to go to the U.S. military airfield on the West Coast and await clearance. On landing, I opened the cabin door and smiling army men greeted me, asking for stateside newspapers. We always carried two bundles of the *New Orleans Times Picayune*, so their request was easily granted. Accepting an invitation to have "chow" at the army mess hall, the passengers disembarked and I left the door to get my purse. When I returned, the steps were gone and waiting below were several men in army "fatigues". There was nothing "tired" about them. They helped me down by bodily handing me from one to the other, saying the steps had to be used for another aircraft. I slid into waiting arms. Ah, the sacrifices one had to make to be an airline stewardess.

Traveling often to Guatemala, I bought clothing, tablecloths, towels, leather purses and shoes (which never fit properly and ruined my feet). As crew, U.S. Customs only allowed us $10 worth, duty free, per trip. We either paid on the excess, brought in a little at a time, or "fudged" on the price. Customs was never fooled but were generous with us.

On one of my last trips from New Orleans, Roger met me

with his motorcycle and we went shopping in the market. Seated behind him I carried a heavy, woven blanket I had purchased, as we scampered around corners I could not see. At the hotel we met friends in the lobby with talk that Guatemala might close as a crew base. Gloomily we discussed where we might be transferred. Hap came in from her trip and, trying to forget the changes that might affect our lives, we went to the El Patio restaurant, located around the corner from the Palace Hotel. It was furnished in Spanish Colonial style and barefooted, Mayan women in their immaculate, native dress, served delicious local dishes.

Returning to the hotel, a departing stewardess warned us that someone was trying to break into our room, using an object to pry at the latch. Hap and I did not take her seriously, but no sooner were we in bed when a metallic noise was heard at the latch. We called the desk, and roomboys were sent but claimed they saw no one. Later the noise was heard again. We sneaked to the door, that was not flush to the floor and had space at the bottom to show light from the patio. We could see two black sock feet. Hap grabbed her high-heeled shoe like a hammer, ready to pounce. This time Hap said, "Okay, you've had your fun, go away." We heard no more. Wanting to sleep and still feel secure, we shoved two chairs and a chest of drawers with a lamp atop, to block the door. In the morning there was banging at the entrance, force being used against the door, and a crash of the lamp to the floor. In walked Frannie and Ginger. "What the hell's going on in here," Frannie cried. When we explained, Ginger commented.

"Don't tell me that man is back. He's a diplomat from South American. He's tried this before, pretending it's his room and he lost his key. The hotel knows who he is but they're afraid to accuse him. They say he's harmless."

"In a pig's eye!" said Frannie. "Just let him try that when I'm here and I'll teach him a little 'diplomatic' lesson. Anyway, why doesn't he just knock?" I never heard if the "Diplomat" came back again.

On my next trip I was scheduled to fly to Miami from Merida, as I was due my semi-annual emergency class review. An overnight in Merida enabled me to see more of this old Mexican city. The henequen fiber from the agave plant grown in the Yucatan had once prospered the area. My crew and I drove about in a horse drawn, open-carriage "taxi" on a pleasant, balmy night. Colonial style buildings lined the main plaza. Old mansions graced the area from its days of opulence. A quiet dignity lay about the city, which had relinquished its economic success when synthetic products uprooted their market.

On departure at the airport, I met a former Miami roommate, Jean Weber, who was on flight to Panama. I had left some things at her apartment and decided it was a good time to recover my possessions when I reached Miami.

"Here's my key. When you leave, put it in my company mailbox," said Jean. It was all neatly arranged, we thought. Unfortunately, right after Jean left, my schedule changed and I had to return to New Orleans. This meant that Jean would get back late at night and have no key to enter her apartment. I told the Miami skipper of the dilemma and he offered to take the key and put it in Jean's mailbox. The arrangement seemed fine. The only trouble was the skipper forgot about it. He went home with the key nicely tucked in his pants pocket. All so perfectly explainable, all so innocent—except to his wife who emptied his pant's pockets before sending them to the cleaners. A year later I met this pilot who said, "You girls almost caused me a divorce!" Blame Scheduling.

NEW ORLEANS, FAREWELL

Chapter 9

Meals aloft were pre-cooked, placed in round ceramic bowls and held in metal thermos containers. The dinner menu between Merida and New Orleans consisted of filet mignon steaks wrapped with a bacon strip. Americans, who had wartime rationing of hard to find, expensive beef, particularly appreciated each one. However, unused steaks were to be thrown away by the Department of Agriculture. Of course. The family dog jumped excitedly at a paper bag in my hand when I came home.

Salads and desserts were generally the type that did not require refrigeration, an improvement to come with later aircraft—dry ice was used extensively. No alcoholic beverages were offered. Coffee, tea, and juice were favorites, since plain water was seldom palatable, if indeed safe to drink. Entrees southbound were mostly chicken, causing pilots to "cackle" as soon as the cockpit door was opened to admit their trays. Later there would be a requirement to serve a different entree to each pilot, in case of food poisoning. It was seniority that won the beef and another reason pilots were anxious to promote to captain.

The day after Christmas of 1945 I left on flight, and that was a mistake. I was coming down with a cold but to cancel around any holiday was an unpopular thing to do. The captain of my flight was a cigar smoker. No, he was a cigar puffer. That did not help my sinuses. However, the captain was usually treated with respect for his position. Not that he was considered as "next to God", but rarely were his likes, opinions or authority questioned. It was considered proper and polite to call him Captain Jones or Smith, whatever his surname. A captain would not be called by his first name, at least not in public, and certainly not in front of passengers. To be friendly, he would be called "Skipper", and more frequently was.

It happened that the pressurization on the Boeing was not working well. With ear tubes clogged upon higher altitudes, I was more than just uncomfortable. The engineer knew I was having difficulty in equalizing the pressure upon my ears and tried to adjust his instruments to lessen my pain. Chewing gum can help, even moving one's lower jaw horizontally, or yawning, but nothing worked for me. I was one who felt effects just riding in an elevator.

I flew many trips over jungles that grew the sapodilla tree that produced the milky juice for making gum. It was normal procedure to offer gum when checking passengers' seat belts. This was done for years to prevent inner ear pain. A little blue box with a snap-lock cover held the tiny gum cartons and was as important as masking tape. The former helped keep the passengers out of pain. It would take an entire chapter to reveal the many uses for masking tape on the aircraft. Alleviating earaches was not one of them.

Sympathy was expressed regarding my ear pain and, to distract my thoughts, the crew pointed out a large reef in the Gulf of Mexico, north of the Yucatan Peninsula. It was pale yellow-green and emerald colored water surrounded by the deep blue. This coral reef, several miles in diameter, is just below the water surface, clearly visible from the air. But no diversions lessened my torture. When I returned home, I learned I had damaged an eardrum and had to take time off. I grew a lot wiser when it came to flying with any sign of a cold.

One of my last flights to Guatemala from New Orleans will be remembered because the only passengers I had were a baseball team and seven Catholic nuns. During the night, the team "shot" craps on the galley floor and tried to hide a whiskey flask. The nuns sat stoically reading their prayer books. I asked half the team to sit while the others played because there was too much weight in the rear of the aircraft. "We're dragging our tail," the pilots cried. When we met with turbulence, the baseball team became deathly sick, one by one. The nuns I can still see sitting upright, holding their prayer beads, not a pea-green face among them. The air cleared as we flew over Flores, a town completely covering an island on an inland body of water near the Tikal ruins. Aloft, I tried to help grown men overcome sickness in flight. When we landed, the nuns disembarked without a falter; the ball team could not have walked to first base.

A few times in Guatemala we went to the movies. Films had dubbed-in Spanish voices or captions were used. I recall "Desert Song", "Frankenstein", and "Road to Morocco". One day Ginger and I, with a few pilots, went to see "A Medal for Benny". When the show ended and lights came on, we noticed we were the only women in the theater. In a slow moving aisle of men, towards what Ginger and I thought was the exit, we walked into the men's lavatory. We took a quick about-face, stumbling over two men behind us. In the lobby, the amused pilots asked, "What happened to you two?"

Based in New Orleans, flying from March 1945 through February 1946, I made 48 trips to Guatemala, 7 with shuttles to Mexico City, 13 Merida shuttles and one Miami Ferry flight. Total airtime, 837 hours. This did not include the time spent on the ground with passengers during delays. In April, Hap and I were transferred to Brownsville, Texas, from where we would take trips as far south as Medellin, Colombia. We planned to live with another stewardess, Martina Catalan, who offered to share her apartment. Life with the airline was changing, as it always would.

BROWNSVILLE

Chapter 10

At the mouth of the Rio Grande River lies Brownsville, Texas; seaport and border town between the U.S. and Mexico. In the spring of 1946, the tallest building was the nine storied El Jardin Hotel. Skyscrapers did not always determine size in Texas. Brownsville possessed a large friendliness. It was also a base where PanAm began flights in the western sector of its Latin American Division.

Hap and I were fortunate to share with Martina Catalan, who had a cooler than usual upstairs apartment. Martina spoke a fluent, Castilian Spanish. Her folks were born in Spain, though she was pure American. Martina introduced us to some of the local bachelors who took us to the Boca Chica Beach to swim, enjoy surf fishing, and treasure seeking through what washed up on shore—usually sand crabs.

We also frequented Matamoros, across the Rio Grande. On the Mexican side the Immigration and Customs officials would not rise from their chairs in the shade. They waved us through with a smile and a "Buenos Tardes!" On return, the American officials were cautious in their check of identification and purchases. Americans had to be gone for 24 hours from the Border States to be free of duty on Mexican articles, but there were other reasons to cross the river besides shopping. Brightness of color abounded in Matamoros. Shops and street vendors covered all corners, both good and not so good. There was outdoor and indoor music and entertainment, and resturants, some good and some not so good.

Nightlife of dancing and mariachi combos made Matamoros a lively place, albeit more enticing than comparatively quiet Brownsville.

On my first flight Martina checked me out. We left on a DC-3 in early morning. By the time the sun came up we were over barren, rugged mountains. At Mexico City we left two deportees who, Marina informed me, had "misbehaved" in the States.

"Why not just take them across the bridge to Matamoros," I asked.

"They'd only swim back again. This way they get a free trip and our lov-e-ly company," Martina replied.

From Mexico City we flew south to where banana groves blanketed the land. Then we cut inland over green valleys between volcanoes, and low enough to see Mayan Indians run out from their huts and villages to watch us fly overhead. Soon Guatemala City appeared and it was like coming home again.

There was no limit or restrictions to "duty time". One could be called for working a flight whenever needed. We no sooner retrieved our suitcases before we were assigned a shuttle to Salvador. No passengers traveled outbound, but 21 golfers were returning from a tournament; men more interested in seeing their golf bags safely loaded in the cargo hole than their suitcases. They probably would have preferred to drive balls back to Guatemala, with Lake Atitlan and the volcanoes surrounding it as golf hazards. The village of Rabinal, crouched between mountains, was the signal to descend into the valley of our destination.

On next departing Guatemala, we had a delay. Martina kept everyone's spirits up. She showed transit passengers around the airport shops and helped to translate. Suddenly she approached me and plopped a baby in my arms with a "needs changing."

"Where's its mother?" I asked.

"She's outside in the fresh air. Which would you like, sick mother or wet baby?"

The baby was a bit damp, but had I not asked to be a stewardess? After waiting for several hours, the flight cancelled and we went back to the hotel. In the evening, with Martina and her date,

Roger and I had daiquiris in the San Carlos Hotel lounge, a place distinctive with Mayan decor. Martina never drank anything stronger than lemonade and was always the life of the party. Afterwards we went to dinner at the home of our newlyweds who had married in Panama while on a trip together. They seemed so content, settled in a house with their German Shepherd, "Tarzan". Little did any of us know that in a few months we would all have to transfer to another base, and once again find new living quarters.

On this night a taxi strike had developed, so with our escorts we piled into a city bus that had one tire smaller than the other tires. It was a bumpy ride all the way. We amused ourselves by trying to sing with voices that stuttered with the bus movement. "Tampico" and "Linda Mujer", popular songs of the day, received our torturous renditions. The huge doors to the hotel were closed when we arrived, as they were always shut past midnight, but after banging and bell ringing, a sleepy headed baggage boy admitted us. Still singing, and a little loud getting back to our room, I called out, "We made it!"

"Si, como no," Martina laughed, with her favorite Spanish expression. In the morning we learned our Brownsville manager was in town, with a room across the hall. At the dining room for breakfast, he wore his usual stoic expression. I believe we awakened him the night before, but not a word was said.

Next was San Salvador again, 113 miles from Guatemala. Martina called this flight the "Buckle, Buckle, Better Stay Buckled Run". We encountered turbulence all the way. Landing in Salvador could be a scary experience. Near the end of the single runway was a steep cliff that dropped several hundred feet to Lake Illopango. The plane's descent gave the impression it would hit the cliff, not glide on to the runway; however, the little DC-3 would land safely. Likewise, if the plane left Salvador to take off over the lake, it might dip below the steep cliff edge, as though it would fall into Lake Illopango; but the little DC-3 would pull up and away.

Between Salvador and Tegucigalpa, Honduras, though only 128 miles, were replete with volcanoes. One had a yellow-green lake in its crater with a sulfuric bubbling; another, a chartreuse lake, of a color no paint box could duplicate. Izalco emitted a few fireballs, and smoking Rincon was a beacon for ships at sea. We landed on Tegucigalpa's dirt runway. During our 30-minute stay, TACA, an airline competitor, was the only other plane there. Airports in Central America were comparatively quiet in 1946.

Shorter flights did not always indicate a comfortable journey. There was less time to seek altitude and level off. The closer you were to the ground, the more air currents would disrupt smooth flying—especially in the mountainous terrain. Managua, Nicaragua, our next stop, was only 142 miles from Tegucigalpa. The Managua Airport at that time had "Pan American World Airways" in huge letters across the front of the building. Beside the entrance was an iron bell on a metal-legged pedestal, to sound for boarding. Here in Nicaragua, PAA was recognized for expanding international air travel, as well as assisting in the building of airports and runways.

Leaving Managua, I must give recognition to some of the outstanding volcanoes—Talica, whose cloud expulsions stretched for miles over the Pacific Ocean, as if the earth were smoking a cigar. Momotombo towered over little Momotombito nearby—two perfect peaks, like mother and a baby. The larger one often warned of possible activity. Omotepe could be timed to belch its discomfort every seven minutes. At great height, volcanoes would hardly show more than a pimple on the earth's surface. During piston times, they were seen in all their majesty and power.

San Jose, Costa Rica, last stop before Balboa, is an idyllic spot of delightful climate and flowers that abound all year. The country seemed quite progressive with more paved highways, dams, and concrete bridges. I could only see this from the air, and the La Sabana Airport, for we continued on to Panama.

PANAMA

Chapter 11

It was so hot in Panama I could only think of the milk shakes and ice cream that Martina had promised would be ours in the military commissary of Balboa. Before landing at the Tocumen Airport, the Canal Zone was pointed out in the distance. We were not allowed to fly over the Canal and passengers were told "no photography". WWII was finally over but caution was still being taken. The Canal Zone, controlled by the U.S., was a separate section from Panama, but Balboa was partly in both. The U.S. military was in evidence and wherever American troops went, so went ice cream and milk shakes.

We stayed at the Hotel Tivoli in Ancon, dubbed "the fire trap" because of its wooden structure. Smoking in bed was indeed risky and ours was a match carrying generation. This night I was awakened by a burning smell. Martina and I shared a three-occupant room from which we leaped up and out to a smoky hallway. Dottie Mack came from a nearby room crying, "It's okay now!" A wall light extended over the basin mirror in the bedroom, which the girls would cover to keep from disturbing anyone asleep while they dressed for a flight. (It always seemed our flights departed late at night or in the early morning hours.) If someone left without turning off the light or removing the towel, it just got hotter until it burned. Notices were soon placed everywhere; "Towels must not be put over basin lights . . ."

Sleep was unthinkable after that incident, as we had to exchange and analyze news on the latest marriages, love affairs, rumors, etc. We finally dressed and, with others from Brownsville and Miami, left the hotel to see the city. Balboa did not have the scurrying of activity, as did Guatemala. With the heat and humidity, lethargy was prevalent, but understandable.

The old section still held some colonial style buildings. For the most part, the wooden structures appeared as though a good storm would blow them away, if fire did not consume them first. I was in Panama on a later trip when a huge blaze destroyed many homes. Standing on the veranda at the Tivoli Hotel, it looked like a bomb had been dropped. The poverty of the people was disheartening, particularly in contrast to the Americans encamped in the military area.

For lunch we went to the Army's clubhouse in Balboa for an American hamburger, and that night to "El Rancho" for dinner. The latter was located on a rooftop in Balboa. We had been advised not to penetrate certain parts of town, particularly at night; however, we ventured to the "Club Realto" to see The Moon Girls in a floorshow you would not exactly write home about. Compared to other places, it held a mild show. Nightclubs in Balboa had some wild and risque entertainment, apparently a profitable draw for the military.

From Panama I had a David shuttle, pronounced "Da-veed," which seemed to be a lucrative run for military men on leave. It was a desirable area for animal hunters. One passenger left his gun shells in Balboa and begged us to turn back. Though being on time was not as demanding as later years; once aloft, we could no more oblige him than the honeymoon couple who left their marriage certificate in a seat pocket.

Soon the restrictions flying near certain areas of Panama were lifted. Flights would arrive over many Panamanian islands that revealed huge gun installations, still partially hidden by camouflage of natural floral growth. We crossed forested territory with large craters where the military had practiced bombing. Other areas showed firing ranges for gunnery exercise. The jungles would eventually take back everything.

Lightweight, valuable cargo pieces were often given to the steward/ess, who were held responsible. One such package I had received in Panama was supposed to go to British Guiana. Only my flight went elsewhere and I failed to notice this while signing a dozen commissary papers. The wires that crossed for that error—another reprimand.

My trip was to Medellin, Colombia. After first flying across the "bottleneck" that connects North and South America, we landed on a dirt runway at Turbo in the middle of the Colombian jungles. Airline employees assigned there were happy to receive the latest newspapers. What impressed me was a huge sloth and anteater that were kept as pets on the airport grounds. The sloth sat lazily against a tree where it had been tethered. It was as large as a bear, with the most vapid expression seen on any animal, a face like a turtle, a monkey's body, and bird-like claws with three, long curving nails. The anteater used its slender snout and tongue to dine by its built-in vacuum cleaner. Two local boys showed me some snakes they had killed. They laughed when I said, "Ugh", but I gave the lads some sweet rolls from the galley, to which their eyes got big as craters. Our boarding passengers had delayed us because in order to get to the airport they had to come by canoe.

We continued on to Medellin, barely flying over the jungle trees. Though low to the earth, we were still 8,500 feet above sea level. Suddenly the plane dropped off into a long, enclosed, deep valley where-in lay Medellin. The contrast to outside the valley reminded me of the story of Shangri La. The city was a color painting with flowers and farmland that held grazing, solid white cattle speckling the hilly countryside. We returned to Panama with boxes of orchids in every part of the aircraft, including empty passenger seats, all packaged for shipment throughout the world. Our plane looked like a flight for orchids only. I was convinced that the valley of Medellin was the most beautiful spot on earth.

OVER AND OUT

Chapter 12

One day I was called to the cockpit and found the captain flying the airplane in his undershorts. It was a warm day but we were high and cool enough, I thought. Before I could leave, he asked if I had a needle and preferably dark thread. Yes, it was part of ship's equipment. I was handed his trousers with a jagged tear.

"Well, I guess you can't get off the plane looking as you do now," I said.

"Nor can I make an emergency landing because of it," he added.

My problem was to carry the trousers back to the cabin where I could repair the damage. Closing the cockpit door behind me, I clutched the pants like a ball but still had the uncomfortable feeling that every passenger knew exactly what I carried. I raced down the cabin aisle to an empty row of back seats where I engaged in my assignment until a passenger came by going to the lavatory. The pants were quickly tucked under the seat but once out of the lavatory the passenger wanted to talk. As we got closer to landing, the cockpit bell sounded and I went forward again. In answer to "where are my pants, we're almost there," I replied, "you've got to put on the Fasten Seat Belt sign or I'll never finish." The plane throttles were pulled back and the sewing completed, a make shift job, but at least the trousers held on to him.

Our pilots were everything from Bible preachers to Don Juans, artists to ex-football players; they were an assortment of personalities. One "dark and stormy night," after hearing the frightening sound of hail hitting the fuselage with the sound of machine gun bullets, I went to the cockpit for encouragement on weather conditions. What I did not expect to see were two kotex pads (the kind from small boxes serviced in our lavatories) stretched out on the front window ledge. The co-pilot began to wipe his window as he said to me, "Defroster isn't working. These things do come in handy." Beyond that cockpit door were men as resourceful as they were unpredictable. Of course the girls found other uses for those pads too. As regulations required that hair be worn above the collar for sanitary reasons as food handlers, some "long hairs" used what was called a "rat", a soft cushion material upon which their locks could be rolled. The pads in those little boxes came in handy as temporary substitutes.

On a trip to Medellin, I purchased some conquistador stirrups, supposedly the genuine article. They were of heavy bronze and could have pointed or blunt toes in fancy etched designs. Even if some Conquistador did not wear them a few hundred years ago, and were only a means to the Yankee dollar, they were a conversation piece. A pair made an excellent wall hanging or used as plant holders. Mine never made it to home.

Walking through the terminal building in Balboa with my stirrups in hand, I was stopped by an army major who asked me to meet his colonel in the airport office concerning an important matter. He sounded so serious. To my surprise, the colonel wanted my conquistador stirrups and offered me anything in the Army PX in trade. Sorry, but I wanted my stirrups.

While in the colonel's office, a call came through to inform him that two B-17s had collided aloft while searching for a missing P-38. It seemed a good time to leave, as I held tightly to my stirrups. I thought that was the end of it. Later I received a phone call from the colonel asking me to dinner. I declined. Roger had flown in from Guatemala and I was to dine with him. I did remember seeing a 35mm. camera in the colonel's office that was not easy to acquire during those days after the War. Thinking to get another pair of stirrups on my next trip, if the colonel conceded his camera, I agreed to a swap. He did, but I never returned again to Colombia. As for conquistador stirrups, they are about as rare as Conquistadores themselves are.

Aboard my northbound flight, Hart Preston, a *Time* magazine correspondent, was a passenger. He had come from Peru, about which he wrote an article in a subsequent issue. As I had left Panama without snack trays and was forced to serve my passengers using empty breadboxes, I hoped that would not hit *Time*. Fortunately, Machu Picchu took center stage.

Before leaving Mexico City, I discovered that five people who boarded were not destined for Brownsville. One of my passengers was Jorge Negreto, the Mexican singer and movie star. There was a delay and much excitement and confusion at the airport over Negreto, idolized as the Mexican Frank Sinatra and mobbed in the terminal building. Movie stars sometimes caused disruptions. Frannie had a flight when a famous American movie star became so warm sitting on the aircraft awaiting departure that she removed her blouse. It was a scorching hot day, easily 120 degrees inside the cabin. The star sat fanning herself with her blouse, exposing her well endowed, upper half, clad only in an underslip that Frannie thought was prettier than a sundress. Waiting on the ground, the aircraft was suddenly spirited with more male employees who had found duties to perform. Two maintenance men came aboard; one with a pair of pliers, the other carried a light bulb. Two commissary employees came with a small box of sugar. When two cabin cleaners appeared, one with a broom and the other holding a dustpan—that did it. Up to the cockpit went Frannie, asking when was "takeoff" as the cabin was being flooded with possible stowaways. The captain replied, "We're going now, but tell Miss (the movie star) that I can't leave without my takeoff kiss."

Frannie related, "I reached across the throttle panel and gave (the pilot) a big smooch, telling him, 'Okay, now you've had it, let's get the h— out of here!'" The airplane took off, banking so sharply that faces pressed to windows as though they would fall out. Then it banked the other way before flying level.

"See how your kiss reeled me," the pilot said jokingly later.

Back in Brownsville, I received news that my father was ill. Permission was granted to go home, and I was given the opportunity to return to New Orleans via Guatemala, as a crewmember on emergency leave. It was one more reason to feel grateful for being a PAA employee.

GOODBYE, TEXAS

Chapter 13

When I returned to Brownsville from New Orleans, Martina informed me that we were invited to a barbecue given by her friends, owners of a large ranch. We were shown true Texan hospitality, complete with mariachi music and succulence steaks. Such opulence made me think of my parents who tried to teach me to be thrifty. I wrote home to proudly tell them I had saved $200. I was earning $190 a month, with a $10 raise semi-annually. My father sent me a certificate, fifteen shares of PAA, worth about $500. It was a birthday present with a note saying, "let this be a start". That certificate would become ever precious to me.

My living in Brownsville lasted four months. A decided sadness clouded over friends when crew bases were shut down. Progress dictated this had to happen. Like Key West, Florida, Brownsville had been a starting field for PanAm's flights through Central America, but Houston, as Miami, was the larger draw for connections. With DC-4s flying further and faster, there was no need for foreign crew bases near the States either. Martina stayed in Texas. Hap wed her sweetheart from the "Casa", who was transferred to Rio. Besides the new Houston base, some went to PanAm's Pacific-Alaska Division in San Francisco. I chose Miami. My flight time from Brownsville had averaged 85.20 hours per month.

One of our last gatherings at the "Casa de Lobos" in Guatemala was the night of the Joe Louis-Billy Conn fight. We listened on the radio that carried big events from the States. Prize fighting was not my preference, but I did win $15 on a pool bet of the fight. I will forever hold dear Roger in my memories, as he was one of the best friends I had during those days.

The only landing I have not mentioned was Tampico, Mexico. Besides seeing many oil fields, I recall a passenger who complained of a lost gold tooth that he had left on his meal tray. Commissary in Tampico searched every tray without success. I had to file a "lost claim" report when the passenger said it was broken off by something in the food. He bore a gold, toothy grin, revealing lots of spare "nuggets". Well, now, I wonder?

When I got transferred to Miami, it was hard to believe that over a year had passed since I trained there. On arrival at the 36th St. Airport, I waited for Frannie to come for me. There was much activity compared to quieter Central America. PAA held a predominant spot in the Miami International Terminal, with planes lined up destined to Buenos Aires, Panama and Nassau. I watched the actor Edward G. Robinson check in for a Havana flight. He was not the ugly man pictured in the movies but had a sense of humor and was friendly and smiling.

Waiting for Frannie, I sat and reminisced over my first days in Miami. Our training was in the Coconut Grove area, close to the Dinner Key Airport. The latter was used by PAA for its seaplanes, whose days were numbered towards the end of the war when they flew New York to Lisbon via Trinidad. If weather was really bad in New York, the seaplanes were held in Dinner Key. We were given time from classes to visit those impressive seaplane "Clippers". I could not imagine an aircraft being larger.

My daydreaming was interrupted when Frannie arrived. She was driving a car that belonged to her latest boyfriend. As we drove by Biscayne Bay, I reminded Frannie of all the LSTs and destroyer escorts that were moored the last time I was in Miami.

"They're gone now. It's all over," Frannie dejectedly reported. "Remember when Miami Beach was so crowded with military using the hotels for "Rest and Recreation"? Why, you could hardly walk down the beach without stumbling over some gorgeous guy."

"Which reminds me," I asked, "What ever happened to Clyde Whatshisname, whom you met at the Embassy party in Guatemala? You know, the one you were going to marry as soon as he proposed?"

"Oh, HIM? I changed my mind." Frannie answered and slipped into silence.

To switch subjects, I spoke about our latest raise in pay and recalled the day when we started flying at $140 a month, with free uniforms—as well as shots in tetanus, typhoid, and small pox. We laughed together and mused over being paid to be part of so much fun. Then Frannie told me about the stewards trying to form a Union. "Oh, I don't know about that," I replied. "I have no complaints."

Our address was a couple of blocks from the "old" Orange Bowl Stadium; so close we heard the shouting in the stands. Five of us lived in a downstairs duplex. Around the corner was an ice cream parlor that served the best hot fudge sundaes. How much I wanted to gain weight, particularly in the upper part of me, where Frannie had no problem. My roommates were an assortment, born or lived in the States as well as Latin America. Our cooking varied from western chili to southern fries, northern chowders to spicy Spanish dishes. Between flights we enjoyed sitting around in our nightwear until late morning with a pot of coffee as a battery charger, discussing every subject from various passengers to company personnel, personal ideas to opinions on men, of course. Carrie, the eldest at 25 years, was given the highest regard for her "aged" experience and knowledge. Oh, how I wanted to be "twenty-five."

My friend, Jean Weber, of the lost key episode, was "semi-engaged" to a Philadelphia intern (Whatever semi-engaged meant.) While visiting her family, Jean went to Philadelphia to see her old sweetheart before returning to Miami. On the train she sat next to a man who was also going to Philadelphia for rehearsing the wedding ceremony with his intended. When Jean and her new acquaintance reached the "City of Brotherly Love", they decided they were not in love with their respective paramours, but with each other. They decided to marry. They did, and moved to Quito, Ecuador. But back to flying ex-Miami. . . .

MIAMI FLIGHTS

Chapter 14

From Miami I first flew to Havana and Nassau on DC-3s, sometimes twice in one day to one or the other. A DC-4 flight took me back to Guatemala via Merida on which I had an exceptional passenger, a little Dachshund. Some DC-4s had a cargo section between the cockpit and passenger cabin. The dog was crated and placed in this area to avoid freezing in the cargo hole. He was so shaken from fear that I begged the captain to allow me to hold him. "Just for a minute," I pleaded. The minute grew longer as the little fellow cuddled, licked my arm, and had soft brown, expressive eyes. I was ready to quit before giving him up and asked to keep him in the warmer cabin. Permission granted I took the dog down the aisle while the co-pilot carried his cage, which we strapped in a back empty seat. For the rest of the flight the dog was mascot and friend to all. The event was omitted in the Log Book.

My initial trip to Rio de Janeiro began with a shuttle from San Juan, Puerto Rico, to New York City. DC-4s were used, which carried 54 passengers and two cabin attendants. My partner was one Jorge Lopez, an "old timer" who treated me kindly, but the captain made it clear that he did not favor women as crewmembers. I was to realize that PAA had truly been a "man's company"; women were still under scrutiny.

Our flight stopped at Camaguey, Cuba, and the Dominican Republic, before Puerto Rico. The captain gave me intimidating orders that promised a difficult trip. Fortunately, my old friend, Harry, from the "Casa" in Guatemala was on board. Harry, with his full red hair, gentle manner, and soft Georgia accent, was so different from the captain. Riding to the hotel in San Juan, the skipper announced there would be a "de-briefing" session upon arrival and all were to be present. When I asked Harry about the "rights" of a captain to demand our appearance, during rest time he and Jorge laughed.

"That's a crew party he's inviting you to," Harry advised.

"This means Captain Lyon has accepted you as a member of the crew," Jorge added.

"I won't go!" I said to Jorge and Harry. "I will take no more of his bullying." I was adamant and a "no-show" to the gathering.

It was a company ruling that no crewmember could drink alcohol within 24 hours of a flight departure. We were within legal limits. Drinking was a relaxing way to unwind, though maybe not a healthy one.

. In Puerto Rico we stayed at the Condado Beach Hotel on the oceanfront. There was no beach but a rough surf crashed against a rocky shore, waves of which kept me awake. It was the constant pounding of the water that was disquieting, as though an ominous warning. Sunshine brought calmness the next day and, before Harry departed, we strolled the area climbing rocks, taking pictures, playing volley ball, and enjoying the swimming pool. "This is great," I commented. Harry reminded me I was yet to see Rio de Janeiro.

I flew on the Clipper "Endeavor" for LaGuardia with the same crew, minus Harry who had proceeded to Brazil. New York at dusk revealed miles of lights and the outline of Manhattan skyscrapers. With the "Fasten Seat Belt" sign lit, Captain Lyon ordered that I come to the cockpit immediately. I unbuckled my seat belt and hurried forward, expecting an emergency, only to have him point out the Empire State Building. I wondered what had gotten into him.

We drove into Manhattan, piled in two taxis, which took an hour with all the traffic. Our hotel was the Collingwood, a half block off Herald Square on W.35th; an old place once used by Hollywood stars. I think I know why they left—the garbage truck before dawn created a racket louder than any street siren. I could sleep no more, so I dressed and walked to a coffee shop near by. The only place open; it gave me a clear picture of New Yorkers on a workday morning. The countermen and customers exchanged quips with no voice restraint. Food orders were taken fast, in a vernacular communication I could not even understand (There were no Menus.). I did not give an order immediately, so the counterman moved on. The brusque manner and accent was new to me. All around were people with heads buried in newspapers while consuming coffee and bagels. It seemed there must be big news, maybe another Titanic sinking. I was to learn that coffee, bagels, and newspapers in the morning were "de rigueur" in New York.

The counterman returned with a cup of coffee before I even spoke. Then he asked how I liked my eggs? I had not said a word about eggs. I often wonder what would have happened if I had ordered "grits". The whole scene typified New Yorkers as I came to know them—sometimes noisy, always in a hurry, often impatient, never too trusting, but mostly hiding a soft heart they believed dangerous to reveal. To me it was another world. That evening Jorge and I enjoyed the acclaimed musical, "Oklahoma".

As to male flight attendants, they were a mixed variety. Enjoying travel was an incentive, though some were professionals in the position. Others considered the job as a contact for future importing businesses or travel agencies. One became a priest; another started his own restaurant. Others became teachers or changed to management jobs. A few would activate and direct labor unions.

On flight departure I found Captain Lyon had mellowed to be most solicitous. He knew I liked to take movies so invited me to film our takeoff from the cockpit. I gratefully stood behind the pilots, filming the race down the runway. Heavy with a full passenger load, and fuel to carry us to San Juan, I was unaware that anything had gone wrong until I heard the captain say, "I've got it!" as he held the controls. Of all the luck, we had an engine failure on takeoff, a rare but dangerous time for such an occurrence. The captain had to make an instant decision whether to try to stop the plane, or continue. His judgment was based on what he felt was the only thing that could be done—get the aircraft in the air, as he would not be able to safely stop it. He strained to this objective with hands holding the wheel firmly, measuring by feel when the plane could lift all that metal and humanity. He could not pull too hard, nor give in an inch. The sound of the three engines' struggle was deafening, the tension almost painful. Gradually the huge craft began to rise, as we barely edged out over the seawall. Hugging only a few feet above the waters of the East River for an interminable time, as though we might drop in at any moment, little by little the plane winged into the air, creeping up for what seemed forever, until we felt the coolness of altitude. Perspiration peaked, but calmness in the entire crew, particularly the captain, gained my complete respect and admiration.

Once aloft I informed my passengers that we had to return to LaGuardia. We could not arrive immediately as we were too heavy to land safely. Fuel had to be dumped over the ocean. This gave some passengers plenty of time to bemoan the delay, and for me to ponder if I was a jinx in the cockpit. When we returned to the hotel, this time I attended the crew de-briefing party. It took place in the Collingwood Bar where other crews were present and the din of conversation centered on flight experiences. As I entered the room, Captain Lyon stared at me and smiled softly. This gave me an unexpected pleasure, but a strange foreboding as well.

RIO DE JANEIRO

Chapter 15

The following day I had a different cockpit crew for an eleven-hour flight to San Juan on the Clipper "Bonita". While in the galley, Jorge and I sang melodies from "Oklahoma". Somehow my spirit was not in the singing, yet I refused to believe my feelings. Could I possibly be missing that "Lyon" and his taunting manner?

Our stay in San Juan was short, leaving early the next day for Port of Spain and then on to Brazil. It was another eleven-hour flight, plus a couple of hours in Trinidad at the Piarco Airport. As we crossed the Equator, just north of Belem, the pilots forced a dip in the plane's glide to pretend we were crossing "over the Equator". The initiates would sign a statement for their membership "into the Empyrean Realm of His Exalted Majesty, Jupiter Rex". The passengers would later be mailed certificates to this effect.

Belem was once an active and affluent metropolis as a port for the rubber industry, until this pursuit was moved to the East Indies. The city lies at the mouth of the Amazon River, whose tributaries are so wide it took us a half-hour just to fly across them. The delta is really a confluence of the Amazon branches with other rivers meeting the ocean, spread out like fingers with currents in various shades of muddied water. Discolored flows extend for miles over the ocean before being absorbed into the Atlantic's blue.

While the males of my crew stayed at the PanAm staff house, I was accommodated at the Grande Hotel, to share a room with the stewardess on the northbound flight. After a period of chatting, I went to bed under the mosquito netting. Above was a ceiling fan and a table between us held bottled, drinking water. It was the only safe kind, though it tasted like Alka-Seltzer. When I awoke it was almost night. My first thought was "Where am I?" With nights spent in different countries, one could wake up a little confused.

It was 8:30 hours from Belem to Rio de Janeiro, a city as well known for its landscape as its carnival celebrations. We landed at Galleao Airport, located on an island just off the harbor, which required taking a short boat ride to the city (until a bridge was completed). A highlight was seeing a little Beachcraft plane park beside us on the tarmac. Out stepped Tyrone Power and Cesar Romero, famous movie stars of the era. As I stared at these handsome men from the plane, I cursed the fact that the windows were too dirty to see well and wrote a discrepancy in the maintenance section of the Log Book. From this excitement, the motor launch that carried us to shore, zigzagging between ocean going vessels, had an engine failure. The boat crew tied up to a rusty old barge to await rescue, as we waved to large and small ships sailing by. Maybe I helped a little by pointing my thumb like a hitchhiker. Some things Brazilians never missed, even from a distance. We got towed in to shore.

At the Riviera Hotel, the stewardess quarters were located on a high floor facing the Copacabana Beach and fabulous views. The well-photographed, black and white tiled sidewalk, with its waving, interlocking design, could be seen for blocks as it followed the beach. It was spring in the Southern Hemisphere; the ocean was a bit chilly but that did not stop us from lounging on the sand or taking a quick dip.

I met Hap and her pilot husband, Bob, who were now based in Rio. For the first time since Guatemala days, along with Harry, we were together. When Bob left on a Buenos Aires trip, I was driven around to see well-known spots—Sugar Loaf with its cable car, and the famous statue of Christ. Blocks of unfinished or unoccupied business and apartment buildings gave a haunting effect. There were areas of poverty where people lived in the flimsiest of huts and unsanitary conditions. Harry said that the whole of Brazil was going through a depression, with the tourist trade being slow to resume since the War.

Later we sat in the oceanfront patio of the hotel by a bubbling fountain. It must have been a popular gathering place, as many Brazilians occupied tables. Seated a while, I noticed a group of men glaring our way. They were like stone statues staring in a deliberate fashion and I could feel their eyes boring a hole in me. I was informed that this was a male custom in Brazil, particularly towards women who were alone or, in their opinion, a group in need of another man. Hap had grown used to this "custom", and laughed it off. (Still, it was nothing compared to Mexico City where we found men liked to literally pinch a woman's backside while walking in a crowd.)

Prior to dinner I turned on the shower and there was no water. NO WATER? The patio fountain was active and the ocean washed ashore. I called the desk clerk and was told that during certain hours of the day water would be turned off, due to a critical shortage. Here was one of the most desired cities to visit, a hotel next to a world famous beach, and I could not get enough water to clean my teeth. My plight was not half so bad as of a stewardess on the next day who was soaped up in the shower at the time the water went off—before due time too. She removed the soap with bottles of drinking water. So it was in 1946.

The next day I left on the Clipper "Dauntless" for Buenos Aires. Unfortunately, we returned to the airport "due maintenance" and sat there for several hours. Scheduling decided we should take the northbound flight, so we boarded the Clipper "Ariel" bound for Belem. I was disappointed to miss seeing Argentina.

As for frequent aircraft delays due to maintenance problems, I do not think I had many trips on piston planes that were without a delay somewhere, other than on the reliable DC-3. PanAm was quite sensitive to keeping a favorable safety record and the pilots were truly conscious of taking precautions. When troubles arose, PanAm aircraft did not have a St. Louis, Denver, or a close place to land for help. We crossed oceans, jungles, deserts, mountainous terrain, even unfriendly territories, and thousands of miles where no airports existed.

I returned to Miami from my first trip to Rio. The second day back, my roommates and I attended a meeting of PanAm flight attendants who gathered to discuss possible Union affiliation. Being connected with the C.I.O. did not seem palatable. Would the Union understand us? They would "fight" for us, we were told; discussion went on and on, pro and con. Much ended in argument and we went home feeling more disloyal than satisfied.

BUENOS AIRES AND BACK

Chapter 16

Finally I was scheduled to go to Buenos Aires, a seventeen-day trip. However, a San Juan/New York shuttle again preceded flying into South America. I spent two days in the big city, enjoying the Ice Follies, the Museum of Modern Art, and a store called "Macys, Next to Gimbals". In an age before shopping malls, the latter was as exciting as a toy shop to a child. In the evening I joined friends to hear "Bob Crosby and His Bobcats" at a popular nightclub.

The next day we flew to Port of Spain, Trinidad, in 11:45 hours before stopping for crew rest. At the Staff House that had been rebuilt by PAA to accommodate crew and passengers since seaplane days, we were serviced by immaculately dressed, young boys in uniform, rigidly observant and quick to handle our requests. One boy would stand behind each seated diner at mealtime, in personal assignment. They were the descendants of people from India, indentured many years ago to work in the fields.

Trinidad was overnight before flying on to Belem. After a brief stay at the mouth of the Amazon, we flew the Brazilian coastal route. We stopped for fuel at Recife, a picturesque little town with a beautiful beach, and then overflew Bahia, after which was named the famous song. In Rio I visited the hotel beauty parlor, deciding to sit in comfort and have my hair washed without worry of sufficient water.

"Madame, how shall I style you so?" I was asked.

"So," I replied, pointing to a picture on the wall—an upsweep hairdo. I was treated as though I were a rich American with nothing but time and money. Later the hairdresser looked at me with pride, saying, "May you have a lovely evening." Then I rushed up to my room to get some sleep before my flight. Bobby pins kept my new waves in place but I could not wait to toss that uniform hat in the overhead rack of the aircraft.

There was no such thing as bidding for flights, with or without seniority. You went where Scheduling sent you. Buenos Aires, Argentina, generally called B.A., was a favored trip. The flight time from Rio, with a stop in Montevideo, Uraguay, was just short of seven hours. I arrived in October, their springtime, and stayed at the City Hotel. Here was a metropolis on a grand scale with impressive boulevards, buildings, monuments, and the same quick pace and diversity of ethnic backgrounds as New York. Buenos Aires, not Latin, European, or American, yet a mixture of all, is strictly Argentina, with its own style and character. Though Latin-American countries may have some different words for the same meaning (as the Americans and British with their "elevator" and "lift"), the Argentines articulate the Spanish language their own particular way.

My day began with a dish of the recommended, local strawberries and cream, followed by a walk to observe the sights. I took a carriage ride through the zoo and a jaunt on the subway, whose walls bore artwork en lieu of ads and graffiti. As Argentina is a land of beef and dairy products, our steward led us to dinner at the impressive "Corrientes Once" restaurant. When customers walked in the door they pointed to their choice from an iced showcase holding large slabs of beef. Tables were shown after wine selection. We enjoyed a variance in flavor from American beef, but delicious.

On my next shuttle to B.A., I joined my crew's wishes to go to the horse races. I had never followed the "ponies". Now I could say I had been to the races—in Buenos Aires! "Here they come!" "There they go!" That was it. I could hardly even see the horses. That evening we dined in the restaurant, "La Cabana", where two cows greeted us, that had been handled by a capable taxidermist. Steaks were brought to our table on hand-carry, grill pans with burning charcoals. After a few years of a beef-scarce war, we Americans ordered champagne to celebrate our recovery.

The steward, Dave, controlled the aircraft cabin, justifiably so, as I was new to the area. However, females being senior to men had not been fully recognized, as single traveling women was not favorably accepted in some Latin countries. Although men led the Union, as men controlled the Company, they began to foresee that the growing number of females would make a mark on the airline.

While in Rio I slept off the enjoyable Buenos Aires days. Who but a stewardess would spend all her time in Rio de Janeiro just sleeping? When I extended my energies in one place, I had to catch up on rest at the next stop. Confinement at high altitude for long periods of time, particularly without pressurization, could be exhausting; improper rest was devastating.

In Belem we were entertained by a friend of Dave's who was in the export business. He had an attractive penthouse with a view of the city and entertained us graciously. We watched a beautiful sunset from his balcony. Our host suggested that before dining we should have a drink at a particular spot he wanted us to see.

"A favorite hangout for Errol Flynn," we were informed en route. The taxi driver took us to a quiet neighborhood with one distant street lamp.

"Wait here," said our host, as he knocked upon the door of an insignificant looking building. The driver was uneasy and revved his engine to leave when no one answered. Carol, the other stewardess, and I were both feeling a bit reticent. "Perhaps it's closed," we said. Just then the door creaked ajar and partially revealed an older woman who asked what we wanted, as she looked at a party of men with two girls. Our host spoke to her in Portuguese until the woman conceded to allow us entrance. She backed up to a badly lit hallway while twirling a set of keys around her fingers. This is not real, I thought.

The end of the dark hall opened to a large room with occupants seated as in a restaurant. Tables had red checkered covers and candles. Music came from a nickelodeon by a small dance floor. We sat down trying to act unaffected and blase. Across the room were three elderly men, well dressed in white suits, each with a young female. Our drink orders were taken and delivered by a younger woman who scrutinized the males in our group. Few words were spoken as we each turned our glasses in place on the table. A chubby, "busty" girl in bright orange pantaloons kept her eyes on one of the pilots. First she crossed the room, back and forth, as though she had something to do on the other side, yet moving her body in seductive fashion. The girl who had delivered our drinks talked to another pilot and lightly touched her body against his shoulder. To these women it was as if Carol and I were not there. Each movement of the "girls" was enacted like a stage rehearsal, though almost in boredom. Our pilots nudged closer to Carol and me; perhaps we provided their excuse for being "unresponsive".

Suddenly the Madame appeared with her keys and led a man from the room with his partner, young enough to be his daughter. Their departure was as casual as if they were going to the food line in a cafeteria. From the hallway came the sound of a door shutting. Carol and I looked at each other with the same uneasiness.

We were about to depart when in walked a young girl who astonished us with her delicate beauty. She entered unobtrusively and with such a regal bearing and gentility of manner that, had she been seen anywhere, her appearance was noticeably outstanding. She was simply dressed, wearing little makeup. Her features held pale skin, clear and youthful, with hair a glistening black. She made no advancement towards anyone and sat alone, seeming in a trance. Only once did she turn her head and look over to our table. I gazed into the most pathetic eyes I had ever seen. Her look expressed a thousand words of despair. She made no overtures, as though she had been ordered to show herself, then disappeared as quietly as she came.

Who was she? Where did she come from? Later we were told

how young girls, often of aristocratic families, could be branded, ostracized and abandoned if they lost their virginity, committed adultery, or loved anyone not accepted by their family. Whether or not this was her plight, I will never know, but I cannot believe that "house" was her intended, or desired, destiny.

The next day we flew back to San Juan for the warmth of the swimming pool. I shall always remember that trip and the tragic eyes of a tortured soul. She epitomized the luck of circumstances, deserving no honors, but no discredits either.

SAN JUAN—NEW YORK SHUTTLES

Chapter 17

Just when summer was upon Rio and Buenos Aires, I was assigned shuttles to New York. I had hoped that my seniority would improve and enable me to return below the equator. However, in San Juan I could enjoy the swimming pool and take pictures. This time I filmed the Morro Castle, which sits high on a rocky cliff at the entrance to the harbor. From the parapets one can envision the galleons sailing towards the island centuries ago. The clear air and bright sun offer excellent color photography.

Before PAA qualified to fly via Bermuda, our route to New York was non-stop over Charleston, Richmond and Washington, D.C. This made the flight a little longer, but the layovers too. In the big city I had the good fortune to see the play "Harvey", with Josephine Hull and Frank Fay; then the King Cole Trio and Stan Kenton's orchestra. To browse through Fifth Avenue stores was "the" thing to do. So with uniform overcoats in the cold, Libby McPherson, a Miami roommate, and I went shopping for needed apparel, new bathing suits.

On one departure from New York, an experience occurred with Clipper "Aurora" that could not have endeared our passengers. We returned to the terminal three times because number three engine failed—once, from the end of the runway and twice, after feathering it in the air. We retreated to the hotel and departed the following day. A different aircraft, the Clipper "Defiance", took eleven and a half hours to San Juan and not one passenger from the day before had cancelled.

Arriving at Puerto Rico with roughness in my throat, I feared flying again with a cold. I shared a room with a stewardess who was being treated for dysentery. When the doctor came, he gave us the same pills. Whatever the medicine, it cured me, and the dysentery girl lived to survive what was really an inflamed appendix. I have often wondered what those cure-all pills could have been, for antibiotics were still in the experimental stage.

The next day I left to go north. It was November. The weather was colder in New York and fog settled in. We arrived over the airport and waited with other aircraft in "stacks", circling until granted permission to land. Immigrations, Public Health, and Customs took hours to expedite the traffic jam. LaGuardia Airport had become too small to handle the volume of flights. Passengers sat in the plane until entry rooms cleared within the building. A generator was attached to the aircraft to operate the heating system and prevent the waiting passengers from freezing. At times the generators would break down, or there were not enough for all aircraft.

The field closed several times before we were able to leave New York again. It was back and forth, returning first to the Henry Hudson Hotel, or the Biltmore, then the Collingwood. Driving to and from the airport was more tiring than the flight itself. On the last airport arrival, the captain peered through the fog saying, "I can only see the tail of our plane from here, hope to h— we can take off." When we finally did leave LaGuardia, we had to feather an engine over Philadelphia and return again. We used another plane and still arrived in San Juan with rough engines.

"Why so much engine trouble?" I asked the co-pilot.

"Would you believe we've been using Army surplus engines, and none of them are any good," he responded. It seemed to me that with all the assistance PAA gave the U.S. Army during World WarII, we did not deserve favors like that.

On a subsequent shuttle to New York, I met friends of Libby's and went to see Charlie Spivak at the Hotel Pennsylvania. I remembered this band from a prom dance in school days. (Spivak was known to travel from campus to campus, particularly where there was R.O.T.C., training students for the armed forces.) Prior leaving for San Juan, I saw Lunt and Fountain in "Oh, Mistress Mine", followed by a walk around Times Square. New York was growing on me; it oozed with attractions. When I finally returned to Miami, I wrote my parents that now I was called a "Purser", and would make $250 a month. I had also received a retroactive check of $212 after a Company/Union settlement.

My next trip was with the roaring Captain Lyon. His attitude had changed, showing concern about the slightest problem that I might have. He ordered that he be kept informed of "whatever might be difficult for the flight attendants". In New York, my crew and another went to "Captain of the Seas Restaurant" for dinner. Somehow there were enough raw oysters and swordfish steaks for all of us. Up until that time I had only enjoyed oysters fried or in my mother's pie and stew. Eating them raw was the captain's idea. "From Louisiana, and you don't eat raw oysters!" he bellowed. So I tried them and was hooked. After dinner we saw the movie, "The Razor's Edge" at the Roxy Theater, with Tyrone Power. It was a fun evening for all.

In San Juan I tried another new adventure. On the top floor of the Condado Beach Hotel was a gambling casino. I had grown up in New Orleans within a mile of a Jefferson Parish casino, without having been there. This night I did not want to hear "never had raw oysters, never been in a casino, and you're from New Orleans!" (How I wanted to say, "But I've visited a *whore* house," as I thought of my experience in Belem.) While the pilots dropped dollars at the crap table, we girls won on the roulette wheel. Later our chagrined and envious skipper said, "Don't you know you're the bait? Good-looking girls draw the suckers, so they give you a few dollars. Those tables are fixed!"

"My skill and ability caused me to win," I replied. The "Lyon" laughed and unabashedly kissed me. "Oh, damn!" I thought, alarmed at the enjoyment of it.

In New York it was snowing. This was a bigger thrill than raw oysters. Where I grew up, it only snowed every 30 years. I just had to walk in the snowflakes. "Wait for me," sounded a familiar roar. I feared to hear that voice, yet could not deny it delighted me. We walked together through the snow, as he held me to prevent my slipping and talked about his college days. The freezing cold gave me an undeniable earache, so he insisted we stop in a nearby coffee house to get warm. There he led me to a partially enclosed booth. I felt pleasure with his nearness and warmth when he did not sit opposite, but beside me. However, there was that awful foreboding feeling.

"Captain Lyon . . ." I started to speak, as his arm around me replaced the cold.

"Please, call me Norton," said my skipper in a soft voice, so unlike his usual vocal tone. He kissed my wet cheek where a snowflake had fallen. With my chin in his hand he turned my face near to his.

"Yes, Norton," I whispered. "But please don't kiss me again. Please. You see, I know—I mean, I'm aware—I—well—I . . ." How could I say that I knew he was married—it might sound so childish, and he did not mean anything by that kiss, I tried to tell myself. At that moment the waiter came. I looked towards the outside window and saw it had stopped snowing.

Back to San Juan I met Frannie who told me of another disappointment she had with the opposite sex. I was unable to tell her I was feeling "confused" myself. We played Gin Rummy as we shared a pitcher of martinis, a drink that potently affected me. Enjoying our "girl talk", we planned on room service and retiring early. Frannie related how she met some tennis players in Barranquilla where a worldwide tournament was held. One of the famous players took Frannie's heart, until she learned he was married.

"Oh, Frannie," I said, "Don't you know when they're married you've got to run—yes, run, get away. . . ."

"I know," she replied. "You run until you trip over something that turns out to be your own stupid heart. Then you fall and break your . . . head."

Just at that moment the telephone rang and it was "Flight Ops" looking for a volunteer to work a trip to New York. Someone became sick within an hour of pick-up time. No one could be found to take the trip until Frannie answered the phone.

"Draw a card for who goes," said Frannie, jokingly.

"No," I answered, "I'll take it."

"You can't, you've had too many Martinis. We'll tell Flight Ops the truth."

"No, I want to fly. I can't explain it, but I must leave from here now," I adamantly insisted.

"Who are YOU running from?" Frannie asked.

I left and slammed the door. It was not the smartest thing I ever did. I met my new crew in the hotel lobby where they had waited for me. "Well," I said, bravery showing through the martinis, "I guess I'm pretty important." Later it was the crew who gave me coffee. I will never know how I survived. Working the galley I truly suffered in the swaying tail of that aircraft.

A week before Christmas I left New York for San Juan and landed instead at Washington D.C., where it took two days to acquire new engines before ferrying to Miami. We stayed at the Willard Hotel and hoped for an end to maintenance problems. In the meantime, it was marvelous to see the Smithsonian Institute. On arrival in Miami I had accumulated enough time to go home for Christmas.

REBELS AND RADICALS

Chapter 18

My brother finally came home after years of destroyer duty on the Pacific Ocean. It seemed I had not seen him since childhood. We recalled the days we went sailing on Lake Pontchartrain, when we tried to pick up watermelons that fell off barges crossing the Lake. The melons would float, roll around when you tried to get a hand on them, and were harder to capture than using your teeth to get apples from a water barrel. Our father had purchased an old cat-boat half buried in the sand at Biloxi, Mississippi. He rigged it, painted the hull, and launched the boat himself. My brother learned to sail before his days in the Navy, but being in the engine room of a destroyer was a little different.

I was fortunate to get another trip to New Orleans with a two-day layover, working my way on a DC-4 trip via Panama. When I left New Orleans, we stopped in Guatemala for what became a frightening experience, witnessing a militant attitude from the moment we stepped off the airplane. Customs men spoke in a wretched manner, pounced on our bags with double inspection, and refused to let us take anything to the hotel. Our luggage had to remain in quarantine for further spraying, they said. I was told my camera would be confiscated, as I had no "papers" for it. "Take my clothes, but not my camera," I thought. Men in uniform raced around in irrational movements, making loud comments.

"What's going on?" I asked the captain. "It's like a revolution around here."

"That's about the size of it," he replied. "But don't anyone raise a fuss. Stay calm." PanAm ground employees hurriedly put us in a taxi.

At the hotel I bathed and put my uniform back on again. At least I would be dressed for whatever might happen. Nothing more did occur and I awoke the next morning still in uniform. I did retrieve my camera, but my heart felt heavy when the plane took off. The United States had offended Guatemala in some way.

"The trouble has to do with bananas," said our co-pilot.

"Bananas!" I cried.

"Yes, bananas. I believe our government sided with American fruit companies in their disagreement with the folks here. They're pretty riled up over it."

Just as the crew represented the airline, Pan American was a badge for the United States. Even the airline name was symbolic. Whatever our government politics or policies, PanAm received the heat of any foreign disagreement. Our DC-4 had a heavy load on leaving the area of discontent, including children squeezed in as "babies". More people remained, unable to get a seat. We landed in Managua and then on to Panama. From Balboa we returned to Miami via Barranquilla, Colombia, and Kingston, Jamaica. Passenger loads were full and we were kept quite busy. When our pilots pointed out Errol Flynn's yacht sitting in the Kingston harbor, it was the only moment of diversion.

Further unsettling news greeted me in Miami. When I walked into the house there were suitcases, boxes, and foreign purchases scattered everywhere. I learned we had to vacate our duplex and find another place to live. The landlord wanted a lease, which in our case was prohibitive. We were never sure where we might be in 24 hours, much less six months. Libby and Babs decided to transfer to New York. The Latin American Division had opened a crew base to handle flights from the big city to South America, via Puerto Rico. (This caused dissension with those who preferred to live in Miami and did not want to lose Rio and Buenos Aires trips to another base.) Carrie, Frannie and I found a furnished cottage for $150 a month, complete with fruit trees we never got to enjoy.

Our glorious life did have drawbacks—always the uncertainty of where we would live next. No sooner was I unpacked when I was called to work flights out of New York on a temporary assignment, until sufficient permanent transfers took place. Thinking I would fly to South America, I arrived to learn the trips were still only as far as San Juan.

After one shuttle, I spent three days in New York. There was much snow and flights were either delayed or cancelled. I met Babs and Libby who were adjusting to their new base. Babs, quite knowledgeable of the area, introduced me to her friends who were members of the New York Athletic Club's water polo team. We double and tripled-dated; taking in spots all over Manhattan. One night we saw the musical, "Burlesque". New York held a plethora of things to see and do. I was ready to transfer permanently. Carrie decided to go to San Francisco and Frannie to New York. I said, "Me too, I want New York." We submitted our bids.

On one of my last flights ex-Miami, I arrived at the airport to see that the skipper would be the "Lyon Captain". I trembled from the weakness I felt around him, but was unavoidably elated too. As an interim stop to Puerto Rico, our flight included Port au Prince, Haiti, where the natives crowded the airport fence to sell their wares, particularly the beautiful woodwork. When we boarded the aircraft to leave, number two engine refused to cooperate. The night was spent in Haiti waiting for a magneto to be sent from Miami.

Port au Prince was so hot it would make Panama seem like a refrigerator. We stayed at the Grand Hotel Oloffson, located high on a hill overlooking the city at sea level. Built as a home for the President of Haiti, it was later bought by a Norwegian ship captain who converted it. Our rooms opened to a veranda where old bamboo rocking chairs lined the balcony. It seemed the only cool spot in town. Even the swimming pool was too warm. We all sat rocking in the light breeze that barely existed, ordering rum drinks from little Haitian boys. They spoke both French and English with a lilting, Creole patois. As the evening progressed, the boys' services were dismissed and each crewmember left for his room. When I stood up to leave, Captain Lyon asked me to stay until he finished his drink. I chastised myself later because I did not want to leave him. The two of us sat there in the darkness, looked out upon the lights of the city, and listened to rhythmic drums beating in the distance. The lights were less electric than burning fires used for cooking. One by one each flickering fire disappeared, as fireflies in the night. Only the cicadas were heard.

"The fires are going out," I said, in a weak remark to break the silence.

"But not mine," he replied, as he moved to the railing and faced me. For seconds I could not move.

"Oh, Norton." I rose to leave, run away, or fall towards him—perhaps all three. He made the decision for me. I could no more deny my feelings than prevent air to my lungs. At the end of the porch a screen door squeaked upon opening. The co-pilot came out to smoke a cigarette. It was just the interruption needed to regain our "sanity". We parted with a quiet "good night". Alone, I cried, "Oh, God, this can't be happening. Why?" Then, as though the Captain of the Universe was not aware, I prayed, "Lord, you know he's married, don't you?"

The next day we ferried the aircraft to San Juan. As we had no passengers, I sat behind the pilots in the cockpit while we circled Christophe's Citadel. This Haitian castle is 50 miles from the ocean, high on a hill. With its incredible architecture, it was built by a man who called himself Henry the First, and ruled Haiti like a king. He did not last long, committing suicide—no one had bothered to attack his fortress. I watched Norton manipulate the aircraft; captivated by his strong hands controlling all those switches, gauges and equipment, as though I had never seen them handled before. My mind was not operating on all cylinders. I had even left my camera in my suitcase.

From San Juan with a full passenger load, for which I was grateful to be kept busy, I arrived in New York. I met Libby and Babs who had located an apartment near the Soldiers and Sailors

Monument; a place for me to live too, as soon as my transfer came through. The apartment was reasonably furnished, a temporary situation, as the owners were away in the Adirondacks for only four months. We could all be married within four months, if not transferred again. Or we could die with broken hearts.

L.A.D. NEW YORK

Chapter 19

By May of 1947 I had moved to New York. Our place on W.89th was large enough for seven stewardesses. That is, there were six beds and the last one in got the couch. Only once was this a problem as we were not all home at the same time. The apartment was spacious with three bedrooms upstairs, a huge living room, and a library empty of books. The long, dining room table had a foot buzzer that called to whomever was in the butler's pantry. Last one seated was the designated butler. We took turns being cook and house cleaner; the clarity of that plan of equity lasted about a week. Someone always had an excuse—going on flight or tired on arrival. Few days were spent without a party or guests, which made life fun but difficult to get sleep. The arrangement did not last four months; we learned that the percentage of women living together in harmony decreased with the more involved.

Rio and Buenos Aires trips were expected with the LAD-New York base that never materialized. Instead, we went back and forth to San Juan like a yo-yo. It was not the most desirable trip, as many Puerto Ricans did not adjust well to air travel. Sickness aloft was ever present, weather was not always cooperative, and the frequency of troubled engines was a plague upon us. For my June vacation, I went home.

My parents were slightly worried about my many moves. "Settle down in one spot," said my father. "Put your roots somewhere." As much as I loved and revered him, he was not the type of man with whom I could easily discuss my inner feelings. My father always had my best interests at heart, but he was a very practical man. My mother could laugh or cry with me; however, she was of another age, with an innocence that made me want to protect her from any pain I might cause her.

There was one variation in my flights—Bermuda shuttles. Bermuda was the honeymooner's paradise. Flying over, the plane filled with gaiety, champagne, and moonstruck lovers. Returning, the cabin could be much quieter. On one trip I carried a pair that argued all the way home—"Strike one!" Another couple hardly said a word to each other the whole way back—"Strike two!" Most held hands and/or slept all the way. I also had the well-known radio and film stars, Fred Allen, and his wife, Portland. They were not obvious comedians as they carried serious reading material. I learned from celebrities I met that most good comedians *are* intellectuals. I also enjoyed meeting Arthur Murray, the famous dance instructor, a delightful man, modest, sensitive, and so timid I wondered how he ever asked anyone to dance. The only time we could have a layover in Bermuda was if the weather was a problem or aircraft maintenance was required. The first time I stayed at a Bermuda lodging, the termites let me know that I was in their dining room. Perhaps the whole place has now been eaten away.

In San Juan I met Bob Hope. My stewardess and I were to fly on the aircraft from which he disembarked. He showed his famous "eye for the girls", with complimentary remarks, as he stopped to talk to us. It was five in the morning, yet he was as entertaining and alert as ever on film. I have heard he pays four writers for his jokes but I do not believe he needs any. Hope is a natural comedian. He took the captain for $150 playing gin rummy and made him write a check to charity.

On another flight from San Juan I had the Herbert Hoover, Jrs., a lovely couple, who were low key and unassuming. On the same plane was Henry R. Luce, editor of *Time* and *Life* magazines. He was not a man to befriend easily and was left alone. Arriving in New York, he was perturbed at having to adhere to the same customs regulations as others and angered when those who met him could not handle this for him.

Back again to Puerto Rico, I was checking in at the Condado Beach Hotel when handed a note that tersely said, "You're wanted in the bar. That's an order." It made me smile because I knew of only one person who would say he wanted me, in command form. En route to the elevator I passed the bar entrance and saw crewmembers gathered together with the "Lyon Captain". Our eyes met and could not conceal a mutual feeling. He motioned for me to enter but I indicated that I would have to change from my uniform. In the elevator a voice within me sent a warning. Another voice said it would not hurt to be together in a group. An uncontrollable part of me denied any reasoning.

By the time I came downstairs again, the crews were waiting on the sidewalk to leave for dinner. Since Norton was not with them, I walked back to find him. He was sitting at the bar with a tall drink in front of him and another one I learned was for me.

"Norton," I said, "they're waiting for us. The taxis are coming."

"I'm not hungry. Sit and join me in a drink."

"I'm not thirsty. Please let's have dinner?" I saw he had enough to drink.

After a moment, feeling exhilarated but drained of strength, I moved to leave. He paid for the drinks and caught up with me just as the taxis arrived.

From dinner we all returned to the hotel lounge. I parted from the group to sit and play a few classical pieces on the piano. Norton sat beside me on the bench. After listening quietly, he said, "I might have guessed this about you." Words came from his lips so incongruous to his nature. He began to recite poetry, verses of hopeless love. I wanted to cry. There was no rhyme for the aching in my heart.

I returned to New York to enter a dark apartment. Only the light from the hallway showed the switch. When I flicked it, I heard, "turn off the light!" In the flash before doing so, I noticed several of my roommates looking out the window. When I walked closer I saw what they were observing. Across the street in the apartment building opposite ours, with window blinds open on this hot night, was a couple slowly removing each other's clothing as they intermittently embraced.

"Ooo, step three," giggled one of the girls. Then as the woman slid to the bed, the man drew the shades.

"Damn!" shrieked Frannie, "Just when it was getting good." At that moment Libby came downstairs and remarked, "Would you really watch other people in the sex act?"

"Who's for a late night snack?" asked Frannie, as she walked to the kitchen.

DECISIONS, DECISIONS

Chapter 20

We left our place on the West Side. Four of us moved to Jackson Heights, an area on Long Island closer to the airport but not too far from Manhattan. Frannie was not one of the four. A hometown friend in the Air Corp visited me and asked if one of my roommates would accept a blind date with his buddy. Frannie was available and the four of us had a magnificent time going to the Copacabana, 21 Club, and spots in Greenwich Village. It was a fantastic evening, but when we returned home, Frannie became strangely too quiet.

"What's the matter?" I asked.

Softly she said, "I'm going to marry that guy."

"Oh, Frannie. Not again. Rest on the idea, will you?"

She did mean it; she did marry him. In fact, I walked her to the altar as she whispered, "damn aisle's longer than a runway." The nuptials took place in a small church of lower Manhattan with only a few people present. Frannie had no family but wanted a church wedding. "Gonna get my man in a church, by God!" she exclaimed. She wore a blue suit-dress and looked more beautiful than I had ever seen her. When she left I missed her, even her profanity. She settled to the life of her husband's military career.

On several trips I had trouble getting back to LaGuardia because of the weather. We flew in stack arrangement, circling at different altitudes with soupy overcast. Visibility could be so poor the wing tips were obliterated. On one such arrival I went to the cockpit to confirm the crew's liquid needs and heard cursing to make even Frannie blush. Through contact with ground control, the pilots had heard that there was a small airplane in the vicinity with defective instruments and was unable to identify its location. It was possible for any of the stacked airliners to have a midair meeting with the lost craft. To complicate matters, our captain accidentally left the switch on to the cabin speakers, inadvertently letting the passengers hear what was going on. We had to calm a few people as we rocked around in the rough air. It seemed an interminable time until landing safely.

When next in San Juan, the sickness of a Miami attendant enabled me to take her trip to Belem, a 10:30 hour flight. I was hopeful of a chance to fly on to Rio and perhaps enjoy their Mardi Gras. Instead I was able to see a Belem street festival with my crew, where we joyously participated with the crowds. With so little sleep, only as a young person could my body have taken the punishment I gave myself in staying awake. On return it took almost 14 hours to get from San Juan to New York. Bad weather had forced a landing in Washington D.C. Immigrations and Customs did not expect us and were most distressed over our 4 a.m. arrival. Government formalities always took place at the first port of entry to the U.S., not Puerto Rico, and our flight had originated in South America. With a full load, mostly passengers who did not speak English, we waited for the officials to come to the airport and "accept" us legally. Hours later our plane finally reached LaGuardia.

In 1947 there would be 25 inches of snow to paralyze Manhattan and much of the East Coast. Libby and I were invited to Massachusetts for Christmas with Babs and her family. We took the train to stop near their home, a 170-year-old house in the country, decorated with the spirit that resembled so many pictures of Christmas in New England. Babs' mother greeted us with milk and mincemeat pie as soon as we arrived. She had baked nine pies that morning and prepared the finest Christmas dinner. Later we waded through waist high snow to see lambs in the barnyard, warm in their natural covering. I asked to help shovel the house entranceway but after a foot of that, I lost interest; the drifts of snow must have reached over half my height. A thrill to remember was our ride across the fields in a horse drawn, 19th century sleigh, with bells on the bridle. How little time separated our swimming in Puerto Rico to enjoying the snow in New England.

A couple from Boston, trying to drive to Florida, got stuck on a nearby road. Babs' parents kindly offered them a room for the night. It was in their car that we attempted to drive back to Manhattan, both on the Merritt Parkway and the old Post Road. When the car spun out of control, we were glad to get to the train, the only available transportation that was moving anywhere.

My 1948 New Year's resolution was to leave LAD New York and transfer to the Atlantic Division for new, glamorous routes. However, I was informed I had to speak a European language. My high school French was almost forgotten and Spanish was unacceptable. PanAm did not fly to Spain then. I knew how weak my Spanish was but decided to "hit a long iron" and file a Union Grievance. My contention was that Spanish was indeed a European language, in which I had qualified on being hired, and many passengers spoke Spanish who crossed the Atlantic. I won my Grievance but could not transfer until July.

One spring morning I received a call from the "Lyon Captain". He was an avid fan of the Brooklyn Dodgers and had three tickets to see the afternoon game. I was asked to join him and a friend. "Ah," he said, in a happy way, "not only will there be three of us, but thousands at the game, so I cannot possibly attack you." I had to laugh and agreed to go. When we met, the friend was a "no show". But it was a thrill to visit old Ebbetts Field, have hot dogs and cold drinks, listen to the yelling fans, the crazy Dodger band in the stands, and watch the great play of Jackie Robinson, Duke Snyder, PeeWee Reese, etal. Norton roared in his excitement and, before I knew it, I was screaming too. One thing puzzled me and I asked, "why do the fans cheer a Dodger when he makes a hit, but boo him when he doesn't?"

"It's the Dodger way," he said, "but you still love the Bum. Remember that." Suddenly a chill wind blew across the stands and I unconsciously shivered. Norton placed his arm around my shoulders to warm me. Eventually, when the Dodgers moved to the West Coast, the Brooklyn fans lost the team they worshiped. Would they ever forget their "Beloved Bums", and sever the pain from their hearts? They were to draw my empathy, for I too would know the feeling.

ATLANTIC DIVISION

Chapter 21

When I left the Latin American Division for the Atlantic Division in 1948, I had accumulated almost 2850 flight hours. The Atlantic Division had its own management and operating procedures, which in some ways made it seem like two companies bearing the same name. The Pacific-Alaska Division was the third part, which also had its own individuality. Crew uniforms were the same, though the women in Atlantic had black accessories (purse and shoes) while LAD had brown. Oddly enough, in the Atlantic we could wear short sleeve blouses that were not acceptable in the warm climates of LAD. Emblems on hat pins and breast wings bore a crest of the world, while those of LAD had a likeness of Central and South America (PanAm's original emblem). In Atlantic we wore fur-lined boots to walk across snow and icy tarmacs. (Aircraft were still boarded outside by mounted stairs; no covered tunnels or loading bridges existed. Large umbrellas were used to escort passengers during inclement weather).

Besides attending classes, to be able to fly with experienced pursers was a great help to learn the Atlantic Division. However, the inequity of male cabin attendants always being the one in charge, regardless of seniority, encouraged more females to attend Union meetings and expedite changes. If the Union took equal dues, we wanted equal regard. Transition to full acceptance of female pursers, without discrimination as to certain flights and areas, eventually came about. It took longer before having female supervision in the Atlantic Flight Service office.

One day I contacted my mother's cousin on Long Island. I had promised to do this but had procrastinated. Now I took the Long Island train and was met at the station by her husband, a retired Navy admiral who had commanded a large ship during World War II. My cousins asked if I had met Juan Trippe, President and founder of PanAm, and other leading figures of the airline. "Haven't had the pleasure," I replied, and thought how I probably never would. At least my "adventurous spirit" was complimented.

My first trip across the ocean was a flight to London in the Lockheed Constellation, affectionately called the "Connie". This was a sleek-bodied, triple-tailed aircraft with lines like a sailfish. It was pressurized and could carry passengers more comfortably than the DC-4. The crew had cockpit bunks and a large navigator's table, though their front windows were smaller than previous aircraft. Aft of this was the galley, enclosed in front of the passenger cabin. Flights were provisioned with frozen meals that came in two huge, rectangular containers—without affection, called "coffins".

One passenger on this flight was a government courier. Valuable papers were in a briefcase handcuffed to his wrist. Although he had permission to carry a gun, it had to be identified and kept by the captain in the cockpit, as were all weapons. Our route was up to Gander, Newfoundland, which served as a crew layover station as well as a fuel stop, 4:45 hours away. We left New York at night, but it was daylight on arrival. Being July, and quite far north, days became much longer. The flight was over many lakes, rocky shores and woodlands, far different from the Southern Hemisphere where I had been accustomed to flying. Hotel accommodations were former military barracks at the Gander Airport.

Gander has mostly a wintry weather, but this was a nice spring day. The crew invited me to join them in trout fishing. They were well prepared, bringing rod and reel from home. I knew nothing about rod casting, but at least I knew something about sailing. We rented a homemade rig, a large rowboat with jib and mainsail, an oar for a rudder, and ventured the waterways. The winds were so strong we only used the jib, or we might have crossed the Atlantic by boat instead of plane. We did catch some beautiful trout. Until then, I had only bayou-fished with hook, line, and bamboo pole. The trout were brought to the barracks kitchen where we cleaned them for our dinner.

In flight again, off the coast were several huge icebergs. As three-quarters or more of them were located below the surface, they were surrounded by a yellow-green color. Even from great height they appeared cold and awesome. The flight to London took just over ten hours. We first saw land about 50 minutes from Heathrow Airport.

The British allowed a special crew bus to take us from the aircraft to the customs area, and then in to London. There was no freeway and the drive into the city on the Great West Road took more than an hour. The gearshift on the bus had a grating noise to awaken anyone who fell asleep. Every mile or so we circled a roundabout, a small park area with a fountain or statue that slowed our travel. The long drive did enable me to see the city and people who were still economically strapped by the recent world conflict. We passed empty office buildings, closed stores, some with broken windows. It was a dismal sight that matched the overcast sky.

As London was five hours later than New York time, it was always a difficult decision whether to retire at their bedtime or to give in to body fatigue and collapse upon arrival. If the latter choice, it was possible to rise in the middle of the night wide-awake and hungry. It was 1948, and the dining room was not open 24 hours nor did late room service exist—at least not at the Green Park Hotel where we stayed. This led to our removing leftover snack food from the aircraft.

The hotel was located on Half Moon St., walking distance from Piccadilly, the theater and entertainment district, and across Green Park from Buckingham Palace. PanAm had provided a convenient location, but for accommodations it was lacking—our rooms had no baths. We had to walk up and down a maze of short, winding stairs and cold corridors to go to the toilet or shower.

There was no soap; you brought your own. The toilet paper was worthless, slick, and like gift-wrap tissue.

On my first visit, promptly at 7 a.m., there was a knock followed by a key opening the door to my room before I could ask who it was. In walked a husky looking woman with mop cap, carrying a tray.

"Mornin', 'ere's yer tea, miss."

"I didn't order tea," I said, a little groggy.

"Comes we yer room, miss."

Well, I had heard the expression "when in Rome . . .", but now I saw that when in England one better like tea as coffee was "chicory au lait"; the genuine was still a luxury.

As for London weather—it was many trips before I saw the sun, if only for a couple of hours; however, this historical city had so much to offer. Transportation was the underground subway, called the "Tube", and some of the old square-shaped, black "cabbies" that still roamed about. But I preferred the red double-deck buses. The ones with open, second-levels were ideal for sightseeing. You had to make your way up the spiral stairs in the rear while the bus was rolling. A conductor picked up fares after the rider sat down. In a couple of trips I learned how to safely climb those stairs and find a seat without falling.

Evidence of WWII was present in blocks leveled by the bombings, particularly around St. Paul's Cathedral. These areas were cleared and used as "car parks". Some partial building structures still stood, although most of the rubble had been cleared away. The skyline was a mass of chimneys. From years of burning coal for heat, buildings had that dark, smoky appearance which later on would take several years to completely clean. Fires from the bombings had only intensified the situation. People in the streets did not seem to be dressed in much better than rumpled, drab clothing, by American standards. Suits had been washed instead of dry cleaned for so long. Noticeable was the deplorable condition of people's teeth. Limited diets during years of war had taken its toll. The British had endured hard times during the conflict, and they held my great admiration for their moral strength.

The London "Bobbies" walked with our crew to show directions. We took a ride on the Thames in a boat that had been used for the exodus of troops at Dunkirk. Many school children were present wherever we visited—the Tower of London, Westminster Abbey, galleries and museums. I was impressed with the behavior of the youngsters, who were orderly, disciplined, and stood in line waiting their turn with remarkable patience.

In England, as the teapot was worshiped, tea drinking was a ritual. At 4 p.m., films were stopped in the theater and stage performances ceased. Lights came on and tea was sold down the aisle. In food shops you might get sandwiches smaller than the palm of your hand, with an invisible sliver of cheese, the proverbial "toe-ma-toe" and sprouts, but always plenty of hot tea.

During my first crossing in the Atlantic Division the flight time round-trip was just short of 30 hours. Back home, although plenty of soap was available, we could never wash the battleship gray out of our lingerie. The dust and dirt of New York put a permanent dark color to anything white. Thus it was, in the big city, on our side of the Atlantic.

Before my next flight, my brother visited New York to participate in a Navy Reserve meeting. He and a fellow officer took Libbie and me to the Stork Club. We met Sherman Billingsly, the owner, who impressed all the ladies with the gift of a vanity case. From dinner until after midnight, the food was excellent and the orchestra commendable for dancing. The bill was rather impressive too. It was a place to see at least once in a lifetime.

ACROSS EUROPE

Chapter 22

To be scheduled for Prague, Czechoslovakia, a new flight for PanAm, was particularly exciting. Prague was under Russian influence but somehow our government was able to get approval for PAA to fly there. I eagerly departed, loaded with suitcase, company briefcase, and two cartons of cigarettes said to be worth gold for purchasing merchandise.

Hurrying across the lobby at LaGuardia Airport, I twisted my ankle. I refused to believe that anything could stop me and continued despite the pain. It got worse as we flew to Gander. Eventually I was using the seat backs as crutches to get down the aisle and had to return to New York in agony. No Prague trip was ever offered to me again.

On my next trip across the Atlantic, we did not stop in Gander but Sydney, Nova Scotia, due to weather. If Sydney closed, we landed in Stephenville, or Moncton, New Brunswick. On one trip we landed, in a little place in Maine, so early in the morning that the cafeteria was empty of employees. I got permission to use their kitchen to fry eggs, bacon, and serve a hungry group of passengers and crew. (The captain signed the check.) We obtained enough fuel to fly as far as Shannon, Ireland, a duty free port that was extremely popular. Besides the marvelous meals in the airport dining room, which everyone looked forward to, the woolens, linens and lace were bargains; whiskey and liqueurs were a third less the price in the States.

In August of 1948, I flew to London when the 14th Olympiad

took place at Wembley Stadium. To partake of this event, our crew took the London Underground, the British subway, which later became an "overground" in the suburbs. Being American became quite obvious while on the train. I never realized how loud we sounded in comparison to the English, who sat silently reading or dozing as they held their black umbrellas. Going to the Olympics put us in an exulted mood but we quieted down when we realized the train was like a library we were disturbing.

First to the stadium, we saw the Men's Discus qualifying meet. Harrison Dillard did not race that day, only warm up. There was little excitement at the Stadium. The Britons did not cheer or yell for anyone. They softly clapped and said, "Very good". If their contender missed, they still lightly clapped and quietly said, "Too bad". We left to go to the pool for greater activity, where we saw the Men's 800 Meter, Swim Relay race in which the U.S. came in second to Hungary. We gave the boys our cheers. The next event was a Water Polo match between Belgium and Sweden. All I could see was one team trying to drown the other and end up in a tie anyway. In the afternoon was the best of the show—the U.S. had a young man by the name of Sammy Lee, whose dives off the high board were phenomenal. He brought home a few gold medals.

Back in New York, Libby had landed on a flight ahead of me and was being held in Customs. I learned that she had stood up to the customs men in their attitude towards the aircraft liquor check. From flights over the Atlantic, any opened bottles (broken seals) were confiscated by Customs, as they were tax-free fifths and could not be used again. Two customs men had taken some unopened bottles, broken the seals and removed them, under the pretense the bottles had been used already. Libby complained of this dishonest act. She was escorted away, with head held high, and "detained" two hours before being released—but she made her point.

Our little quartet was soon to break up. Carol decided to return to the Midwest and marry the hometown boy. Libby met a doctor with whom she wished to share her life. Babs, with the dancing eyes and broad "A" accent, planned marriage with one of our pilots. There were not many single pilots left. When women were taken on as flight crew, the single men were "gobbled up" almost before they could say, "Fire two!"

A childhood friend, Ellie Marshall, came to New York and I introduced her to our service manager. She was hired immediately. Ellie was over the height limit but was an attractive, blue-eyed blond, who made her viewers look at anything but her feet, upon which she wore flat shoes. We decided to find an apartment together until I was called for a Calcutta trip. PAA was going all the way to India, using five pilots, two engineers, a navigator and two cabin attendants. This time I was not going to race across floors and break anything. I was going to India—a 15-day trip in which I would accumulate 88 flight hours.

With hardly any time to see the changing of the guard at Buckingham Palace, I left London for Istanbul on the Clipper "Hotspur", a seven-hour flight. Though the "Connie" flew higher, we were able to clearly see the snow covered Alps, the Parthenon over Athens, and a ribbon that was the Corinth Canal. Istanbul took me within a waterway of Asia. From Istanbul's Airport, our driver spoke one language—SPEED. Again I encountered the reaction of taxi drivers to pilots. If a car had wings, ours would have taken to the air. Almost three days were spent in this interesting city. Without a daily round the world flight, we stayed until the next plane arrived.

The Hotel Konak entrance featured shoeshine men and boys with their small brass kits polished like gold, as valuable to them as a cowboy's horse. It was an old hotel; the lobby held the ancient caged elevator, rising from center floor.

Istanbul is built upon hills, with the surrounding Bosporus Strait dividing Europe from Asia, the Sea of Marmara, and the Golden Horn, which connects the old and new part of Istanbul by crossing the famous Galata Bridge. We visited the Sultan Ahmet Mosque (called the Blue Mosque for its coloring). As required before entering, shoes were removed. So many sandals looked alike, I wondered how people retrieved their own. Our American shoes were not hard to find. Youngsters almost fought over the watching of them, not only for the coins they were given, but to study our different footwear. Only men were inside the mosque, bent over in the low bowing, head to floor posture on prayer rugs. We viewed the magnificence of the place, including the fabulous dome. A short distance away, St. Sofia, originally Constantine's church, revealed Christian murals once effaced by the Moors, but now restored by the Turks.

We ran to catch the double-coach streetcar, one red for 1st Class, the other green for Second. It was not crowded, except I discovered that Turkish men seemed to be experts at pretending it was packed and they were forced to move closer—to women, really close. (Where was that wine bottle opener when I needed it?)

The next day we took a train to Florya's beach on the Sea of Marmara. The train circled the ancient wall that had enclosed Istanbul before it was called Constantinople. Once a Roman wall, it extends out to the Bosporus with its Norman towers. In Florya we were able to swim and picnic on unbelievable, blood red melons and citrus fruit. Dinner in Istanbul was at the Park Hotel. From a table on the outdoor, awning covered, narrow balcony, many blocks high above the tiered city below, we watched ocean going vessels maneuver on the Bosporus. We were in Europe, looking across to Asia. When the sun descended, the water glistened like gold.

ASIA

Chapter 23

Before PanAm established layovers for crews between Istanbul and Calcutta, we worked the entire route with airport stops at Damascas, Karachi, and New Delhi, an 18-hour flight plus at least an hour on the ground at each landing. There could be nine men in these long-range crews who alternated flying, navigating the aircraft and using bunks next to the cockpit. For the flight attendants, there was a rear seat on the port side, if not sold. Trips like these made for a stronger Union in Flight Service—wanting better rest facilities, more ground employee help, or more pay, preferably all three.

Between meals the purser handled the paper work with Baggage Declarations, Landing Cards, Health and Immigration forms for each passenger. Every country required ship and cargo papers, in particular, the General Declaration. The latter listed the crew, their position and place of birth, aircraft itinerary, and passenger number. Questions on the document were probably taken from ocean-going ships' forms, i.e. "Anyone incapacitated, diseased or deceased?" And, "Did anyone become sick *abroad*?"

India's independence from the British Commonwealth came a few months before my first trip there. Crews received Yellow Fever shots in their routine inoculations, required for admittance to a country that had never been subjected to the disease. India took precautions to prevent any more diseases than they already had, but I believe the last Yellow Fever epidemic in the States was in the previous century. However, the most important form when traveling to the Far East was a slip of paper in a pocket on the bulkhead by the main cabin door. It stated that the aircraft had been sprayed with DDT prior leaving the States. Without that paper for Karachi, we could be quarantined or hospitalized. (There were crews who had experienced both.)

Disconcerting sights increased fatigue as the taxi crossed Calcutta. People were living in what seemed mankind's lowest degradation, the slums called the "Bustees". Humans ate, slept, and "eliminated" in an open area of the most squalid conditions. Humidity carried odors so strong that the car windows were necessarily closed into suffocating heat.

In Calcutta we met the Pacific-Alaska Division crews who flew in from Hong Kong via Bangkok. This contact completed the round the world service which PanAm was first to start in 1947. (Being "first" became a PAA slogan, as an American pioneer airline overseas.) We arrived at the PanAm layover facilities, an old home complete with our own dining room. The "bearers", with red lips and tongues from chewing betel nut leaves, directed small boys to struggle with the heaviest bags. The little fellows smiled when sympathy was expressed, and tried to lift the bags higher to show their strength.

Calcutta streets crowded with "holy" cattle, carts, women at public water pumps, hawkers, some crippled and gaunt, and a few of the well dressed Brahmans, the priestly Hindus. The caste system of India, to which one was born, was prevalent. The Indian shopkeepers were not easy to bargain with. They set a price they generally stuck to. If, after setting a price, one was foolish or the loser, it would never be the Indian. After purchasing a few brass objects and silk scarves, I took pictures of cobra snakes, lured out of baskets by their owners playing a weird piping sound. People began to gather, staring at Americans who stared at the snakes. A tethered bear was urged to dance—for a few rupees. The poor, rope-tied animal looked pathetically defeated and humiliated in an act we did not encourage. When the crew and I walked away, fortunetellers followed and persistently tried to coax our interest. Finally one said he could name our engineer's wife as proof of his powers. We were amused until he said "Martha", which her husband admitted was her real name that he never used. It was more frightening than startling.

On return, I hoped to see the Himalayas from the air but we were too far off the track. Over Iran, Iraq, and Syria, were hours of desert country, with no sign of life. I thought about the plane that had crash-landed on the sand below, a year before, in which several passengers and all the cockpit crew but one lost their lives. Flight attendants and the one pilot were able to get most of the passengers out of the plane before fire destroyed it. (That one pilot went on to become the writer/producer of the original "Star War" series on TV, Gene Roddenberry.)

We spent three days in Istanbul, and I slept at least two of those. I did make a trip to the market to buy a sultan head, meerschaum pipe for my father and an after-dinner liqueur. U.S. Customs allowed crew members one bottle of spirits per trip without duty.

Between Istanbul and London, we landed in Brussels long enough to have a meal so delicious that, in contrast to London's food fare, gave rise to thought. Belgium was a country that had recently come out of a terrible war, mostly as a captured territory, yet it seemed to have no dearth of meat, fruit, vegetables and dairy products, to say nothing of rich desserts.

Flying over the English Channel, I looked down at the water and thought of my childhood first love, whose bones lay in his B-17 somewhere below. After a raid over Germany in 1943, he almost made it back safely. Almost was not enough. I remembered when it was from him that I had my first kiss. He did not kiss me—I kissed him. I still see his surprised face when he said, "Wha'd you do that for?" We were nine years old.

Returning to England was back to fish, chips, and tea with thumbnail sandwiches at four in the afternoon; a really good meal in England was hard to buy at that time. I met Ellie on her first trip. We visited the famous Wax Museum, the Tower of London, and had our picture taken on Raleigh's Walk with Beefeater guards in their Tudor costumes. We joined other crews in visiting a local pub where activity extended around the popular dartboard. The English frequented the same pub to meet their friends, as if it were a private club.

September was my vacation in 1948. I flew home on Eastern Airlines and enjoyed sitting on the screened porch with the folks. After some restful days, I was ready to fly again—it was a disease!

BY WAY OF ROME

Chapter 24

Politics was a subject that never really interested me. In my home state, poilliticians did not always have a very honorable reputation (except when they made speeches), and they all seemed to belong to the same party, as did most of the people. It seemed so incongruous. The other party only put a hand in an oven if they tried to interfere, or get elected. As a youth I only knew of Franklin D. Roosevelt as President, a man whom everyone so revered, how could there be another party? When he died in 1945, I was flying over Mexico and was called to the cockpit to be given the news received by our radio operator. Now in 1948 there was a Presidential Election with Harry Truman opposing Thomas Dewey. On departure from London I heard that Dewey had won. By arrival in New York the votes had swayed to make Truman President. I liked Harry. He called a spade; a spade.

Ellie and I looked for a place to live in Greenwich Village, long known for its writers and artists, beguiling us to believe this was the most glamorous place to be. We were fascinated with the 19th Century townhouses having ivy pots on the window sills, gardens to the rear, and bright painted doors with brass knockers; however, the closer to 5th Avenue, the more expensive. We asked a policeman for directions in response to an ad in the *Villager* paper and he walked us to his real estate friend. In this way we met our landlord to be, Mr. Bertia, who learned we would be flying to Rome, his native home. Apparently this seemed beneficial to him. We wanted a place with charm and character, particularly with garden and fireplace. Surprisingly, he had an opening on Perry Street near Sheridan Square, where we could take the subway to the airport. The apartment had little character but lots of charm. The yard was a wreck, the inside needed painting, furniture was sparse, but it did have a fireplace and a usable refrigerator and stove. Our landlord owned several buildings that he rented more or less, as was. For us he found a bed, a couch, and a chest of drawers. All we really saw was the patio and the fireplace. There was running hot water (if you waited a while) and the toilet flushed. With plumbing in order, all we needed was fireplace wood.

No sooner settled, I was called for a Calcutta trip while on "Standby". When the phone rang I was in the shower.

"This is Scheduling. Need you for a CCU flight in two hours. Ready to go?"

"Well, not at this particular moment," I answered, as water dripped about me. "I'll get there as soon as I can."

I always kept a suitcase packed with essentials, so clean clothes were all that was needed. I had barely unpacked from moving. At the airport I ran into Norton. He looked terribly tired. For an instant it flashed through my mind an urge to soothe that tired body, but I just as quickly suppressed the thought. When I dashed off, I felt dejected. Though never a solution, my trips curtailed a particular loneliness.

As it was the end of October, flights went directly to London. This did not always happen, depending on the winds and time of the year. After a day in London, we took off for Istanbul via Brussels. All went well until over Italy the plane suffered a cracked cylinder. If one has to lose an engine, what better place than near Rome? We landed at this treasure of the world and spent thirty-six hours awaiting the plane's repair.

I was immediately enamored of Rome. A day was spent visiting the Vatican with Saint Peter's Basilica, the Sistine Chapel, the Roman Forum, and the Colosseum. At the latter place the flight engineers debated how the Romans possibly held water for sea battles in the arena. We walked over to view the balcony where

Mussolini had stood a few years before, making speeches with his jutting jaw. Seeing Rome hurriedly is like turning the pages of a good book before reading all the lines. That night we went to the famous "Biblioteca" restaurant, located in a cellar with candlelight tables and a violinist. Iced clams, still in their shells, were rolled to our table on a cart. One clam was so fresh, I swore he winked his bi-valve at me. They were live, for to touch their shell they would close.

Rome was departed with bottled wine in straw casements, a cameo for my mother, doe skin gloves at $2 a pair, an Angora sweater, and tooled leatherwork. The wine never made it back to the States; it was consumed at Istanbul in a "de-briefing" party.

At the Damascas airport I purchased Mother of Pearl inlay boxes for Christmas gifts and a black leather belt with silver thread design for myself. With no layover there, it was off again, flying over Syria where camel caravans were seen to make slow moving ribbons across the sand. Next was Karachi—then the Palam Airport at New Delhi. On departing the latter we had a real scare. The plane was speeding down the runway when brakes were sharply applied, bringing us to a wavering, screeching stop. The sensation was as though the aircraft was a whip being snapped horizontally. A cow had walked on to the runway; hitting it would not only have endangered our lives but I could see the newspapers, "PanAm plane kills sacred cow." By the time I arrived at Calcutta I felt I had walked across Europe and Asia. It was one place in all my travels I believed I had reached the end of the world; however, with renewed rest, I was ready to fly again.

Back in Istanbul, after a boat ride on the Golden Horn in delightful weather, my crew and I watched as Turkey celebrated the Anniversary of the Republic, which Ataturk had proclaimed 25 years before. Red flags with the moon crest were hanging from every building, and waving in streamers across the streets.

From London we carried a full load of G.I. wives and children, in a flight to New York that took 17 and a half hours. There were nine babies and seven youngsters. It was a constant parade of diapers, bottles, and children's needs all the way. Indeed, we did work hard on our flights.

Ellie had our apartment more in order when I arrived. She found an old kitchen table and cut down the legs for a perfect coffee table in the living room. Well, almost perfect, as it did require periodically replacing a match folder under one leg. The neighbors in our building were an assortment of individuals. There was a newly wed couple two flights up; a writer who later published several books and her husband, an editor with *Time Magazine*; and a handsome, unmarried fellow who did not seem to have a steady job but regular girl friends. A retired lawyer, called the Mayor of Perry Street, lived one floor up. His redheaded niece, who often visited him, had her sights on grand opera but was relatively unknown. Uncle Syd, as he insisted we call him, gleamed with pride over "Bubs". (She later became famous under the name of Beverly Sills.) The closest I came to the operatic stage was when Ellie and I tried to become stand-ins or "props" at the Metropolitan Opera House, but were refused. They only wanted boys.

We lived around the corner from The Village Vanguard, a nightspot where many people got a start in the entertainment world, such as Eartha Kitt and Harry Belafonte. Comedian Wally Cox had a lengthy stay there. Two blocks away was a famous steak house on Broadway, and down on Charles Street was a cozy little Spanish place, great for Paella, which Bing Crosby claimed was his favorite. N.Y.U. was a close walk. The Washington Arch at the foot of 5th Avenue opened to a small park filled with students studying, children playing, babies in buggies, and "artists" of all types. Greenwich Village was like a small community, with the subway or bus to go any place in the metropolitan area. Living there was truly a memorable phase of my life.

NEW YORK, NEW YORK

Chapter 25

When PanAm started service from New York to Caracas, Venezuela, via San Juan and Curacao, the Constellation was used, flown by Atlantic Division crews. Curacao, Dutch West Indies, was the crew layover stop in the pastel colored town of Wilhelmstad. The Hotel Americano, on the dockfront near the famous pontoon bridge, took care of PanAm's crews. The bridge opened for as many as 50 ocean vessels a day, gliding by in a natural waterway, one of the deepest in the world. It was so close to my window I could almost speak to the people aboard. A huge ocean-going vessel would appear to be driving down the street.

Wilhelmstad was a free port with bargains in attractive shops. Particularly nice was the Delft china. The open street markets were redolent with color, including pungent tropical fruit that women carried in baskets upon their heads. It was an ideal trip to relax, swim, or watch constant activity around the channel. The liner "Alcoa", out of Mobile and New Orleans, docked there during my stay, and encouraged ocean travel by inviting visitors. We did not go swimming in the Caribbean directly. The Curacao Beach Club enclosed an area of the sea to keep out the barracuda. It had high coral rocks from which to dive into the water and bright green water where swimming was done with "friendly" tropical fish.

Although this was a Caracas flight, we landed at the foot of the mountains in a place called Maiquetia. Passengers had to take a harrowing trip by car up a winding, 17 mile, mountain road to go to Caracas. The road had a dangerous reputation for safe travel.

On one return trip I boarded the New York subway and had to stand, setting my bag beside me. When a seat became available, I sat down and the rocking of the train took away my alertness. Near the 14th St. stop, I looked up and saw that my suitcase was gone. I believed that I would never see the bag again. In the evening I received a phone call from a stranger saying he had found my bag and would I meet him on a corner of 23rd St. at 7 p.m. He hung up before I could get his name. Ellie and her friend, Phil, insisted that meeting him alone was too dangerous. They hid themselves close by when I tried to keep the appointment. I waited an hour and no one appeared. The next day another call came from this person, who claimed I had waited at the wrong corner and suggested we now meet in Queens. This time he came with my suitcase. I expressed my gratitude just as Ellie and Phil appeared beside me. Not until we got home was it noted that, though nothing was missing, no nametags remained anywhere. "How could he know it was my luggage, with no identification?" I realized.

"He's obviously the one who took it," Phil replied.

There was one thing in the suitcase, which I told no one about—a notebook of scribbled poetry, a feeble attempt at verse, a pouring out of my heart with unrequited love. The notebook was all that was missing and I never saw it again.

Ellie and I enjoyed a camaraderie of acquaintances and college friends with whom we partied, played bridge, and attended the theater. For Christmas of 1948 we decorated our apartment with holly and mistletoe. The mantelpiece had southern pinecones, needle sprigs and loquats sent from home. Holding these were beer steins from Germany, and Turkish mugs from Istanbul. Christmas cards were stuck to the window panels, placed over cracks and kept out the cold. My parents shipped a box of delicious, Louisiana navel oranges, not well known because so few are grown. Ellie's mother sent jams, preserves and large western pinecones. Friends and neighbors came over to join us in our Puerto Rican rum punch. It was joyous.

The day we went to see Tullulah Bankhead and Donald Cook

in the stage play of "Private Lives" it started to snow. Phil and Ellie built a snowman in the yard. Our garden had a vine-covered trellis, edged with white snowflakes to make a sparkling view. Four inches of snow fell, but did not stop the tinkling bell of the Salvation Army people on the streets. Ellie and I put on our uniform boots and walked by shop windows that encouraged the Season. At Washington Square we threw snowballs and felt like the children that we watched playing football using a rubber hot water bottle. We visited stewardess friends also living in Greenwich Village. One of the girls would later be killed in a plane crash, but all was happy then. We took the bus to Radio City and watched ice skaters on the outdoor rink, and the huge lighted tree.

The next day Ellie left on a trip to Africa. My mother was happy when I wrote that her cousin in Connecticut had asked me to visit for the Holidays. On Christmas Day it snowed again and Cousin Fred met me at the station. He sounded so jolly and different from his serious-minded sister on Long Island. Robust, Cousin Fred, wearing only a scarf and a sweater, met me wrapped up like I was going to the Pole. He drove to a beautiful home, which I complimented as we went up the driveway. "Oh, we don't live there. We live in the barn in back." Fred watched my face and then said, "We rent the house; the barn as a home is our own idea." The barn was far more charming. Houses converted from barns were as much the rage as apartments with gardens in Greenwich Village. My cousin's home was warm with early American furniture; a kitchen holding polished brassware, hanging from iron hooks attached to an old wagon wheel mounted on the ceiling; collections from antique stores and potted plants on the long front window sill. Fred's wife, Mitzi, had a welcoming sense of humor and made me feel at home. They were such a compatible couple, always teasing, yet praising each other. I envied their happy relationship and wondered if I would ever find such bliss. My room in the rebuilt "hayloft" had a high four poster bed, holding comforters and quilts of early America. Their son, Paul, who was still in college, came home to show me a small pond where children with their dogs played, skated, and slid across frozen ice; a childhood I had only read about. The next day we talked so much I missed my train. I was encouraged to take the next train, then the next, then—Connecticut impressed me, and the beauty that snow made of Christmas.

In March Ellie was given a Public Relations assignment at Washington D.C. She represented PanAm as a stewardess in the christening of the new Boeing Stratocruiser we would later fly. Margaret Truman bounced a bottle of champagne off the nose of this large piston aircraft, the last propeller craft PanAm would use before the jet age.

I was off to San Juan where, after a brief stay, I was called to return to New York on a DC-4, earlier than scheduled. The pilots were already at the airport. The steward and I raced to the plane and were met by a commissary loader who laughingly said, "Hope you got enough hay." This did not make sense as we walked up the stairs. Inside we were shocked to see special compartments holding well-secured horses. "Not just horses," said the steward, "These are thoroughbreds."

At that moment the co-pilot walked up, chuckled and said, "Can't you two take care of horses?" I must admit they were beautiful passengers.

PORTUGAL AND SPAIN

Chapter 26

On return I met my illustrious "Lyon Skipper" in Flight Operations and was shocked when I saw him. His pallor revealed an improper care of himself. I knew he liked his libations, but not even his strong body could take persistent ill treatment. I did not know whether to feel guilty for desiring him or for avoiding him. All I had asked to do when I left home was to travel the world and meet its people. Well, I was seeing it, in all its beauty, excitement and frustration. I was miserable from the terrible suffering that comes from wanting to be near someone, despite all ethics that say it is wrong.

Norton and I took a boat trip around the New York harbor. It was our romantic ocean cruise in a couple of hours. We passed the Statue of Liberty but did not really see the lady. We held hands among millions of people who neither knew us nor cared. We stopped at the renowned Oyster Bar in Grand Central Station, to relish on what he once teased me for never having tried before. As the Master of All Decisions had control of Scheduling, Norton and I were rarely in the same place at the same time. I tried to tell myself it was just as well. I could not decide which was worse, to lose him or my self-respect. When Scheduling called me, I hoped it was for a long flight to Africa or India. No, it was to Barcelona.

One of my passengers was a darling young man who persisted in talking to me despite the fact that I was trying to serve a meal. He followed my every step, until finally he blocked my path to say, "Would you be my sweetheart?" I told him if he would eat his lunch, I would think about it. He replied, "I'll give you my teddy bear if you tell me now." He was six years old, so sweet I cried to see him off the plane.

Santa Maria in the Azores was our island stop before Lisbon. Near the airport, motel quarters were former army barracks that included laundry service, good food and even a fireplace. The lounge held poker and bridge players, and various board games. The field outside was large enough to play baseball. PanAm even supplied bicycles for us to see the countryside. The Azores was as pretty as an Irish county and, just as typically, had rock fences dividing properties. The oxen-driven carts on the narrow, winding roads had wooden wheels; the farmers still used these animals to pull their primitive plows. We were enticed to walk, when it was not too windy, to see sheep grazing on the hillsides, women thrashing grain, and children carrying home their fishing catch. The village of Villa do Porto had an old church it was said that Columbus had attended. From the high cliffs, reached by bicycle, we could look down to the ocean waves crashing against the rocky precipice, an artist's paradise. I only took one trip about the island by bicycle, which was English made with brakes on the handlebars. At first my foot automatically went for the non-existent pedal brake. On one turn in the road, I pressed the hand brake too hard and flew over the handlebars to crash land. Somehow I felt I had deserved the injury but I continued on flight the next day, bruised but still bearing.

Lisbon, a beautiful city on the Tagus River, has much to photograph. We took a tour about town—up the slopes to see clear views, and a sight of the Belem Tower that had watched ships come and go for centuries. We drove to the ocean shore to meet the fishing boats, sailing rigs with painted pictures or designs upon their bows. They were pulled up on the sand, side by side. We arrived in time to see the fish being placed in crated boxes by the men, layered in stacks with rock salt poured on by the women. As each crate was filled and sealed, another was pulled up and the layering continued. People burst into song and laughter while laboring. Fishing nets were stretched to dry, and made ready for the next day's venture by the elderly who repaired the tears. How many centuries had this same event occurred on these very shores?

The next day eight crewmen and I piled into the company station wagon and were driven to Sintra, the famous palace of Portugal, now a museum. Sintra is more a fortress than a castle. It was built and styled by the Moors. Unfortunately, the interior was closed to visitors due to maintenance work, but we did get to walk the parapets. Driving back to the city, we stopped to eat at a restaurant where we were the sole customers. An early urge for food was upon us. Due to it being a different time zone, it was hard to tell the stomach it must adjust to local hours, so we awaited our meal orders over bottles of wine. As in other Latin countries, wine is preferable to hard liquor, and there is always plenty of it. Still waiting, and consuming more wine, we found our way to the bandstand in the empty dining room. One of the pilots was able to play all the latest hits on the piano. Unable to discuss with anyone my tremulous heart condition on hearing love songs, I was in the mood to be cantankerous when I found the drums. The piano and drums did not harmonize, which hurried the waiters to bring our meals.

The hotel in Lisbon was not the best of accommodations. It was attractive enough, with tree-size, potted plants throughout the hallways, to appear more like an arboretum. We were still the post-war pioneers, for again the rooms were without baths, as our quarters in London. (Palatial palaces had no baths either, centuries ago.) Located down the hall were bathing facilities. There was hot water, if you knew how to light the pilot light "gizmo" on the wall. Even properly flared up, you might accomplish what intended, if the smell of gas did not asphyxiate you first. However, it was best to be dressed when striking the match. I thought I had the heater lit properly until I heard an explosive sound. With my uniform raincoat (which we used as a bathrobe to save space in our suitcase) I ducked into the hallway and hailed a passing flight crew for help. He laughingly obliged.

"What would you women do without us," he reminded me. Ah, yes.

In the morning the fishmongers, women with baskets of fresh fish upon their heads, awakened me. They walked down the street shouting their arrival. The words to their soliciting cries made no sense to me, but with eyes closed I could recognize them again. They reminded me of New Orleans where I had heard similar sounds on the street—the chimney cleaners calling "Chim—SWEEPS", the dark women and their "Straw—BEA-ries", and the unforgettable, "Baa-nan-aas! Dime a duz-un!" All now in the past.

We left Lisbon, flying to Barcelona, but landed in Madrid awaiting an engine change. Our stay was only long enough to have a nice dinner (at the Spanish hour of 10 p.m.) and then sleep before a morning departure. Breakfast in my room included rich, juicy oranges with pulp as red as tomatoes. From the Madrid Hotel we drove to the airport around the Plaza de Espana with its monument to Cervantes, as revered as London's Trafalgar Square, or the Arc de Triomphe in Paris. Because of this delay, I returned to New York without seeing Barcelona beyond its airport. Voyages in my life held various detours.

ACCRA

Chapter 27

In April of 1949 I had my initial trip to Africa. For 10:30 hours we flew from LaGuardia to the Azores, where I also played my first game of poker. The pilots not only held a serious game but a rather "deadly" one. I lost ten dollars in two minutes and bowed out in two seconds. I never saw men so intent, sitting in a circle like gentlemen vultures waiting for the kill. No pleasure there, I joined a softball game outside.

In 12:50 hours we flew from the Azores to Dakar, which three years earlier had become part of Senegal. Previously it was French West Africa. As the aircraft food always consisted of frozen meals, PanAm tried to serve local, fresh egg breakfasts, taking passengers' orders. It was an attempt to please individual taste; however, this was unsuccessful because all it took was one—just one—rotten egg, and the odor throughout the cabin, to say nothing of the explosion of the egg all over the galley, ruined the idea. In my experience—once was too often.

Africa, with its mysterious aura and distinct character, is the most difficult continent for me to describe. It has to be seen and felt, to try to understand. Accra, as the capital of the Gold Coast, was part of the British Commonwealth. (The country would be renamed Ghana when it became independent.) Customs men in Accra, dressed in black shorts with red sashes and pillbox hats, were efficient, courteous, and spoke English in musical tones. The Lisbon Hotel, with walk-up front steps to a screened entrance, was located across from the terminal building and the only public lodging around. The lobby was a meeting place for missionaries, geologists, hunters, merchants and those on sabbatical or safari. Introductions took place upon entering. No one stayed a stranger to anyone.

When Jonathan, employed to care for the stewardess quarters, carried my luggage to a two story, wooden building, we walked a dirt path between large mud mounds as high as seven feet, standing like ghosts in the dim light. I was told they were termite hills (which seemed perilously close to our wooden barracks). In the distance I could see nothing that resembled the settling of human beings. The atmosphere was truly intriguing, with a silence that drew my attention. Suddenly I heard creatures in the distance whose sounds I recalled from visiting the zoo. The hotel kept a guard all night at the base of each building (one for men and one for women) to discourage four legged creatures. Exhausted, I fell asleep under my mosquito netting.

In the morning I joined my crew in the dining room. Most of them were eating fruit and drinking coffee, but two held bottled beer. "Beer! For breakfast?" I was told that if I drank the water I might go home on the next flight, possibly in a box. I had never acquired a taste for beer but, without reliable water, I developed a desire and affection for Dutch Heinekens. Nothing could be eaten that was not boiled or peeled. Even those precautions gave no assurance. We took quinine pills for malaria; however, for dysentery, good luck was the only sure preventative. We ate mostly fruit or canned foods. Avocados from Accra were the best ever. With or without lime juice I could live on them, and almost did. I had heard of the food situation in Accra before leaving New York and brought three giant-size chocolate bars. They began to melt to a messy liquid. I also learned that cold cream, lipstick, and rouge had the same fate.

PanAm had two flights a week to Johannesburg, South Africa, so our layovers were lengthy just waiting for the next aircraft. The company provided a station wagon for crew preoccupation. This necessitated acquiring Gold Coast Driver's Licenses. I got one mainly as a souvenir and learned to drive on the left side of the road. Another English custom observed by the Britons in tropical climates was the wearing of all white or khaki outfits, mostly shorts. One fellow always carried a riding crop, but I never saw his horse!

Merchants along the roadway sold the popular, wooden, native heads and elephant bookends, all carved in heavy, polished ebony or mahogany. Crews purchased coffee tables and hide-skin seats with wooden elephants on each side for the legs, as well as sandals that never wore out—the soles were cut from old rubber tires. Cotton shipped to England was made into brilliant, printed material and sent to the Gold Coast. The more colorful, the better favored. I ordered shorts and shirts made from this material, though they had buttons placed, as for men, on the opposite side.

We usually had the ocean beach to ourselves, outside of a few native children who romped in their birth clothes while their mothers sold us coconuts. The ocean could be frightening, but breezes were the drawing attraction, when they existed. It was not so much the roughness of the waves that were forbidding, as the sand dunes that would build up under the water where least expected, and a fierce undertow that could drag a swimmer out to sea. A few months before I arrived, a pilot dove into the surf and broke his neck on a sand dune. He lived long enough to return home and see his family one last time.

While sitting in the lounge one day, I was introduced to Bill Welmers, who was in Africa studying languages and dialects for a research institute in the States. He had the same assignment previously in China, Japan, and Ceylon. Bill had just come in from the bush country to shop and had stopped in the lobby for cold beer. His hobby was to identify by accent where any American was born and bred. Bill guessed correctly everyone in the room but one, naming my father's birthplace for me.

On the last day, I was resting when a caller below my window asked if I wished to see the Accra wharf, as a ship had just arrived. I dressed and joined the crew to drive to the ocean, but not to any docks. Ocean-going vessels laid anchor about a half-mile at sea.

Native men rowed out to the ship in heavy boats battered by the surf and little by little brought the cargo to shore. It was like a small army of rowboats going out empty in one line and returning laden in another. Oarsmen on each side held black painted paddles shaped to a three-pronged, silver blade, like a devil's spike. The men fluttered their tongues in a strange cry with every stroke of the oars; the chanting set their rhythm.

I had my camera ready as the first boat arrived, but without audio to catch their vocal sounds. The crashing surf appeared as if it would overturn the craft with its cargo, larger than a grand piano. As the boat was dashed ashore, several of the men got out to secure it. Though their bodies were very dark, we saw that they were naked. Suddenly the overseer ran out and advised them of the two American women present. The oarsmen casually wrapped cloths around their waists. Behind them was another boat roughly hurled upon the beach by the surging water, but I left before upsetting the men's routine.

JOHANNESBURG

Chapter 28

When the second flight of the week arrived in Accra, we took off for Johannesburg, South Africa, stopping first at Leopoldville, in the Belgian Congo—or so it was called in 1949. (Later the Congo would be "liberated" by a dictatorship and called Zaire.) Here we stayed long enough to eat in the airport dining room. With an 11:55 hour flight between Accra and Johannesburg, this meal was a treat. The Belgians had brought their expertise in food care and cooking, including creamy pastries. We went from extreme caution in Accra to positive gluttony in the Congo. Apparently while the English were concerned for what the Africans wore, or should wear, the Belgians placed importance on what was eaten. C'est la vie!

At last I arrived in South Africa, the bottom of another continent. We circled to land, flying over gold mines with their mounds of earth diggings to resemble volcano peaks. Johannesburg, at an altitude of 7,000 ft, was only about 50 years old. It was May, and their fall of the year. One of my passengers was Louis Erisman, a professional photographer, with whom I discussed our mutual camera interest. He was on an assignment to film various African tribes in moving color. Louis had been an army colonel during WWII and had filmed the atom bomb as it dropped on Hiroshima. This time he was going to one of the gold mines where there was to be a showing of tribal dances in native costume, or rather minimum wear with fascinating adornments. He invited me to join him. I was to regret having my 35 mil. rather than my movie camera. To carry both was so cumbersome; I alternated them each trip.

The tribal dances were spectacular. Men in multi-hued, warrior-styled dress, exhibited amazing and some startling performances. Their chants mesmerized spectators and their throbbing body movements were in perfect rhythm. They had come from miles around to compete with other tribes. From the gold mine we drove to watch the white man's miniature car and airplane racing. This seemed so unimpressive after the tribal dances—one a culture, the other a hobby. Following a pleasant barbecue at the home of South African friends of Louis', I was returned to the Carlton Hotel. Unfortunately, I never had the longer layover in South Africa, which enabled crews to take a side trip to Krueger Park.

Back to Accra, a dance was taking place at the hotel. After flying from Johannesburg, which we affectionately called "Joberg", I was tired and went to bed. I tried to drown out the music from the party with cotton in my ears. All was more open in this hot country, so it was difficult not to hear the sound. The windows were screened openings in the wall, the cut away portion on hinges and propped ajar by a slat of wood. Suddenly I saw my mosquito net moving in waves around the bed. I looked over the side as a huge rat scampered away—not a mouse, but a monstrous thing with a long tail. I yelled at it, and Jonathan came running up the steps.

"Missey okay?" he asked. The animal had long disappeared but it was a comfort to know that Jonathan was there. With no telephone in the room, I dressed and went to the office to register a roommate I did not care to have. I was advised that "ladies who keep crackers in their quarters. . . ." Then I walked over to the party for a lukewarm beer to put me to a sleep in which tigers would not have awakened me.

In the morning I heard whistling up to my "window" by Rick, an adventurous steward. He asked if I was interested in going to the bush country with our new friend, Bill Welmers, the anthropologist. (Just give me time to dress and get my camera.) In the dining room we grabbed a pineapple, avocados, bananas, and lots of paper napkins. For liquid nourishment there was the only safe kind available, beer—like a whole case. That seemed all we needed. Using Bill's truck, we drove for hours over an asphalt road, which turned into a dirt road, then no road. Rick and I searched the countryside for an animal that might jump out from behind a tree. Bill could identify flora and fauna and drove to visit a particular tribe. We passed several villages and observed people in their cone-topped grass huts. The cleanliness of their communities was impressive, casting a decided purity about the land.

Suddenly we came upon a village having what was obviously some sort of celebration. People were gathered and many were dancing alone to a beat of hollow tree-drums. We stopped and walked to observe closely. Rick suddenly grabbed me, saying, "Let's show them how we cut a rug." He started to jitterbug, laughing as I tried to follow. We began to draw a crowd. More people came out of the "straw works" and naked little kids peered from under their mother's skirts. It seemed a hundred human beings suddenly appeared. A big man, dressed in a flowing blue robe, who must have held a high position, since everyone stood aside for him, motioned in a friendly manner for us to come nearer. As we did, I could not resist taking camera shots of the dancers. In an instant, what had been shouting and feet beating the soil, there was dead silence, but for the click of my camera. I looked over to see an angry-faced man in blue holding his hand up. In the unbelievable stillness, he walked towards me and grabbed my camera. His strange words were harsh. Bill understood the dialect and explained that the chief wanted my camera.

"Oh, no," I cried. Bill offered a pack of cigarettes and some shillings if my camera was returned. While they looked over the money and cigarettes, Bill told us to back away slowly and get back to the truck. This we did, running the last few steps. Rick started the engine; Bill was right behind us with my camera.

"For God's sake! What did we do? Why the sudden change?" we asked.

"It was a funeral," Bill replied. "They believed you had taken the dead person's soul in your camera. I gave them the film." Me and my camera! We drove back to Accra.

On return to Lisbon, I was advised that I would leave with a special group of priests and monks going to Tokyo. They were Catholic dignitaries, including the Bishop of Barcelona, Jose Lopez Ortiz. The excursion was to commemorate the trip to Japan 400 years earlier by Saint Francis Xavier, founder of the Jesuit order. These passengers were a group of gentle people, almost childlike in their excitement over flying, this being a first for most. The pilgrimage carried a relic from Rome, which was guarded carefully. Rick asked if we could see it. When the monk proudly opened the box, I was aghast. It was a shriveled-skin, skeletal hand, sealed in a glass, airtight casement, that of Saint Xavier's himself who died in 1552. Such a "relic" was very precious to these people, as the beliefs of the Africans in the bush country was no less important and sacred to them.

IRELAND

Chapter 29

In the summer of 1949 I had a trip to Ireland in which I did not just airport stop but spent three days. We first landed at Goose Bay, Labrador, with packed snow in June. It was the closest I had come to the North Pole. Here the children, fur-wrapped like bunny rabbits, walked to a school near the airport. The teacher clanged a cowbell to call them. It was cold, but dry. I wondered if those youngsters had ever seen a swimming pool.

Over Greenland, a perpetual ice cap, with the smallest of settlements on the southern edges, the mountainous white stretched for miles with no place to land if we had to. These frigid sights from a great height made me shiver, even in the warmth of the plane.

Flying low over Ireland, I saw evidence of the superstition for which the people sing—visible fairy rings, trees planted in circles. I was told they were for the "little people" to hide within and dance without being seen. Well, no one has been able to disprove this idyllic idea, just as no one can say why so many Irish have red hair. Even the Irish dialect, a lilting, charming way of speaking, can be difficult to understand sometimes.

Ireland was rainy and overcast, though warm compared to Goose Bay. We were provided for at the Ardhu (pronounced Ardoo) House, an old inn located near Limerick, south of the Shannon Airport. The days were so long that we could play croquet until past midnight. Though summer, it was cool enough to have a roaring fireplace. Rooms were serviced with hot-water bottles to warm the bedding; however, the sheets were icebergs from the shores of Greenland. If the water bottle kept my feet warm, the rest of me was cold. If it kept my back warm, my feet would freeze. The solution was to return to the huge fireplace in the lounge where I met others with the same thought. We played bridge until the wee hours of the morning, over hot tea and scones.

The next day was warmer but still a "soft day", an Irish expression when moisture sweeps the atmosphere and tickles your face; a misty condition that could last for days. We took a ride to Cratlow Castle, the remains of a dwelling built hundreds of years ago. It was only left with the "keep", one tall section the width of about six cows, nose to tail, that I judged from the animal standing by it. Ivy crawled up the walls and over to the inside, as the roof was gone. It had a dirt floor, maybe always did, and the fireplace alone was half the size of the hall. With little imagination I could see armored knights gathered around. Along a winding, partially crumbled, stone staircase, the clashing of swords could be envisioned, or bows sending arrows through slots in the thick walls. Ireland was filled with medieval ruins built to withstand battles, which gave in to the ravages of time, if not their warrior defeats.

I attempted to play golf again, which I had not tried since Bermuda. Ireland's fairways were beautiful, the winds chilling. Sheep or goats, which had grazed there long before golfers, were the lawn mowers. When my ball landed amid an animal's tribute, I gave up and returned to the hotel for hot tea.

Back in New York, Ellie and I had another roommate, Millie, who had brought back two Alsatian puppies from England. The apartment became a little smaller. Just getting the dogs out of England on the aircraft was a feat in itself, not easy to explain, but she did it. (Millie was "half" American and "hoff" Brit.) She thought the yard was perfect for the pups, but the pups preferred the apartment and grew by leaps (big leaps) and bounds—almost boundless. It got a little "hairy" in a puppy way. Eventually Millie married and took the puppies with her.

Sometimes our group of friends would meet at "The Fraternity House", a bar and lounge on 3rd Ave. and 17th St., where college and post-grads gathered to drink and sing school songs. The walls were filled with autographed pictures of the famous and the brew was generally beer. Ellie and I decided to have a party at our place. Phil ordered a wooden keg of beer that was propped on a kitchen chair. Beer drawn from the barrel was so smooth it made bottled beer taste artificial. We had lots of Turkish mugs and "Toby" types from England. Ellie made the salad from whatever the refrigerator would emit. I made spaghetti with that wonderful Irish cheese. Only on payday could we afford meat. The night was warm enough to use the patio. The guys and gals showed up via the subway. No one owned a car in Manhattan. Mary came with bread rolls; Esther brought wine for those who did not like beer; Larry brought some ground meat to go in my spaghetti; Jim brought his good humor. Our group was a happy bunch, mostly college grads—Harvard, Yale, Columbia, N.Y.U., Ohio State, Vanderbilt, and one from the Manhattan school of hard knocks. We had one or two newcomers—a starving artist whom Ellie met in a bookstore and a Harvard classmate Phil met in a bar, who was hungry and without a job.

In the middle of this gaiety, the phone rang and it was my "Lyon Captain". I was happy just to hear his voice and invited him to the party, insisting he come and meet my friends. The evening went off well, though with a rather quiet, observing Norton. On his leaving early, I walked to the outer door with him. He held me, saying, "Always be happy, just as you are tonight." Then he left. I sat for a few minutes on the steps and pondered over his abrupt departure. I had tried hard not to reveal to my friends my true feelings for Norton, but—"Oh, no," I thought, "could I have deceived him too." Suddenly I had a sharp pain in my chest. I recalled Norton's words before leaving, and the finality of his tone dawned on me. I raced out the front door and down Waverly Place looking for him. He was nowhere. "He's gone. It's over." I said to myself. There was no comfort in facing the truth.

ITALY

Chapter 30

Of all the countries in the world to be both beautiful and enchanting, to produce more great art, music, history, food, wine and fascination, I would have to put Italy far up on my list. I had the good fortune to fly one of the charter flights in which PanAm took oilmen to Basra, Iraq, by way of Rome in June of 1949. Our outbound layover was five days in this fabulous old Roman city, when lira went a long way. My DC-4 crew and I decided to use our per diem and go to Naples, Pompei, Sorrento, and Capri. Flight Operations gave each crewmember $40 for the Rome stay—$8 for each day to cover meal expenses. We used this for transportation, the Sorrento and Capri hotels, the boat rides, and the return to Rome. Our per diem was sufficient for everything. We saw few tourists and needed no reservations.

A three-hour train ride took us to Naples. Whatever "class" coach it was, we sat with the people of Italy in an appreciable and interesting ride. The Italians brought bread, cheese, wine and fruit to eat as they traveled; something we neglected to do. They noticed this, as a little girl generously offered me an orange. En route, Italians displayed no embarrassment in exercising their vocal chords with singing, solo or together.

At Naples we were told the pickpockets were the most astute in the world, so we took care in boarding the train for Pompei. Our plan was to see the ruins before going to Sorrento. Good workmanship had been put into the depots built under Mussolini. He did well there, as the bright tile work, Roman in character, was impressive. At Pompei we engaged a guide who spoke English and claimed he once lived in Brooklyn. "Didn't all Italians once live in Brooklyn," said our co-pilot. Our guide laughed and asked for the latest news "back in the States".

Pompei is a marvel for historians and archaeologists. Its dis covery so clearly tells the story of Roman life centuries ago and the devastation as well as preservation after the 79 A.D. volcanic eruption. The ruins had been covered for centuries by the lava and ash from Mt. Vesuvius, still a threatening volcano. Excavation had revealed streets with ruts from ancient carriage wheels, dwellings with once elaborate atriums, wine shops with some unbroken kegs, and opulent public bathhouses. One disclosure had a room with paintings on tile walls showing it might have been a "house of the earliest pleasures". We saw the open theater, and the museum, which held dental and medical equipment similar to those used today—and before the Dark Ages that came later in history. There were marble works, gold jewelry, knitting needles, and preserved bread and eggs. The human and animal corpses were statues sealed in the lava, which caught them in their last moments of agony. It was an eerie, tragic sight.

Leaving the ruins, we were met by buggies with fancy colored fringes and horses with painted blinders, all seeking business. Our guide said goodbye with a military salute, (as he had given the Allied soldiers a few years before). From Pompei we took the train to Sorrento, passing orange groves along the waterfront. Such beauty made me wonder how anyone could ever leave Italy. But then everyone could not stay in the Hotel Minerva with a room overlooking the gorgeous Bay of Naples, as I had. Each of our rooms came for a price that would be unbelievable today. My "suite" had once belonged to a German general during the War. The hotel was high upon a hill that the city climbed. From my balcony I could see Capri, Vesuvius, and the boats at the dock. All this for $2 a day, a cheap room price even for those times. We had dinner on the terrace amid the gardens. My crew could not have been nicer, though each of us probably thought of someone at home we wished had been with us in this romantic place.

Breakfast consisted of Cafe Expresso and an abundance of succulent fruit—large sweet cherries, peaches, oranges, tremendous size figs and plums. We rode to the wharf for the ferry to Capri on a sparkling, sunny day. At the dock, the water was such a clear, blue-green color that small fish could be seen swimming near the surface. The boat's muscular seamen, in short pants and red head scarves, sang arias from operas, along with special Italian songs, piped over the loud speaker, as they threw back the casting lines.

Before arriving at the Isle of Capri, the summer palace of the Emperor Tiberius was visible high on a cliff. Flower and fruit vendors greeted us as we hired a taxi to drive up a road with overhanging bougainvillea and high hairpin turns to the main piazza. From there the Hotel Ercolano was a short walk away. No streets existed off the main square, only cobblestone walkways, about 8 ft.wide. The hotel was built into rock overlooking the water. My room actually had the cliff rock jutting into the wall; the building was constructed to fit nature, not the reverse. It was once the home of the writer, Kafka. Other famous people having homes in Capri were Mussolini's daughter, Gracie Fields, Ginger Rogers, and the owner of Colgate Company. It was not cheap to live in Capri. Water had to be shipped from Naples. It cost owners 600 lira just to take a bath—about a dollar. But 600 lira was a lot of money to the Italians in 1949.

We took a small boat to the famous Blue Grotto. Our barefooted guide who did the rowing, also sang arias. (We wondered how many of these people were operatic extras.) The water was an indigo color and many caves graced the shoreline. When we reached the Blue Grotto, it had a small entrance and the boatman pulled upon a chain to admit us, as we lay flat on the boat bottom. The cave inside is 60 ft. deep. The opening, mostly below the waterline, is so large that the light coming through under the water is what creates the blue iridescent glow. Hands placed in the water appear a silver color.

Eventually we drove to Anacapri to see the famous rocks of Faraglioni. I bought watercolor pictures, sandals, a cameo ring, and some coral rosaries for my Catholic friends. Located here is St. Michael's Cathedral, known for its tile floor of the Garden of Eden. Apropos! Capri *is* a Garden of Eden.

Back in the central piazza we enjoyed dinner at a sidewalk cafe. The blue dial on the town clock kept our attention, ringing every 15 minutes. Afterwards we took a cab to the Hotel Emperor Caesar Augustus. Sitting 1100 feet above the bay, it had stone steps winding down from the cliff top to the water's edge. Statues of Augustus were at each corner of the terrace, where dancing took place in more opulent times.

The next day a ferryboat took us across the bay to Naples for the "Rapido" express train back to Rome. With one day left before going to Basra, there was time to see the catacombs of the Capuchin monks, the Victor Emmauel Monument (called the wedding cake), the Piazza del Esedra fountain with all the horses spouting water, the Trevi fountain to throw a coin "for returning", and the genius of Michaelangelo in his statue of Moses. The streets of Rome wind about, making it easy to get lost, but a walking pleasure. That night we dined at the famous "Hostaria Dell'Orso" restaurant, believed to have once been the home of the poet, Dante.

Flying over the Tigris-Euphrates rivers, I thought the Gardens of Babylon must have dried up centuries ago. The temperature was 110 degrees in Basra, Iraq. But I guess there was lots of oil under the ground, for our passengers were men who worked the fields. After all the wonders of Italy taking my energies, I spent the short Basra stay resting and reading in my air-conditioned room. Yes, air-conditioning, a luxury that the wealth from oil provided.

Westbound, via Damascas and Istanbul, with another three days in Rome, I covered every art gallery and museum I could find. My eyes were opened to more sculpture and painting than I could truly absorb in a lifetime. Thank you, forever, Pan American World Airways!

FRANCE

Chapter 31

Ellie was a perfect roommate and a trusted friend. She accepted more of life in good humor and had a gift few people possess—being an avid listener before expressing her own views. Anyone she met was studied carefully but was given the impression they were important to her.

One of my hottest New York summers was in 1949. It was stifling, with moments when breath was hard to draw. A speeding car could not create a breeze. Ellie's friend, Tony, a purser originally from Italy, had a convertible with which he drove us to cool off at Jones Beach on Long Island. Tony was not only a handsome man with an engaging accent, but a celebrity among our Flight Service group. He was the purser in PAA's desert crash in the Middle East, wherein he helped save passengers' lives. Phil may have been jealous of Tony but Phil was so broke he was constantly hocking his property, namely his "Mac" raincoat—never his typewriter. Another way to keep cool was in the theater. Ellie and I went to see the play, "Anne of A Thousand Days" with Rex Harrison as Henry the Eighth. Women had "progressed" a little better since those dark days—well, a little.

One night Phil came over with a bulge in his pocket from which he drew a live puppy, an animal he had saved from being destroyed. Ellie adored the little fellow, which she named "Rudy". We realized after naming the puppy that it was a female. She was such a tiny little thing; but her sexual attributes never did form into a male. And Rudy's pedigree was so mixed it was difficult to tell what varieties composed her. Whatever, the "dog" was loved. We had a third roommate who left us, deciding that Rudy made it difficult to sleep when a cold nose was always wanting a goodnight kiss. Rudy never hesitated to jump up and kiss us all goodnight. When Ellie's mother came to visit, we sought Mr. Bertia for another bed. It took a gift of a bottle of wine from Rome, but he complied with a sleeper couch. Now we had enough beds for everyone, including one dog bed for Rudy, who seldom used it.

About this time I was called for one of PanAm's first flights to the Riviera. Over the continent we flew low enough to see Portuguese and Spanish towns, clustered buildings with red roofs, and winding roads that followed original cow paths. With only one passenger we continued to Marseilles from Barcelona. Near the border into France, the plane was flown completely around the Medieval walled city of Carcassone and, before landing at Marseilles, the pilots circled for a sight of Nice and Cannes. Our single passenger was so intrigued he asked if PAA always gave such aerial treats. Well—we tried.

Marseilles was not where we spent the night, but Aix-en-Provence, a place known for its beautiful fountains, trees, and boulevards. We stayed at the Hotel du Roy Rene. It was easy to see how the artist, Cezanne, a native of the area, disclosed his love for landscapes. In the evening we enjoyed a delicious meal where wine was forty cents a bottle, whereas bottled water was sixty cents. For just a few francs there was no difficulty obtaining a license to gamble in the casinos on the Riviera. My license showed the error of saying my "domicile" was "Angleterre", and where the card asked for age, it was blank. (The French would not be so indiscreet to ask a woman's age.) Such was my introduction to France. Perfume was so inexpensive; it was a sin not to buy.

On return to New York, two Siamese princesses boarded, accompanied by several servants, plus an Associated Press writer. From the latter acquaintance I was introduced to several in his New York writer's crowd; one night at a place called the Show Spot where the artistically inclined met. My AP friend had Broadway in mind when he showed me the play he wrote on airline personnel. His portrayal of our life style led me to suggest that he try temporary airline employment for better understanding. He could not leave his job, nor did his play ever get to Broadway. Before I could advise him further, I was off to Belgium.

Brussels impressed me with its foliage, cobblestone streets, and lovely Belgian lace work. Another popular product is their delicious chocolate, which I purchased from a lady wearing wooden shoes. (I could never find any shops that sold wooden shoes.) In London I met friends from New Orleans living in England and brought them the Belgian chocolate, a treat for their two young sons. The boys were attending school in England and were wearing student suits, typically English. Their home in the London suburbs had a large yard in which the father was not able to encourage his sons to like American baseball or football—only soccer held their interest. When I was shown about the kitchen, I was amazed to see that the refrigerator had one small tray of thimble-size ice cubes. No wonder the English drank their Scotch without ice; they had no ice. Now if we could just convince the Brits not to serve breakfast toast in those cooling, silver racks.

The biggest news back in New York was the arrival of Ellie's brother, Gary. After graduating from Stanford, Gary was still trying to make decisions about his life before seeking employment. He not only came to dinner and spend the night, but moved in. As Ellie's brother, whom I had known since he wore knee pants, nothing seemed out of order; though it was an era when unmarried, mixed sexes living together was less acceptable. Gary contributed to our household with his cheerfulness and compatibility. He also fixed the French doors to the garden, the yard fence, and stopped the running toilet. He was good looking as escort or companion, a voracious reader, and responsible for turning two orange crates into bookcases. For a while it confused people when Gary answered the phone, but soon our friends knew him too—we were family.

MIDDLE EAST

Chapter 32

In 1949 I traveled to four continents, Europe, Asia, South America and Africa. When scheduled again to Calcutta, a crew layover was established in Damascas, Syria, a place I was anxious to visit. En route I stopped in London long enough to see a legitimate play. Stage plays in London were less expensive than New York and it was easier to get tickets. On other trips I was able to see "The Potting Shed" at the Globe with John Gielgud, and "The Aspern Papers" at the Queen's Theater with Michael Redgrave.

Damascas, via Brussels and Istanbul, was 11 hours from London. We stayed at the O-ma-yad Hotel, called the "Oh-My-God Hotel", by some. In the middle of the high ceiling lobby was the elevator, which crept up slowly. When I arrived at my room, I discovered that the window was an aperture without cover. Strange musical instruments, unfamiliar callings by tradesmen hawking their wares, were heard below in the street. I watched the scene of people dressed in flowing robes, alien and mysterious. Not only was the language beyond comprehension, understanding the mood of the people was equally so. The men seemed not to regard my female presence as a being. I could abide their disrespect, but not the sound of the muezzins in the minarets, with their incessant wailing, forbidding sleep. Yet the enchantment of just being in this strange country overcame that discomfort.

In the morning a guide drove us to country where shepherds dressed as they did in the times of Christ, carrying the "crook" often seen on Christmas cards and tending their sheep flocks. We met nomadic people encamped near the roadside. After a discussion with our guide, we were invited to one of their tents. Men in their aba robes and keffiyeh scarves sat in a circle, cross-legged on woven rugs. They drank a dark liquid while smoking hookahs, "bubbly wubbly" pipes. I could not tell if it was tea or coffee. The men showed resentment when I entered their tent, so I only stayed a minute. Near another tent, the women with all but their eyes covered by burkas darted quickly into hiding. As we walked off, I heard rough language between our guide and the Bedouins. Apparently their hospitality did not include females.

At the airport I received papers to sign for valuables, to verify their tags and see the hatch closed when loaded in the cargo hole of the plane. As I came toward the aircraft, I heard a crash. The loaders had dropped a crated box beneath the fuselage; it was my valuable shipment. I can still hear the tinkling sound of gold bracelets, amulets, and rings, as they rolled over the tarmac. Though it was dark, the gold glittered in the sparse light. Needless to say, this caused a slight delay.

Once more in flight, we headed for Karachi, which had only recently broken from India, with bloodshed taking its usual toll. Pakistan was trying to establish a country of mostly Muslim people, apart from the Hindu of India. Mahatma Gandhi, who tried to keep peace between the people of India, was assassinated only months before.

Our hotel in Karachi was the best accommodation to be had. No Hilton, Holiday, or Hyatt hotels existed. This hotel, considered of European standards, had a large dining room with linen tablecloths, fine silverware, china, wine goblets, and flowered centerpiece. The waiters, dressed as expected for the formal surroundings, served with all the pomp of the famous Savoy. Putting our opinions of the food aside, whatever it was, it was impossible to eat. We requested additional saucers to cover the glasses and cups. One hand had to constantly sweep away the flies while the other held a fork. On the next trip to Karachi I took canned goods, cheese, crackers, and Manhattan bottles off the aircraft.

The most enjoyable memory I have of the area was sailing on the Arabian Sea, to which Karachi is a port. The boat was about 30 feet in length, the sail a local variety. The captain of the boat's crew handled the helm while little boys ran to whichever side was necessary to compensate the shifting winds, or balance the boat in "coming about". The agile youngsters used a single board they shoved from side to side, upon which one lad would crawl out over the water, while the other end of the board was locked in. They delighted to show their talent, particularly in climbing the mast, which they could scamper up barefooted better than a telephone lineman climbs with cleats on his shoes. Sailing was the coolest way to spend the day.

An unfortunate incident occurred at Karachi, which caused a slight disruption at the hotel. We were having pre-dinner drinks in a pilot's "suite" (as we all tried to avoid the dining room as long as possible) when a bearer came in to service the area. (Crews slept at such irregular hours that workers found it difficult to time their chores.) After cleaning the bath, the man picked up some drinking glasses, which he started to polish. Suddenly one of the pilots grabbed this "cleaner" and almost threw him out of the room, while the rest of us looked on in shock. The poor fellow fled as the pilot yelled at him, "Are you mad? Using the same rag on those glasses you cleaned the toilet with! No wonder we get sick around here." (And we could often get sick. I recall one flight when the cockpit door was repeatedly thrown open as each pilot all night literally ran through the cabin to the lavatory in the rear of the aircraft.)

The next day, on leaving the hotel for the airport, we faced another distressing sight. While our luggage was being put in the taxi, the car was mobbed with women in Punjabi clothing. They each carried a baby and held the other hand out with palm up. Arms came through the car windows; some tapped or grabbed the pilots' shoulders. For moments it looked like a riot might ensue. It was so uncontrollable we had to close the windows and bear the heat. Perhaps their agony was greater than ours was, but all that we had would not have been enough for the many there. Our driver informed us that at least half the women were not even the mothers of the child they held. One pilot broke the tension by pointing to a woman's child, "Lady, I didn't do it, honest. I've never been here before!" But the crew was unusually quiet riding to the airport.

The monsoon season in India brought rain and relief from the intense heat. Afterwards there resumed that impenetrable, stagnant atmosphere of highly seasoned food, smoking cow dung, pungent aroma of burning incense, and odor of the masses of humanity. Some of the poor people I saw lying on the street, I wondered if they were alive. I was told that a wagon went around in the dawn hours and picked up the dead; reminiscent of the Black Plague that took many lives during the Dark Ages of history. I could never go down to the Hooghly River where the burning ghats were located. India left me feeling very humble and more aware of human mortality.

Many Hindu people who traveled on the aircraft would bring their own food in cloth bundles. Perhaps our offerings were not acceptable or they sought to avoid airsickness. They would take our fruit juice, hot tea, or maybe bread. Out of Karachi, on westbound return, there boarded many male Muslims whose bundles proved to be prayer rugs. Late in the night I was asked to point out the direction where Mecca lay. To be precise, I went forward to see the navigator. He was standing on a stool to take sights from the stars with the sextant he had attached to a small opening in the aircraft ceiling. When he removed this instrument, a hissing sound came from air pressure released, until he sealed the hole again. His large table held a map on which he charted our course. The navigator, who was our source for learning where we were and when we would arrive, was as popular with the cabin attendants as the flight engineer, our trusty repairman.

Pointing my hand like a traffic cop, I informed the Muslims the direction to Mecca and dimmed the lights for the evening. Later I stumbled over a figure in the middle of the aisle, bent over in prayer on his rug, facing Mecca. The entire aisle was filled with rugs and bodies facing alike. There was no way I could get to the rear of the aircraft. I returned to the forward galley and allowed them their privacy.

THEN DELHI

Chapter 33

In the fall of 1949 my brother visited New York. We shared enjoyment going to see Jack Lemmon's hilarious stage performance in "Mr. Roberts", and "Asti's Restaurant" in Greenwich Village, well known for the waiters and bar tenders who sang arias from opera. Particularly nice was seeing my brother again. The day he left town, Ellie departed on a London trip and Scheduling called me to go to Lisbon. One of my passengers was the movie star, Madeleine Carroll, of the creamy complexion and large blue eyes. She had starred with men like Sterling Hayden and Gary Cooper. I remembered seeing her in "The Virginian" and "The Prisoner of Zenda". She was so petrified of the aircraft that she asked me to walk her to the lavatory. The weather was no help. Over the Atlantic a hurricane brewed, though we landed safely.

At Lisbon my crew and I drove to Estoril, a Portuguese casino and beach town. Few tourists were about and the place seemed for us alone. Nearby was Cascais, where we arrived in time to see a bull fight. This "sport" does not excite me but at least in Portugal the bulls are not killed in the arena. I took some movie film to catch the swirling colors of animal and man. Sensuousness and grace lay in the bullfighter's movements; however, a large part of the attraction was the colorful toreadors, the horses dressed for the event, and the "oles" of the cheering crowd. When the poor bull was tired, men formed a conga line holding on to the animal's tail as he ran, and kept the bull from charging into them. We Americans could not resist an inconspicuous, "Come on Bull! B-U-L-L!"

When I returned to New York, Ellie and I thought it was a perfect time to see the fall colors of New England. Tony offered to take us in his convertible. It was a gorgeous trip, driving upstate New York and Vermont by the Hudson River and beautiful Lake George. A canopy of red, yellow, and orange leaves surrounded us. In Montreal we experienced our first hotel room with television—all in French. Scheduling had tried to call me for a Calcutta trip, so I could not have left Montreal a day too soon. This time I would have a layover in Delhi. Always eager to see new places, I was packed and delighted that Patty Tibbets would be with me. It was an 18-day trip in which we accumulated 80-plus flight hours.

With only twelve hours in London, we flew to Damascas to spend two and half days. This time I enjoyed going to the market to watch metalsmiths, glass blowers, and leather workers ply their trade, as their ancestors had done for centuries. I was told that the glass blowers seldom lived to age forty before their lungs gave out. The callers in the minerets were still "plying" their trade but I was becoming accustomed to the sound.

Delhi, as India's capital, has tree-lined boulevards and rows of foreign embassies in the modern part, New Delhi. The old city possesses ancient mausoleums and the famous Red Fort built in 1647, where the Royal Baths were as large as a swimming pool, amid beautiful inlaid marble. Patty and I looked upon the harem quarters, a single-story building surrounded by a dry moat with a single elevated walkway. It resembled a doll's house and had long been without women once secluded there for the purpose of pleasing their master.

The following day happened to be Sunday. As a good Catholic, Patty wanted to go to Mass. "A Catholic Church in India!" I asked. But there was, and I accompanied her. The priest spoke in English and the sermon was about "paying one's bills." We flew all the way to India to receive such a lecture.

The flight we were to take to Calcutta was cancelled, giving us seven days in Delhi, time to go to Agra and see the Taj Mahal. The crew hired a car, split expenses, and drove about 125 miles south.

The land was barren in many places, as though farmed for many centuries, with the good soil flushed away by monsoons. Our driver, a bearded Sikh, was a muscular man with hair (longer than most women) that he rolled in a bun under his turban. Sikhs, as strong, powerful men, usually tall in stature, are said to be the most formidable fighters in wartime. They are also a cult that rejects the caste system. We drove over a road shared with cattle drivers, carts, and people.

Two unforgettable events occurred on this ride. One was the sight of women walking for miles behind cows, holding a pan to catch fecal droppings before it fell to the road. With a scarcity of firewood, this matter is dried and used for fuel or roofing material. It was hard to believe their desperation, let alone patience. The second happening, I can still hear as well as see. Our driver, on seeing a dog cross the road, deliberately swerved to hit the poor animal. The dog cried pitifully as we sped on. In no way could we help it and the driver was not about to stop. For this inhuman act, the Sikh was scolded in vociferous ways; however, he did not flinch nor seem to care. Dogs in India were not considered sacred, nor animals to cherish. They required food in a land where human survival was an everyday exigency.

In Agra we saw the memorable Taj Mahal, built by Shah Jahan as a mausoleum for his wife. As a "modern" Wonder of the World, the Taj Mahal is an impressive sight, from its reflection in the rectangular pond before it to the stone-studded interior. Our guide was a young Indian boy who, in a singsong, Indian accent, proudly gave us the historical background. I can still see the incongruous setting of the lad in his torn clothing, standing on the top, white marble step of this elaborate edifice, his eyes filled with envy, saying, "Take me to A-mer-i-ka with you." I hope he became notable for his country in later years; he was so bright, but I had to realize he would have little opportunity. On return to Delhi, we stopped to see the four-storied tomb at Sikandra, built of red stone and marble by Akbar the Great, the Mogul Emperor. If it took 12 years and 20,000 men to build the Taj Mahal, Akbar surely needed as much.

Delhi, being more northerly in India, could be cool at night. In our room in the Swiss Hotel, Patty and I had a fireplace but did not request its usage for fear of what material might be burned. We had our own bearer, who called the roomboy, who called his servant to change the bedding, who harshly called his servant to sweep the floor. The sweeper, a pariah of the lowest caste, had a small short handle broom he literally crept around on his haunches to use. He looked like a frog moving around and never once rose from that stooped position, as though his body could not, even if he tried. When we departed, the bearer called for the roomboy, who brusquely called the baggage boy, who loudly alerted the elevator operator. The local "peckin' order", was strictly observed.

Leaving Delhi, my passenger list showed a total of three. On boarding, I found all the aircraft seats had been removed except the last two rows. The cabin held cargo covered with a tarpaulin. Loaders had come aboard carrying what looked like a small brick. It took two men to carry so small an object. When the pilots arrived, I laughingly mentioned this. "Did you try picking one up?" I was asked. Under the covering were solid gold bars that filled almost the entire cabin of the airplane. We were a flying Ft. Knox.

DECADE END

Chapter 34

Ellie and I both had our vacations in November of 1949. We decided to take advantage of a ride on a PAA ferry flight to Miami. With diminished suntans, we were eager to do something about it. Off we went, packed for summer weather, with a room awaiting us at the famous old Macfadden-Deauville, one of the first great hotels on Miami Beach, and the sight of the Miss America and other beauty contests. The hotel swimming pool was perfectly constructed for meets and diving competitions, preliminaries for the Olympics. The top diving board was the highest on the beach, perhaps on the whole East Coast. However, the old hotel needed serious renovation and was condemned to be torn down. Until this happened, we enjoyed what it provided. The first day at the hotel pool we met others taking advantage of the double room for $6 offered to airline personnel.

It was here that I met William, who actually had just been released by PanAm in a pilot cutback, along with others who were low on the seniority list. The Company began to use the Boeing Stratocruiser, a larger aircraft that carried more passengers but required less cockpit crew. There was also the imminent merger with the overseas part of American Airlines, American Overseas Airline. This meant a converging of seniority lists (which would satisfy neither group). Both changes led to the release of some junior pilots. It was sad to see these men given walking papers. Rarely does a pilot find other positions more suitable. I suppose once a pilot, always a pilot. There is an allurement about it that only they can describe.

It was Will who really introduced me to golf. He played quite well and I found the sport challenging. Will was appealing too. He made me think that maybe, and hopefully, I could be attracted to someone again. I was not in love with him, but he seemed to show interest in me and was like a big cuddly bear. We found time to play golf during the weekdays, not a cheap hobby in Miami or New York, especially for an unemployed pilot. Some of the men "laid off" found other employment, but Will wanted to fly and applied for pilot positions with various airlines. Later a charter outfit accepted him, with no surety to the future.

Following my vacation, I was assigned another Rome-Basra trip that left on the 13th to take me out for Christmas. It appeared I would be in Rome for the 25th. First we stopped in Shannon, staying at the Old Ground Hotel in Ennis. I wanted to try golf again, until the weather made me stick to card games by the fire-place.

In Rome I dallied longer in the Sistine Chapel. Michaelangelo does not allow for a hurried observation. The balance of time was spent in Christmas shopping, with so much to choose from, particularly the fine tooled, inlaid leatherwork, suede products, and various artifacts. Once again I went to the Biblioteca Restaurant where those delicious clams were still winking at me. Before leaving the "Eternal City", I enjoyed Verdi's "Falstaff" at the Rome Opera House. The Italians are proud of their operatic productions. The lobby was bustling with the connoisseurs of the art, all making profuse comments between acts. They were as much a show as the opera itself.

In Basra I left a few dollars buying packaged dates for which Iraq is well known. Our layover was none too short for me. The Arabs left me cold. It was their contemptuous attitude towards Western women. (Our faces were in an "uncovered", unholy state, and our legs showed below the knees.) The American oilrig workers revealed in their eyes a need for some "home cooking", but they were not disrespectful. Ours was one of the last Basra charters. I guess the Iraqis were all "checked out" in oil drilling.

This time we stopped in Damascas before flying back to Rome. It was a layover at the Omayad Hotel that will stay in my mind a long time. Too many crewmembers piled into the elevator with their bags and briefcases. Half way up, in the middle of the high ceiling lobby, the elevator halted with a jolt, as though taking its last gasp. It would neither move up nor down. Here was an airline crew, capable of taking a flying machine anywhere in the world, locked up in a cage with bars on all sides like a jail cell. We were higher than any ladder around. Beneath us was a rustling of people, speaking words we could not understand. One of the pilots took a bottle of whiskey from his briefcase.

"Shall I affect the Weight and Balance and toss this overboard, Skipper?" he joked.

"Oh, let's empty the bottle first."

"I'm willing to sacrifice my Manuals," laughed another.

"Yell FORE before you drop them."

The bottle was passed around while we started a chorus in song. After what seemed hours, and while singing, "How dry I am . . .," the elevator jolted.

"Who burped?" asked the Navigator. At that moment a figure came running down the stairs to announce the trouble was being corrected.

"Hooray!" We all yelled. "Fire three!" (Three is the first engine started on the aircraft. When the captain calls out "Fire three", the co-pilot pushes the starter button.) We did eventually reach the upstairs floor, in a rather "merry" condition.

Later at the old bazaar, feeling in the mood to purchase a Christmas gift for each man in my crew, I saw some pretty little caps. The tradesman tried to discourage me from buying them. I could not understand his manner; did he not want my business? One of the pilots laughingly led me away. It was then I learned the caps were for male sons upon their—becoming a man? Oh, well.

Due to a schedule change, I did not spend Christmas in Rome but was "deadheaded" (term used for positioning crews) on the new Boeing Stratocruiser from Shannon to New York. It was the 1027V (V was called Victor). At 10,000 feet in the sky, just SE of the moon, we saw the Evening Star, tremendous in size. The passengers appreciated the sight and joined together singing carols in the lounge. We landed at the new Idlewild Airport (later renamed Kennedy). Arriving sooner than planned, I was able to attend church and hear Handel's "Messiah" sung beautifully at St. John the Devine Cathedral.

Thus ended for me the decade of the Forties. What a ten years, with high school graduation, college, World War II, and PanAm for almost five years. It also marked a period of finding love that I only had to forget. There had been kindly Will with whom I played golf; Larry, the good looking Ivy Leaguer, who took life so seriously he even frowned when he smiled; and tall, handsome Shawn with twinkling Irish eyes. I asked my heart, "Why are you being so difficult?"

By 1950 I had flown 4,325 hours. Mileage I never computed, but it was all by piston aircraft.

BOEING STRATOCRUISER

Chapter 35

The 1950s bared new horizons for PanAm. Merging with American Overseas Airline was a certainty. The new Boeing Stratocruiser, the B-377, was all the rage and deserves comment. This plane was the last of the piston aircraft designed for total passenger comfort, carrying 60 passengers, all one-class fare, and 12 to 14 upper berths. Lower berths, rarely used, were later disengaged due to the number of seat displacements, making them impractical. The cabin door was just forward of the stairwell steps that circled down to a bar and lounge. The lounge led to a cargo compartment and emergency exit with built-in steps; the latter, when opened, would enable one to walk down to the ground. This was the "belly" section of the fuselage. The original configuration (before Economy class was inaugurated by PAA) had a large ladies room on the starboard side and men's room to port. More than one person could enter the lavatories that had several basins, as the WC was a separate unit within. Forward of the lavatories was a more private compartment for two upper and lower berths. The cockpit was spacious but the galley in the tail of the aircraft was the worst part of the design. There could often be a decided "sway" in flight, with or without rough weather. I recall turbulence that caused an unbelievable incident. I had set up trays on both sides of the galley deck. The plane hit an air pocket that caused the loaded trays to fly up and land on the opposite side. Amazingly they did not collide, but merely changed sides. Ripley would not have believed it.

Just forward of the galley was a jumpseat and desk for the purser to handle paper work, note the call lights, Public Address System, and cockpit intercom. Music was piped out for passenger enjoyment. Comfort and food service were the selling points of the Boeing Stratocruiser, which had nicknames like the "Double Bubble", and "Pregnant Duck". The cabin held recliner seats with foot extensions and pullout tables built in the arm rests. Some London and Paris trips had what PAA called the President Special flights. Five flight attendants handled these, with a deluxe cart service using PAA Rosenthal china, with special logo-marked silver and glasses, in addition to the usual transoceanic amenities. Regular flights carried three cabin attendants and were not as elaborate a service as the President Special, but still had a course by course meal service. Martinis, Manhattans, and the best wines were offered as part of the meal. Entrees were dished from partially cooked food in containers that were re-heated in galley ovens. Coffee was prepared in a huge, restaurant-size urn and served using a silver tray, pitcher, creamer and sugar set (with tongs). Along with dessert, the passengers were offered a choice of cheese, fruit, and mints, followed by after-dinner liqueurs. Compared to casseroles, canisters, or container frozen meals, it was considered a nice service.

In February I was still flying the Constellations and DC-4s but had my first flight to Nice on the French Riviera. It was a brief stay; long enough to learn there was no "sandy" beach. The shore was mostly pebbles with a waterfront that consisted of a boulevard with deluxe hotels, and a promenade upon which "everyone who was anyone" meandered. It was winter and little swimming took place, only the casinos were busy. I took a short walk before retiring—such was the brevity of my visit. Regardless of the interesting places traveled, fatigue could be ever present.

In disappointment, I was not called for a Stratocruiser trip but several Bermuda flights and another trip to Damascas. PanAm still used the "Connies" on the RTW (Round the World) trips. One of my passengers was Joseph Cotton, the famous movie star. When he walked on the aircraft, one really felt his presence, a distinguished aura about him. Other celebrities on my flights were the handsome Stewart Granger, Trevor Howard with the unmistakable raspy voice, gentle-hearted boxer, Primo Carnera, and Jersey Joe Walcott, who gave each of us an autographed photo. Tourism was not in full sway; economy fares were yet to come. If not the wealthy, most travelers were sent by their government or employers.

This time we flew so low over Germany that bombed areas from the War could still be seen—not just blocks, but miles of destruction. It did not appear as though Germany could ever recover. The skipper on my flight brought his wife along, with whom I enjoyed shopping and touring in Damascas. In a rented car with guide, we stopped to look at camel caravans laden for journey. The camels were not the sweetest smelling animals, nor the friendliest, but the Syrians let them know who was boss. At the old market I had my first and only experience of a near faint, probably caused by fatigue, or "something you ate?" I was more embarrassed than frightened, but grateful I was not alone. Later I purchased a round copper tray with etched design and a raw-leather tote bag. It was fascinating to walk the narrow, cobblestone streets, pass through the Roman East Gate and walkways where Christ himself had tread centuries ago.

On return, in London, I met my friends from New Orleans who took me about the English countryside where every home, even the most humble, had a flower garden. We drove to the little town of St. Albans to see the old cathedral and a Roman theater still operating in England. Soon I had to return to take my flight from Heathrow Airport, where I learned I would go home on a Stratocruiser. But before leaving London I was able to see the musical, "Annie Get Your Gun", with an English cast that did well mimicking Western accents.

I left on the 1033V, amid a fanfare of people out to see the Boeing 377. The plane always drew crowds. It was also "a bugger to get the kinks out", like a new car. From London we landed in

Shannon, departed Shannon and then back to Shannon before continuing to Goose Bay, Labrador and Idlewild. (The flight engineer informed me that as soon as the Stratocruiser landed and the engines cooled, troubles invariably ensued; if the engines could be kept running all the time, there would be less problems.)

Over the ocean, after the dinner service, the upper births were pulled down for usage. Generally they were all sold—for $25. A ladder was used to assist the passengers into the berths, which had safety belts for turbulence. We kept only the aisle lights on so all could sleep. As usual, the bar downstairs was kept active late into night. When a gentleman came upstairs and asked for his berth, I attached the ladder and opened the curtain. There was a quick closing from the inside that embarrassed me to believe I had the wrong berth. Checking my list, I confirmed it was his. This time I called and asked the person in the berth to please identify. There was no answer. I called again and still no reply. Then a passenger seated across the aisle revealed that a woman had crawled into the berth by leaping from the back of a seat. By description it had to be the Turkish woman who spoke no English. This time I called her name. She opened the curtain and I tried to explain that regretfully, etc. She came down the ladder mumbling. Later she was found in another berth. The same explanation was given, only this time I insisted, "Please, no, no!" When I caught her climbing up a third time, I grabbed her long skirt and tried to halt her, until she started kicking at me. No one volunteered to haul her out of the berth and I had not been trained in Turkish fighting tactics. The berth purchaser relinquished his option (with a refund). He stayed in the bar enjoying drinks (on the house). I thought the sun would never rise (it finally did). My log says that with the turnarounds, the flight time alone was 21.27 hours. It felt longer.

Another time on the Stratocruiser, bad weather forced us to delay during the middle of the night at an airport in New Brunswick. Some passengers roamed outside, others used their berths or just slept in their reclining seats. As long as passengers did not smoke, it was safe for them to stay on the aircraft and the cabin crew would attend them. When ready to depart, I counted noses and was short one passenger. I searched again but finally announced we would be delayed further until the missing person was found. From an upper berth, a waving hand extended through the curtain and a female voice said, "I'm in here!" The lady had not purchased the berth; it belonged to the gentleman with her, whom she had met in the lounge that evening. This may be called "joining the mile high club". The steward got on the Public Address system to say, "Stop whatever you're doing, folks, and buckle up! We're taking off!"

SINATRA

Chapter 36

In May of 1950 I was assigned a 17-day trip to South Africa. With an unexpected, delayed departure, one passenger complained of not being advised before coming to the airport. The passenger was Frank Sinatra. It was rumored that the famous "Blue Eyes" was flying to Spain to see Ava Gardner, the star with whom he was reputed to be violently in love. On boarding the aircraft, Mr. Sinatra arrived in a combative mood. His opinion of PAA was considerably low, as he let me know what he thought of the "oversight". As his whipping post, he left me downhearted before the cabin door was even closed.

Frank Sinatra was smaller and shorter than I had imagined him to be, but his body was as muscular as a boxer. The plane was a DC-4 and Sinatra sat in the front, port side seats across from a woman with a child and a baby. Mothers with babies were usually given the front row where a bassinet could be attached to the forward bulkhead. When the baby started crying and the other little one was crawling all over Mr. Sinatra, I quietly asked if he would like another seat. Bad idea! He not only reminded me that he had requested those seats for the larger space in front, but advised me, "I like children. Why don't you just warm this baby's bottle?" Ouch! We already had a bottle warming in the hot cup.

Later I saw "Blue Eyes" coming down the aisle to our DC-4 galley with a baby bottle in one hand and his other arm holding the baby. He claimed the milk was cold and proceeded to show me how to test the milk in a baby's bottle. I stood there sorrowfully and listened. The bottle had been warm enough when I first gave it to the mother but . . . well, at least Mr. Sinatra was talking to me. A friend of mine had him on a trip and enjoyed a marvelous date with him afterwards. What do I get—a lesson on how to warm and test the temperature of a baby's bottle. I was at 20,000 feet in a confined area with a notable like Frank Sinatra lecturing me. As we drew close to landing, Sinatra came back to the galley holding a full carton of Coca Colas.

"I won't need these," he curtly said. "I understand you will be leaving this flight and I thought you might like some cokes." Then he gave me a forgiving smile. It was the smile that did it. That was all I needed. Perhaps he was the type who could not apologize if he hurt you; he just gave you something. After that, Sinatra flew off to Ava, and I flew down to the Gold Coast to live on pineapples, avocados, and Frank Sinatra's cokes.

In Accra we were usually met by "Trader Dan", who came to the airport to sell his wares. Dan would say, "I'm losing money, but I'm learning English." He followed the Muslim faith, dressed in long, full robes, revealing an impeccable affluence. Dan knew the airline schedule and was prompt on arrivals with fresh new materials. Also well remembered was Jonathan, our "room boy", who was really a man, respected and beloved. Jonathan moved so silently in his bare feet that it was difficult to tell when he was near, but he was always there.

Back in New York the news was that Gary had a job in Connecticut, Will in California, Phil had a "nibble" on his writing, Ellie was studying oil painting, and my brother was to be married in July. I requested Scheduling's help to be around for the wedding, as I was to be a bridesmaid. I could not be home for dress fittings, so I mailed my measurements. At that time I was 5' 4", 113 pounds.

Hopeful of enough time off on return, I left for Beirut, Lebanon, a new horizon for me. On the coastline of the eastern Mediterranean Sea, it was more modern than other places I had visited in the Near East. People dressed in western garb, showed a more progressive spirit, and revealed their European influence. To see earlier times, we hired a car and drove to Baalbek, the ruined city first built by the Romans. Baalbek bore no signs of being guarded or restored. We were the only ones there. The entrance had a long, high-stepping, marble stairway that Hollywood's deMille might have coveted for films. Marble pillars of a once huge temple were 18 ft in diameter; most of these lay broken on the ground. One toppled pillar leaned on another as though it was ready to fall any minute. It had been that way for hundreds of years. The Temple of Bacchus was surrounded by erect pillars, and appeared as it might have a few thousand years ago. Imagine the magnificence of this city in its original ensemble.

From Beirut it was back to Istanbul for a short stop. When the engines were "fired up" again to leave, they were just as abruptly "cut off". A cylinder change maybe? Hours went by. I walked under the plane and looked up at the flight engineer working in his shirtsleeves.

"Chuck, how much longer?

"Can't tell yet.

"I've got to get back for a wedding.

"Can't it wait a few hours?

"Please, Chuck. It's one of those big weddings, the kind with trimmings.

"Well, I'm trying. Hand me that wrench," he said to his assistant.

Night came on. It got dark, darker—and later. A large floodlight was placed to help the engineer and maintenance man as they worked. I walked under the aircraft again, skirting the cowling pieces that lay on the tarmac.

"Chuck," I cried, "Will it be much longer?

"You getting married?

"No, Chuck, my brother is, and the wedding's in Mississippi.

"Well, why didn't you say so. You might make it if you hurry. Almost done."

I was "almost done for" by the time we got underway. When we landed in Brussels with radio trouble, that delayed us again. If my brother only knew how hard it was for me to get to his wedding. I finally reached New York two days late. It was off one plane and on to another with Capital Airlines; the connection was so close. When I finally arrived in Mississippi I did not know if my dress would fit, but at least I got there.

OTHER CELEBRITIES

Chapter 37

Will had a flight to New York and spoke of wanting to get married as soon as he got a "regular" flying job. My feelings were questionable, but we played golf and both of us continued traveling. In the last months of 1950, I worked on the DC-4, Constellation, and Stratocruiser, flying to London, Bermuda, Puerto Rico, Lisbon, and the Riviera. By September, there were strike threats regarding the American Overseas Airlines merger. It took a while before the "marriage" became acceptable; pride held forth for those of both airlines.

PAA frequently had celebrities as passengers. On a flight to the Riviera, we had a gentleman who was "in line" to the throne of Italy. He wore such a strong perfume I had to open all the passenger air sockets for ventilation. Other celebrities crossing the ocean were the well known Elizabeth Arden going to Ireland, Robert Newton on a trip to London, whose performance as Long John Silver in the old "Treasure Island" film has never been emulated. Prince de Ligne, Belgium's Ambassador to India, was the dearest, elder gentleman, kind, dignified, and modest, with not a haughty bone in his body. At the airport in Rome, I came close enough to Mary Pickford and Charles Buddy Rogers, her husband, to learn that Mary had a slight "Brooklynese" accent, unsuspected in her silent films.

My favorite movie star passenger was Claudette Colbert, the lovely lady with the round face and large eyes. With Clark Gable in "It Happened One Night" she won an Oscar and all the plaudits she deserved. Miss Colbert boarded our flight with a refreshing spirit to lighten anyone's life. After complimenting our dinner service, she was aided to her berth that she requested by saying, "when you're not so busy". In the morning she awakened early, opened the curtain and showed the same beautiful smile and cheerfulness with which she retired. Later in the ladies room I caught her cleaning the basins and picking up paper towels.

"Please, Miss Colbert, you mustn't do that." I almost cried.

"Let me help you. You and your crew work so hard," was her reply. I later wrote her of the pleasure it was to meet her. Little did I realize that she would answer with a letter written in long hand.

When my office assigned me to be interviewed by a New York Times reporter for an article about PanAm food preparation, it was the closest to celebrity status for me. My picture was in the paper working the galley in full dress uniform with hat on. This was for publicity, but it amused me because we never worked the galley with hats or jackets. In fact, in those days the galley attendant used a white butcher's apron to keep the uniform clean. As for full dress, I never saw a pilot wear his hat while flying the aircraft, and rarely his jacket. In the movies, even if ditching the aircraft, pilots have their hats and coats on. Semper paratus!

Passengers could make varied comments to break any monotony. Once I was asked if we had a tail wind. I checked with the cockpit and advised the passenger that we did indeed have a tail wind. "I thought so," he said, "I could feel it." Unconsciously I looked back as though there was a hole in the aircraft. Another time, a passenger insisted that we had a rough engine, as he heard it. I, too, had once asked the pilots about the altered drone. It was explained that sometimes engine sounds could vary when changing fuel tanks while in flight. The passenger became more interested, so the pilots received him in the cockpit. Their door was always left unlocked and passengers could enter when invited.

Then there was the passenger who put his hand to my leg in a too personal way as I walked down the aisle in the dark of night. Disbelieving, I ignored this until the maneuver was repeated. Then

I whispered, "Please, sir, keep your hands to yourself." I thought the woman sitting next to him was asleep, but she hauled off and punched him. No, she slugged him. Then she casually resumed her sleeping position without uttering a word.

Once a passenger had repeatedly asked for a Martini. The stewardess came back to the galley and said, "My Spanish isn't too sharp but I can understand when he says 'one Martini', and I gave him another Martini." Later the pilots inquired, "Do we have a passenger named Juan Martini? We got a message about him. He's supposed to be on the Puerto Rico flight." The flight was destined for London.

One night when what seemed a quiet and uneventful flight, I walked downstairs to clean the lounge and found a lone female passenger completely naked, dancing all over the seats. Finding her clothes, it was impossible to get the woman to dress. "Why couldn't she have flown BOAC," I thought. Since we had to think of the passengers who would come down to the lounge as soon as the sun rose, I beckoned the steward to help me dress her. "Not me!" he replied. "That's not in *my* contract." There were no volunteers from the cockpit either. I must add that nothing about her body was particularly attractive. Finally the skipper looked at the junior man and said, "Better get back there and help dress her." What a picture to see a uniformed pilot sitting in the lounge next to a naked woman, casually conversing; however, he was able to coax her into dressing again.

Filling in government forms revealed a few comical passengers. Where "Sex" was asked, some wrote "Not Enough," or "Often". A Health Form inquired where the passenger spent the previous ten nights. One passenger simply wrote for each ten nights, "In Bed," "In Bed," "In Bed."

Perhaps there will never be an airplane that is designed with enough hand luggage space to satisfy everyone. On the B-377s, with berths overhead, hand articles soon filled the closets. One trip, while welcoming passengers at the main door, I saw a huge bass fiddle case coming up the stairs. When I was able to see the owner, I advised him that the article had to be checked with the cargo, as there was no place in the cabin. The man's face dropped and he tightly grabbed his possession. As he held up the passengers trying to board behind him, who were standing on the steps in a chilling wind, I asked him to please stand aside a moment (while I called for help). But no Traffic man was in sight. I felt deserted. When everyone boarded, I was able to rearrange some seating in order to put the instrument by its owner, strapped in with a seat belt. That's how that fiddle crossed the ocean. I could not bear to see a grown man cry.

As most air travelers over water know, flight attendants demonstrate how to don life jackets and identify the location of exits. Piston aircraft did not originally have life rafts attached and inflated automatically upon opening the door. Rafts were stowed overhead in the ceilings and were brought to the door and wing exits in an emergency. We were trained on how to inflate them and make use of the contents; including, turning salt water to drinkable, using flares and a portable SOS called the Gibson Girl. We learned fire fighting equipment and survival tactics in jungles and desert, even how to make a shelter of ice and snow. The handsome movie star, John Carroll, crossed the ocean on one of my flights and offered to be of assistance if ever needed. Oh, how nice. . . .

I spent Christmas of 1950 in New Orleans. The wayward daughter was home for the Holidays with perfume from France, linen from Ireland, brass work from India, woolens from England, and a bottle of Rose Mateus from Lisbon. I had accumulated 5,050 hours of flight time, which is more than half a year spent in the air.

ATTEMPTS

Chapter 38

One cold, January morning in 1951, Scheduling called with a notification. "Your departure tomorrow is now 8:45 a.m., report at 7:30." This meant I had to rise at 5 a.m., leave by 6, and not miss the subway or the bus to Idlewild Airport. Flight time could be 13 to 15 hours. The total time between dress and rest came to anywhere from 18 to 24 or more hours. All was not roses and sweetness.

No matter how much I enjoyed traveling or felt accomplished on the aircraft, my folks believed I had flown long enough and urged me to try and extend my capabilities while still young. In my personal letters were rejections from employers who felt I did not meet their "needs". From an advertisement that said, "Copy-writer, Tomorrow's Vintage," I discovered I was not the right vintage. Another firm, a publishing company, rejected me. I wondered if I was disadvantaged being a woman or because I lacked a college degree, or both. When I did get asked for an interview to a promising position, I was called for a three-week trip. To cancel the interview was tantamount to telling a suitor you could not become "engaged" because you had to go to Asia or Africa.

Perhaps if I had completely left PanAm to look for other employment, I might have made a greater effort; however, it was half-hearted because I really did not want to leave. I had grown up with PanAm and felt as though we were part together. Besides, winter was due, the apartment furnace had broken down, and it was nice to have a paycheck to buy warm clothing. (Our mothers sent us blankets.) Mr. Bertia sent his nephew to repair the furnace but that was like stopping a dam leak with masking tape.

My trip returned via Mindenhall, an Air Force base in England where we boarded 61 airmen returning to the States. We landed in Keflavik, Iceland, but the cold did not bother the airmen who had already packed their overcoats. They were happy just to be going home.

Back at the apartment, I discovered that Gary had returned. Until he knew what he really wanted, he stayed unemployed. Ellie planned to quit flying and attend art school. She had her paints with which anyone who walked in the door was done in oils. Gary had his books, which soon filled the orange-crate bookcases. I took an interest in tropical fish, which obliged me with constant little ones. Gary thought of going to India to join some "gamma gamma" group, as best that I can remember the name. It was a movement of "deep thinkers". He informed me how he admired "sacrifice and denial as a learning way of life".

"Gary, there are many people who don't sacrifice and deny themselves because they believe in it," I added. "They have no alternative. There are millions of those poor souls in India." Ellie would smile and listen. We would spend hours in discussions.

PanAm was finally awarded a schedule to Paris, the world's reputed, most beautiful city. When I was called for a trip there, I asked myself, "how could I think of leaving my life of flying." With a delay in Gander, I began to wonder if Paris was but a dream. I watched the poor Flight Engineer on the aircraft wings checking the gas, gloved hands holding the dip stick in 10 degrees below weather, and almost be blown away by the howling wind. He had no idea of getting another job. This was his life. Passengers finally boarded, and the Traffic "rep" handed me the ship's briefcase. "Have a nice trip," he said, as he pulled the cabin door to close, showing how anxious he was to get back in the warm terminal.

"Hold it!" I called, "There's just one problem."

"What's that?" he asked.

"The pilots aren't on board yet."

We did get to Paris. We stayed at the Hotel d'Iena. February was not the best time for a Paris trip, as I recalled pictures showing people walking in sunshine on the Champs Elysees. At least I got there, and with a three day layover. I even had my own room and bath. The tub was the old claw-leg model, six fect long and wide as a pool. I filled it to the top with cerulean blue water. Whatever created that color, I would not hazard a guess, and I was warned not to drink from the tap. The French never seemed to drink water; wine was their thirst-quenching beverage. I learned that a bottle of wine, a loaf of bread, and Camembert cheese could happily satisfy king, peon, or stewardess.

Cold weather in Paris did not stop me from touring the Louvre, the Eifel Tower, and the Cathedral of Notre Dame. Days could be spent in the Louvre and still you could never see all of it, to say nothing of getting lost before finding the way out. As for dining, one could pick the most expensive restaurant or a neighborhood family place; the latter had more interesting atmosphere and good cuisine. The difference in prices was considerable. My crew wanted to visit the Invalides Museum where the displays are not only historically interesting but it is where Napoleon is buried. For a tomb it is impressive—a huge, marble sarcophagus mounted high in its own rotunda. For the French, Napoleon is their George Washington. For evening entertainment we saw the famous "Follies" in Montmartre, shades of Toulouse Lautrec, with male comics and bare-breasted women flaunting themselves on stage. When we left the famous Moulin Rouge, the "ladies of the night" on the street did not hesitate to accost our pilots as if selling a subscription to *The Ladies Home Journal.* From Paris' Orly Airport we flew to Rome, long enough to enjoy the famous "Ulpia" restaurant. I was not to see Paris or Rome again that spring or summer. Paris became a President Special flight, with selected crews led by male pursers.

Back in New York, Ellie and Gary encouraged me to try snow skiing. I knew nothing about riding slats on snow slopes. We took a tour bus up the western side of the Hudson River to Belleaye Ski Resort in the Catskills, located northwest of Kingston. I did attach my feet to two pieces of wood and took a lesson; however, when I saw ambulances remove several skiers, one after another, who were brought down the mountain with broken legs—*that* finished me. Two good walking legs were imperative to my livelihood. One skier smiled as he was driven away, waved to his friends saying, "See you next year!" I never learned to ski.

In March I had a plane full of travel agents going to Nice, preparing for tourists who would invade Europe in the months to come. It was the start of a greater return to tourism after WWII. I enjoyed telling what I knew of the places we saw. The tour leader offered to hire me if I would live in a small town in Kansas. I was not quite ready for that.

I had accumulated enough time off (or was it, enough dollars) to take the train down to Washington, D.C. and visit friends from college days, as well as Jean Weber and her husband who had returned from living abroad. Lastly, Frannie, who was pregnant with what looked like twins, but was actually just a big baby boy. Though they were all married and living a style so different from my own, I felt fortunate to have such good friends. I could not bring myself to marriage for the sake of being married, I only thought about it.

VACATION TIME

Chapter 39

Towards the end of April, Ellie received a call from a senator of her home state who was attending a political banquet at the Waldorf Astoria. A friend of her family, he had promised to check on Ellie while in New York. We prepared for this visit by placing all "loose" articles under the beds or crammed in the closet. When the Senator and his wife arrived, they learned that Stanford-grad Gary was not employed (by choice), slept on a couch in our one bedroom apartment (by virtue of a home-made curtain) shared with his sister and a friend (me), my tank of tropical fish, and a mongrel dog. Ellie reported her interest in art and her part time job at the Stork Club as a "coat check" girl, where she received fantastic tips from the fabulously wealthy and famous. The Senator left us showing the normal composure of a politician in complimentary approbation.

Around Easter, I received a call from my mother's cousin on Long Island who insisted I come to lunch. She had invited a gentleman she wished me to meet, who was probably given the same story. It was a quiet, uncomfortably classic, luncheon at their country club. The young man was heir to a shipping company fortune and perhaps my cousin was hopeful of a match. I believe the "prospect" attended as a courtesy to the Admiral and was no more relaxed than I was. When time to leave, he offered to drive me back to Manhattan. What I did not expect was a black limousine with a chauffeur. When we reached my apartment in Greenwich Village, my neighbors stared in disbelief as I stepped from this impressive automobile with the chauffeur holding the door. I augmented this scene as long as I could, holding back laughter at the stretched necks from windows.

May was my vacation month. William, who was flying with a charter airline out of San Francisco, encouraged me to visit. My new friend, Stan, owner of a small dress shop in New York, was upset that I did not advise him of my trip so he could go with me. I met Stan months before while shopping. He was handsome, charismatic, and lived nearby. However, vacationing with a man to whom I was not married, was not in my plans. Besides, what would I do with Stan around William, who spoke of marriage?

The charter line that employed Will had a cargo flight departing Newark for the West Coast. I was able to get a free ride upon this aircraft, as long as I served coffee to the crew, who surely carried me as a favor to Will. My seat was a crated box that I softened with my raincoat. I guess it was illegal for me to be aboard, but I did not take time to find out. In a long DC-4 flight, the crated box got harder every mile, with stops in Chicago, Amarillo, Texas, and Burbank, California.

I paid my way from Burbank to San Francisco on Pacific Southwest Airlines, landing at Oakland where Will met me. Arrangements had been made for me to stay with PanAm girls who lived on the peninsula side of the Bay. Will drove over the San Mateo Bridge and pointed to San Francisco. Visibility was remarkable in the clear air. The area was not crowded like New York, though I was told that thousands of people moved to California every day. The girls convinced me to fly to Hawaii too, but first I wanted to see San Francisco. Will drove me through the most beautiful city I had ever visited in the U.S. The hills, ocean, and surrounding bay, even the fog, delighted me.

One dark cloud affected my visit. I attended a party with Will, but as the evening progressed, I discovered he grew quite belligerent with each drink. He became mean and contentious. I asked to leave, as this was a side of Will I had never seen; however, it could have been a fatal departure. On the Bayshore Freeway, he kept his foot on the pedal to reach 80 mph. A slow moving van appeared where we were on line to hit. Will seemed not to see, care, or heed my warning. Slowly, so the car would not go out of control, I moved the steering wheel to miss the van by inches. I never saw Will again after that. I knew he had been deeply in love with another before we met. I realized that I was his attempt to forget her, and I had failed. I could not blame him. In truth, I had probably befriended him for the same reason.

A childhood friend, Holly, and her architect husband living in Monterey, invited me to visit. Their hospitality curbed my sinking spell. Bus service took me south on 101, just a two lane highway lined with orchards. Near the ocean were rows of artichoke fields, then miles of sand dunes around Fort Ord. My friends, who were building a home that gave them a view of Monterey Bay, introduced me to the charms of Carmel, the 17 Mile Drive, Big Sur, and historic Monterey itself. I promised to return again some day.

With my PAA discount, I flew round trip to Hawaii for $50; full fare was $320. It was a nine and a half-hour flight on a Stratocruiser. We landed at the airport with its "ALOHA" lettering on the tower. Every passenger was given a flower lei while welcomed with ukulele music and hula dancing at the foot of the stairs. Our aircraft was the only plane on the tarmac besides a Hawaiian Airlines' DC-3.

The two hotels on Waikiki Beach were the pink Royal Hawaiian, with acres of tropical plants and trees, and the Moana Hotel. They were side by side. Across the street were the Moana cottages where rooms for the stewardesses were located. It was here I was accommodated for $4 daily, a special rate for PAA. Diamondhead, the remains of an ancient volcano, was unobstructed from any point on the beach, looking as it might have when Captain Cook sailed by centuries ago. Every week the "Matsonia" cruise ship (later renamed the "Lurline") arrived from San Francisco around 9 a.m. and departed at 5 p.m. Outrigger canoes greeted the vessel as the islanders had done for ages.

Movie stars Richard Denning and Ian Hunter were guests at the Moana, but more obvious were Spike Jones and his "rinky dink" band. These "musicians" used wash boards, tin cans, and any noisemaker they could turn into instruments. Dressed outlandishly, they were being filmed beside the outrigger canoes on the sand. The stewardesses obliged the photographers with a little bathing suit glamour. The best entertainment at the Moana was under the banyan tree in the patio by the ocean. Live music, singing and hula dancing were broadcast to the States every Saturday as "Hawaii Calls". The program always began with a gentle sound of the surf, heard from a microphone placed by the water.

After this paradise, still the " Territory of Hawaii", I flew to Portland, Oregon, and visited Ellie's mother. She showed me a part of the Northwest that would take no back seat to any area for natural beauty—snow capped Mt. Hood, the Columbia River Gorge, the Oregon coastline. Here too, God must have held a paintbrush as he molded the world.

VACATION ENDS

Chapter 40

Instead of taking a flight from Portland, Ellie's mother drove me south along the renown, rocky coastline, turning inland at Florence, Oregon, for Eugene. We passed fish hatcheries, lumber mills, and massive log trucks. The tall, stately, redwood trees were slowly being cut down. I wondered how long this clearing could go on. We drove through Tillamook, in miles of burnt tree stumps, where a great fire had destroyed the area. Beauty arose with the wild rhododendrons along the coast; lavender and white were their natural flower color. In Eugene I left my kind friend, boarded a West Coast Airlines flight to Medford, Oregon, and from there took Southwest Airlines to San Francisco. It was truly a "loggers run", as we stopped at little towns and carried lumberjacks in and out of the areas. "Hop scotch" flying in a small plane was familiar to me from my DC-3 days.

At the San Francisco airport I met Betty Horn, another stewardess. During WWII Betty was a WASP pilot and had participated as well in various airshows. Attractive, of petit build, she was a veteran to the mechanics of flying. Betty was planning to fly to Bishop, California, to meet some military pilots for a fishing trip in the Sierras. Would I like to go? Oh, yes.

The next day we drove to the area of the old San Francisco airport where Betty kept her Cessna. After the preliminaries of flight advisory and course plotting, we left the ramp and lined up with the larger aircraft for takeoff. Airline pilots smiled and waved from their cockpits, as they looked at two girls in the tiny plane.

When we rolled down the runway, I shall ever recall the sensation. Unlike an airliner, it felt as though the plane was a feather being gently lifted to the heights. We flew over the Santa Clara Valley and crossed east at Pacheco Pass. It was VCR (visual flight rules) at 2, 4, and 6000 feet. Near Fresno the airport reported thick clouds and icy conditions where we planned to fly over the Sierras. Betty turned south to cross at Porterville. The snow capped Sierras looked cold but beautiful. Visibility improved but we needed 10,000 ft to get over the mountains. All was going well when, midway over the Sierras, Betty calmly said, "The carburetor's acting up. It's icing. We either go back or try to make Bishop." I could only gulp. It looked rugged down below. Betty elected to proceed, and landed safely.

Waiting for us beside their plane were three of the "flying fishermen" we were to join. One of them was Chuck Yeager, the famous army pilot who had gained fame by being the first man to break the speed of sound. This day he piloted a beautiful plane, almost as good looking as the handsome grin he wore. He and his crew had known Betty and her flying exploits since the war. Two other Army pilots joined us, driving a van with necessary equipment. We drove to the town of Bishop to get fishing licenses, where there were more people on horseback down the main street than automobiles.

Up into the mountains, the van was parked near a rippling creek. The men had brought army sleeping bags which I found hard to believe could be so warm while snow and ice were visibly near. Camping and fishing gear, and fur-lined jackets were available for all. One man carried a guitar that he set into motion singing cowboy songs as soon as a campfire was lit. He was an army fire chief, as well as a grandfather (whom we all kidded had qualified him to be our chaperon). I slept well, zippered in the sleeping bag with my face to the sky. The beauty of the high country is a catharsis for the soul.

In the early morning I smelled ham and eggs and was the only one not "up and about". I quickly joined the group; not wanting to be considered an inept city girl. I learned we could take all the water we wanted, but not wash anything in the creek. "The water must be left clean," advised a forest ranger who came by. "It flows to serve Los Angeles."

Located at 7000 ft, we hiked near Crowley Lake to Rock Creek where the men cast their lines all day. They were serious fishermen. I had no luck with my pole, so I stretched out by the rocky stream to feel the sun and look upon this great country. Betty nudged me to say that I should put my hand in the water and feel how cold, if I were to roll in. Somehow the fish were not biting; it was steak and beans for dinner, which the men prepared on the grill. They had their own system about everything and insisted on doing the cooking and clean up. Betty and I sat back and enjoyed the food and guitar music.

The next day we hiked down a 1000ft gorge to another stream. At one point we crossed on an old rope bridge that swayed frighteningly. The chief advised me not to look down at the rushing water but keep a firm hold and just watch where I put each foot. While others fished, Betty and I climbed a rocky cliff and thought of the American Indians who were there first. I believe we found a spot where once they might have used a protected, cave-like cliff. Fire burns on the stone appeared ancient, not of recent igniting. It was a perfect lookout point. Since our fishermen friends were real frontiersmen; they found Betty and me by our footprints and the twigs we broke. On return we found deer and coyote tracks which had crossed our own. This time some fish were deprived of their life in the stream and nothing compares to fresh trout, grilled in the outdoors.

The next day Betty and I thought how nice it would be to take a shower. Talk about grubby feelings, it was worse than being in the same uniform for thirty hours. Maybe others were thinking the same. Chuck liked to fish and took his friends to these mountains whenever he could. He also knew someone who had a cabin nearby with modern facilities. We drove there and took turns to a welcomed shower. Pioneers may have survived without such luxuries, but how did they ever bare those ticks?

On return to San Francisco in the Cessna, we climbed to 12,000 feet. We took forty minutes to cross the snowy mountains just south of Yosemite, overheading Millerton Lake. Above the valley, Betty asked if I would like to fly the plane. (Who me?) I was never interested in flying as a pilot. However, I felt I had to say, "Yes, if you tell me what I should do." I did not want to seem unappreciative. Betty's instructive comments were, "Keep your vision peripheral," and "Left wing up, right wing down, watch for traffic 180 degrees!" With my hands frozen on the wheel, each finger had to be pulled away separately, to disengage me. Being a pilot—not for me.

Before leaving California, I visited Patty and her husband in Berkeley. Their home was high on the hill with a gorgeous view of both cities and bridges. We drove to see the redwoods at Muir Woods, across the Golden Gate. Over the bridge, it was partly engulfed in fog and partly in sunshine. I had a vacation that so impressed me; I kept this new horizon in the back of my mind as a place to see again.

My return to New York was on a PanAm ferry, the 1040V, which I was lucky to get because these flights rarely occurred. I arrived to find Ellie engrossed with painting, only a few of my tropical fish had died, and Gary was constantly reading with his feet up on the coffee table. Stan was still upset with me; Larry had moved to Queens; Phil must have sold something he wrote as his raincoat was out of hock. He and Ellie were eating out—mostly paella at "Nino and Nella's" restaurant. It was getting serious between them. Scheduling gave me a trip to Frankfurt, Germany. I was ready to go again.

FORMER AOA FLIGHTS

Chapter 41

With PanAm's crash in Monrovia, Africa, there were no survivors. The stewardess was a particularly cheerful and popular individual, whose laughter and southern accent could be heard long after she was gone. Her mother lived in Louisiana and spoke Cajun French. It was difficult to explain what had happened to her daughter. It took days for anyone to hack through the jungles to where the crash lay. Only the stewardess jacket with wings attached could be identified. When these tragedies occurred, we could only hope it happened so quickly that the victims never realized their fate.

The merger of Pan American Airways and American Overseas Airline meant flying to Scandinavia and Germany. It was so soon after WWII, I pondered on what to expect in the latter country. After first stopping at Prestwick, Scotland, and Amsterdam, we stayed at the Monopole-Metropole Hotel in Frankfurt. I hoped my German name would influence the desk clerk to give me a room with a bath. No, only the pilots got a room with a bath.

At that time the German people were not overwhelmingly friendly, not even pretentiously so; however, I recognized that too recently we Americans were their mortal enemies. The hotel was near the famous railway station, the Metropole Bahnhaus, known for its rounded, glass-enclosed roof, blown away during the War. It had to be hard for the native people to smile at us. Blocks of complete destruction from allied bombings were clearly visible. Yet the streets were as clean as if mopped every day. Never did I see a loafer, beggar, or anyone not working. Resignation as well as helplessness was not their natural demeanor. There was pride and practicality, with some vestiges of arrogance and resentment in the shopkeepers. We may have whipped these people, but they could rise like grass in a desert—with the slightest moisture anywhere, they would make into a spa.

Returning to New York, I walked into the Flight Service office like a German Storm Trooper to insist that women in the crew have rooms with baths. This time I expressed my humiliation in being forced to await a public bath when I needed a shower after hours of handling food. I compared the flight service activities to those of the pilots who sat all the way and only handled their own food. I may have made an impression because on my next trip I had a room with a bath.

With flights departing New York's Idlewild Airport, later Kennedy International, the distance to travel from Manhattan was longer than going to LaGuardia. I had stopped investing in government bonds and saved my money until I was able to drive away a fully paid, blue Chevrolet coupe. It was the latest model but had been used as a demonstrator vehicle, making it a little less expensive. I was so pleased with this ownership. Unfortunately, I had to park in the streets of New York. If I forgot to lower the radio aerial, it would be maliciously broken off. A place to park was difficult too. I had to move the car whenever a white chalk mark showed on the tire. Police "ticket vendors" placed their notices toward a fine, if the car was parked for more than two daylight hours in the same spot.

On my next trip, via a stay in Ireland, little activity seemed to take place except in the pubs. Around the dartboards we shared "stout" and listened to Irish tales. Then off to London where it was a pleasure to see the play, "Kiss Me Kate", that had many raves.

Ellie flew to Stockholm and had a memorable experience. She brought back a newspaper article with a picture of evacuation chutes extended from her aircraft. A galley switch fire had caused an emergency return. Ellie had helped six children slide down the shute to exit the aircraft. No one was hurt but the aircraft had two flat tires from the fast landing.

When I flew to Scandinavia, it was via Boston, Sydney (Nova Scotia) and Keflavik, Iceland, to spend one quick day before going to Oslo, Norway. Cities in Europe being so close together, we flew to several places before being held for crew rest and could only describe the airports. Often, being so busy checking my provisioning, I could not even "go ashore". I would try to just put my foot on the ground and write home to say, "I've been to Oslo, Norway. Tusentakk!" We overnighted in Stockholm at the Malmen Hotel. The June days were long, so I was able to see this impressively built city with canals, called the "Venice of the North". Once again the dairy products were fabulous. What did I bring back from Sweden, known for its unique pottery and lovely crystal? Cheese. (After buying a car I was short of cash.) Memories of Norway are of snow-capped mountains, fiords, and many "Christmas trees".

Back again, I received a call from my mother's cousin on Long Island. She wanted me to meet another man she had invited for dinner. He turned out to be an older, recently divorced, Navy captain. (Why was I being so difficult to—"couple"?)

By the end of July I had a trip to Rome which had become an extension to the Lisbon-Barcelona flight. I had also entered into a period of melancholy, unable to logically explain. How could such an exciting life, with more good fortune in traveling the world than most people ever realize, still have me feel depressed? My father's words of "put roots somewhere" haunted me. I can honestly confess that I began partying too much, from night clubs in Lisbon to the "Quo Vadis Restaurant" in Rome, to whirling times with English friends I had made in Africa as well as London. On and on . . .

LONDON TEMPORARILY

Chapter 42

By summer I heard there were to be London temporary assignments allotted by seniority. I submitted a bid for this wonderful opportunity to see England and fly to Hamburg, Copenhagen, Stockholm and Hong Kong. Before learning the bid results, a trip to South Africa took me away for 23 days. The rent was paid before leaving and due again on return. Months passed like weeks.

In Lisbon, en route to Accra, I joined my crew to a restaurant where no drinks were sold unless one bought a bottle. Drinking water was nowhere to be seen. We settled on red wine, which seemed to be the "going" liquid at other tables. After dinner, as if I had not already walked across the ocean, we hiked the cobblestone streets through curving alleyways in the old part of town. It was almost like seeing the Middle Ages. Our stroll continued until we reached an incongruous sight, a Fairground that had a Penny Arcade of "shooting galleries" with prizes of dolls and furry animals. Between us, we won a toy too big to pack in a suitcase. It was left somewhere in Africa.

The London assignment was awarded to me but first I had a trip to Frankfurt. Tennis stars, Pancho Segura and Bobby Riggs, were passengers. (I had seen Segura play at Forest Hills when he defeated Pancho Gonzalez.) It was a good flight. Their capacity to amuse and entertain matched their talent on the courts.

A PanAm couple I knew living in Frankfurt invited me for dinner. I gave their address to a taxi driver and sat back to watch the sights. We reached a section of bombed buildings in block after block of heaps of granite, chunked as if upheaval from an earthquake. No one was around, making the scene more eerie. A slight fear came over me as I wondered where I was being taken. The driver stopped at what was half a building still standing. The other half was blasted away, exposing open rooms, jagged metal and concrete. It was one of only two (partial) buildings in acres of nothing but rubble. This was where my friends lived. Judging from the inside of their apartment it must have once been a "choice" neighborhood.

My purchases in Germany consisted of a beautiful 500-day clock for my brother and his wife's first anniversary, plus some beer steins and a cuckoo clock. The former clock was so delicate I had to ensure that it be stood upright and was carried gently from plane to plane until my arrival in New York. An Eastern Airlines pilot took it to New Orleans for me, keeping the clock in the cockpit to avoid damage. It was no easy task to bring this gift to the recipients, who did not seem to like it anyway. As for the cuckoo clock, the bird had difficulty making friends too. Even Rudy barked distaste. The clock hands had to be constantly corrected; volunteers to pull the winding chain were scarce.

Embarking on my London temporary assignment, I flew over as a passenger and stayed at the Kensington Palace Hotel. This was the most satisfying hotel in London for crews. PanAm had tried others, such as the Mount Royal and the Anthaeneum. The Kensington Palace Hotel was in a fashionable section, had sizable rooms with baths, and a lobby where we obtained those tiny tomato and sprout sandwiches at teatime. It was opposite the park of the same name, near the Albert Memorial, a monstrosity erected by Queen Victoria for her Consort. However, the "Albert" was a good landmark for locating when to disembark from the red, double-decker, No.9 bus on Knightsbridge Road. Eventually London would open as a permanent crew base, as would Beirut and Hong Kong—well, as "permanent" as anything could be with an airline.

I spent hours visiting galleries, museums, and historic sites. On a visit to Westminster Abbey, where so many famous people are buried or given remembrance, I suddenly realized I was standing on the tomb of Rudyard Kipling. When I jumped away, I heard a soft chuckle and turned to see a robed deacon. He was a Mr. Brown, who gave me a personal tour of the Abbey, complete with his sense of humor. One sight Mr. Brown pointed to was a grave that said, "Tho. Parr of Y County of Sallow, Borne AD 1483 He lived in Y Reigness of Ten Princes, viz.: K Ed 4, K Ed 5, K Rich 3, K Hen 7, K Hen 8, K Ed 6, Q Ma, Q Elize, K Jai & K Charles. Aged 152 Years & was Buret here November 15, 1635." The deacon informed me that the old man died of gout, as though they had been personal friends. I was amused when informed, "This section is only 400 years old but over there it is 700 years." Then he laughingly added, "Careful when you leave, don't step on Dickens." I would have needed a balloon to lift me over the many burial and memorial sights.

On Memorial Day I viewed services when the Duke of Gloucester laid a wreath at the Unknown Soldier Memorial. I walked down the street from Whitehall to where crowds of people stood on the curb waiting for what appeared might be a parade. Suddenly two limousines quickly drove by, after which the crowd dispersed. Someone said, "Queen Mary looks so regal, doesn't she?" Another, "Little Prince Charles is growing fine." They had waited hours to get a glimpse of their Royals. The car went by so fast for me; it could have been Shirley Temple or the Marx Brothers.

At 11 a.m., while crossing Trafalgar Square, cannons sounded. Everything, even pigeons, came to a complete stop, including cars in the middle of the street—all in reverence to the soldiers. It was remarkable to see complete inactivity across a soundless square that always had constant traffic. The stillness was like looking at a photograph. Pigeons were first to break the silence as they took flight together. Unmoving humans must have scared them. It was a chilly day but nothing impeded the British from showing respect for their country and those who died for it.

HONG KONG VIA BANGKOK

Chapter 43

My last trip while based in London was my first trip to Hong Kong—19 days with 76:46 flight hours (London to London). The first leg for 11.30 hours was via Brussels, Frankfurt, and Istanbul, to layover in Beirut; second leg, Beirut to Karachi, 9.10 hours; and lastly, Karachi to Calcutta via Delhi, 6:15 hours. We carried David Duncan, a *Life* magazine photographer, with an enormous amount of camera equipment. When the aircraft got delayed in India, Mr. Duncan would not leave his property anywhere and

Customs would not let him take it all to the hotel. This created a little disturbance, as the Indian officials could be easily intimidated if their authority was ever questioned. Duncan went on to Bangkok to take photographs that would appear later in a *Life* issue with the Golden Buddha Wat (temple) on the cover, but no pictures of India.

The Bangkok airport was 18 miles from town. En route to the Trocadero Hotel we drove through rice fields where dwellings were on stilts; some had miniature dollhouses atop poles in their yards for what seemed to be birdhouses. It was explained that they were provided for evil spirits to live, away from the main house. The King and Queen of Thailand had recently returned from their Switzerland honeymoon; however, we were able to see their impressive Suan Pakkad Palace grounds, as well as the fabulous Temple of the Emerald Buddha, and the Reclining Buddha in Wat Po. The latter, lying on its side, is as large as a train coach. The architecture of these temples is unique to Thailand—roofs with curling, gold-gilded spires reaching to the sky. The Golden Buddha sits in a beautiful white temple and dazzles the imagination. Orange-robed monks with shaved heads walked about the grounds, as they served their religious obligation in meditation and study. Whatever time was not spent resting from the flight, the stewardesses would use to shop for silk material. Thai silk was favored not only because it came in beautiful colors but, even if packed in a crumpled heap, could be wearable within minutes.

When I first arrived in Hong Kong, a British Crown Colony, in 1951, the Kai Tak Airport could only be used during daylight hours. It was a tight squeeze, using a runway on filled-in land over the water. With apartment buildings so close, the plane's wheels could almost pick off laundry on the bamboo poles that extended from windows. The fabulous harbor was an incredible sight. Part of it lay on the island with the city of Victoria, the other part, Kowloon, on the mainland. In the 1950s, thousands of people lived in small spaces, large families in one room. Fortunately the climate is mild, which added to its attractions. Shops lay in an endless stream of signs in Chinese characters, displayed in a checkered conglomeration. Regular ferry service crossed the wide harbor, giving a pageantry of sights. Nothing was too difficult for the Chinese to find, produce, reproduce, sew or cook. You just had to say what you wanted; intense competition produced miracles. Clothes could be fitted and delivered the next day, all hand done with the best materials at unbelievable low prices

The famous Peninsular Hotel was one of few western styles on the Kowloon side. The PanAm stewardesses had a right wing, end room that faced the water, the Star Ferry Tower, Victoria across the bay, the Peak Tram that climbed the mountain, the famous White Pagoda, a moving scene of junks, sampans, green ferry boats, naval vessels from cruisers to aircraft carriers, and cargo ships laden for all ports in the world. It was also a sight to see purchases as one stumbled into the stewardess room; somewhere beneath all the paraphernalia were several beds. No one slept. Everyone was out shopping, eating, or "getting fitted". Years later, the room we used was so expensive it would have taken a month's salary just to touch the doorknob. I was fortunate to have seen Hong Kong in those days of the 50s.

Historically, the Peninsular Hotel ranked with the Oriental in Bangkok, the Imperial in Tokyo, or the Raffles in Singapore. None could top the Peninsular lobby with its Victorian setting, dignified aura, yet informal, friendly atmosphere. There was one elderly gentleman who lived in the hotel and had his own small table in the lobby, with a bronze plaque indicating it was his. He knew PanAm since the "old boat days", and remembered when the last Clipper departed before the Japanese arrived. He always invited us to sit and have a cool drink, happy to have his table used as a place to gather before shopping or dining. I cannot imagine the lobby without him.

One tiny figure was an icon for the Peninsular Hotel for years. When our crew taxi arrived at the entrance, the bellboy in uniform and pillbox hat was a lad of Tom Thumb size. He was always there to welcome the crews and open the door; however, he never seemed to grow any larger—always the same midget boy. One day someone revealed that as soon as the little fellow got too big, he was replaced by another small lad.

In no other place than Hong Kong did we look more like feather merchants. I was to return to New York as a passenger, away longer than a month. This entitled me to $500 worth free of duty, though I did not even spend $300 on purchases during the entire assignment. So with my Thai silk clothing, wicker baskets, china coffee set, embroidered linen, miniature Chinese junk, etc., I left for London.

Flying back between Karachi and Beirut, we had to make an unscheduled stop in Basra, Iraq. The skipper reminded me that if any passenger was Jewish, it should not be written on their landing card. A few months before, when one of our pilots had an Israeli stamp in his passport, the Iraquis delayed the aircraft, threatening to put him in jail as a suspected spy. Crews had to get a new passport if they traveled to Israel. I handed each passenger a landing card and checked religions, as that was one of the questions asked. One man was a Hollywood film director who constantly asked "why" for anything I said. I advised silence on his religious background and told him "why". Then he asked what Faith he should use. "Say you're Presbyterian," I suggested. In the Basra waiting room he announced, "I'm a Ples-ba-terian".

In London I had to wait for a seat due to heavy passenger loads. So I spent time going to the National Gallery and strolling down Charring Cross Road—where second hand book stores were located—browsing myself to exhaustion. Later I went to Harrods store to see all the Christmas decorations, a delightful excursion. In the evening I attended a RAF private club for an interesting time and a delicious steak dinner. At last I saw where good meat disappeared in England, and the RAF deserved it.

When I finally got a flight as a passenger, it became one I would rather have worked back. The airport was crowded with Christmas travelers. As my status was "standby", I did not know until the last minute if enough people had cancelled to allow me a seat. In Shannon I was taken off the flight due passenger load and waited for the Paris flight. (Why did I have to buy that set of china in the basket I carried?) Finally I got on the Paris flight; that is, as far as Reykjavik, Iceland, because the London flight from which I was offloaded in Shannon had a delay in Reykjavik. The Paris flight then had to take some of the London flight's passengers, which meant I was left out in the cold of Iceland. When the Frankfurt plane arrived in Reykjavik, I was put on that flight, then reassigned to the Paris aircraft and then back to the Frankfurt flight. The tarmac was covered with frozen, packed ice, a few "wet" spots, and no place to carry chinaware. I slipped but held up the basket, determined to break my bottom before breaking my china. I swore never to buy anything again that did not fit in a suitcase. On December 7th, the 10th year observance of Pearl Harbor, I landed in New York.

NEW DEVELOPMENTS

Chapter 44

Two assistants to a vice president of PAA, one of whom later became a V.P., sat in the B-377 lounge on a London flight and solicited crew opinions for furthering company revenue. Both of these men were in the Public Relations department, one with System, and the other with the Atlantic Division. When approached to speak, I expressed how I felt PAA could entice more flying abroad by spreading interest to people living in the interior of our country. Though my idea may not have been a novel one, I suggested showing travel films and color slides to organizations throughout the U.S. As tourism began to open up, it appeared that only those living in port cities from which we operated had ever heard of Pan American World Airways.

Times were changing; the Company expanded, trying to promote revenue. Summer travel could mean larger passenger loads but in winter the flights might carry more crew than paying fares. As these were scheduled flights, government regulations precluded cancellations just because of too few passengers. I recall several flights with just a couple of passengers across the ocean. One fare might cover the cost to taxi to the end of the runway. PAA had their problems, with no domestic flights to compensate for seasonal losses. Crews tried to be patient but they were tiring. Flight Service and Engineer unions were threatening to strike. PanAm had to please employees, stockholders, passengers' expectations, as well as meet foreign competition. Running an international airline held many complications. PAA not only had to meet the requirements of our own government for certain conditions, but negotiate with other countries as well. With these considerations went the struggle of PanAm's President, Juan Trippe, to progress towards economy fares.

Just before Christmas I had another trip to Frankfurt, via Gander, Shannon, London, and Brussels, for over 17 flight hours alone. The stops made the total working hours much longer. If it had not been for the world's best mushroom omelets at the Monopole Hotel in Frankfurt, I might never have regained my strength. They were not only delicious but, as part of our "room with breakfast," we could have this meal at any hour of the day or night.

On returning as far as Shannon, I was approached by a Passenger Traffic representative and asked if I would continue on to New York.

"What do you mean?" I asked, since that was my flight destination.

"You're on strike. If you don't take the trip you'll have to pay your own hotel bill and expenses until the strike is over," was the gloomy reply. With this attitude from those with whom we had worked so well all these years, and passengers wanting to get back for Christmas, the atmosphere was distressing. What now, I thought? This was my airline too! I had worked too hard and long to see it self-destruct.

A cabin crew commented. "We'll really hurt the company by refusing to fly. We can stop everything and they'll have to agree to the Union's demands."

Then another said, "Can't we just fly home and strike from there? That can be just as good. Why punish ourselves from being back for Christmas?"

In Flight Operations I requested, "May I see the Union's wire saying we are on strike?" There was none. It was pieces of information from London, New York, Frankfurt, but none from our Union. Maybe there was a strike back in New York, maybe only picketing, or maybe just a lighted match that spread confusion. The

Union heads had said, "You'll be advised by wire when and what to do. Keep going until then."

We were not going anyway. The flight engineers went on strike. Flights cancelled and we spent two days in Ireland. Passengers were accommodated on other airlines. Neither the flight engineers nor flight attendants were denied hotel or per diem; the alternative was a false rumor. Within hours it was over, although "restarting" was like firing up a cold engine. Even a tentative strike can cause very expensive disruptions.

The way back was not easy. Coming in to land at Goose Bay, the crew could not get the gear down (the wheels) and we circled until the sun rose to give more light for landing. Finally the engineers cranked the gear down but could not tell if it was in locked position—the indicator light said otherwise. The captain came back in the cabin and explained that they would first touch and go; that is, hit the runway lightly enough to see if the wheels would hold but still be able to pull up. Having used most of our fuel crossing the ocean, we were light enough to try this. We secured the cabin from loose articles. The passengers were great—so cooperative. When the wheels touched, they held, and we rolled firmly down the runway. Everyone clapped.

Christmas Day I flew to Paris. I suppose if one has to work on Christmas Day, one may as well go to Paris. It would be my last flight for 1951.

DIFFERENT STROKES

Chapter 45

In January of 1952, I was asked to meet with sales and service managers to discuss a promotion to supervisor. After years of male only supervision for the Atlantic Division Flight Service, having females as supervisor became a possibility. My old friend, Ginger Ruiz, and I were both interviewed by several men in the management echelon. We were told that since a decision could not be made between us, we were both offered the job. We both accepted and became Flight Service supervisors in February with a salary raised *to* $400.

Two months of office work followed. I also assisted in stewardess hiring for March as well as April classes and enjoyed being part of a recruiting team. With little confidence as a public speaker, I did not seek class training. This was Ginger's forte, and she would become an excellent and beloved teacher. She also became one of my best friends.

The new DC-6B arrived and we participated in meetings about this aircraft. The Douglas airplane was faster and first tested on the Bermuda run. It was more economical than the Boeing-377 but never as popular. With the DC-6B PanAm inaugurated the first transatlantic, tourist service in May of 1952. The airline president and founder, Juan Trippe, was finally able to initiate economy fares, later called the "Rainbow" class.

In the middle of these developments, Gary returned from acquiring his Masters Degree at the University of Pennsylvania and said he was getting married to a young nurse. This took us by surprise but then Gary was unpredictable. They were married in New York and we held the reception at our place on Perry Street. It was a small gathering; even Rudy joined us for champagne and I took indoor movies.

My first check ride on the line was a flight to London with another member of management. The flight over was pleasant. In London I had dinner with an English friend from the Sales office who congratulated me on my new position. Returning to the hotel lobby, I met the "gentleman" with whom I had flown to London, who said that I should have had dinner with him, an agreement made on the flight over. Of that, I had no recollection. In atonement, I was to join him for a drink in the lounge and discuss our flight—where we spoke little about the job or our trip. When we retired for the evening, he got off the elevator and walked me to my room. On saying "goodnight" I discovered I could not close my door, as he had jammed his foot to the threshold in a sudden quick motion. If ever I felt less in the mood for such antics, it was certainly on this flight. When he did not remove his foot and came in, I tried to make light of it. He grew angry at my rejection, but departed. This unfortunate incident left me with an uneasy feeling that I kept to myself. If I had complained of what happened that night in London, I might have been laughed at and only given support to those who felt females in supervision were a hazard. Damn, I thought, why must women have their capabilities tested as a sex object?

PanAm was becoming more interested in superior dining service—even advertised menus from "Maxims of Paris", aiming to be the best and to challenge their foreign competitors. There were several meetings between management personnel and cabin attendants, which was a hopeful intent to solve problems before disagreements led to picketing or devastating strikes. We had some fine men in management. There could be weak links in the chain of command; however, poor performance could exist in the labor force too. When I was first interviewed for promotion, I had expressed my distaste for the two-sided structure I saw developing in the Company. We were becoming distrustful and combative instead of working together. Ginger and I wanted to see again the team spirit we remembered when we were hired. We started our own column for Flight Service in the PAA "house organ" paper, the *Clipper*. In writing Flight Service news and amusing anecdotes, we hoped to build a family group feeling.

After two trips between mostly deskwork, I had a May vacation and decided to drive to New Orleans in my new Chevy. Ellie, who had left PAA, flew back to Oregon with Rudy to visit her mother. The night before my departure I packed things in the car trunk. At the last minute I decided to put my briefcase in the cabin of the car. That was a mistake. In the morning the briefcase was gone. My coupe had small, push-out windows on the doors. One window had been forced open. I regretted losing my Passport with interesting stamps and visas, my beloved cameras, and my "Short Snorter". The latter was a series of currency bills from various countries, pasted together end to end, with autographs of friends and famous people. Such was a hobby of flight crews, perhaps started during the War. The camera losses brought tears to my eyes, which at first made driving difficult.

I drove on to Washington D.C. to visit Frannie, Jean, and their families, before continuing to New Orleans. On a stretch of Maryland highway, a patrol car stopped me. I was accused of speeding and told to accompany the police to headquarters. I was not told why I had to follow them and felt intimidated, to say the least. I thought they were after the Maryland car that had sped past me, so I had not stopped immediately. No, it was me they were after. Back at their headquarters, I was given the first-degree reprimand.

"You 'arrest' me for speeding on the freeway! I don't even believe I was speeding," I said. To this I got a nasty, "You New Yorkers are all alike. You come down here, break our laws . . ." When I angered at this remark, they threatened to lock me up.

The day was too much. First I lost precious possessions stolen from my car, then stopped for speeding, threatened a jail cell, and lastly called a New Yorker as though I was some horrible creature. I said to the Maryland police, "I'm not a New Yorker. You're judging me by the license on my car. I'm a Southerner and. . . ." They let me go.

I drove through the beautiful state of Virginia over to the Shenandoah Valley where I stopped for gas. It was there that I saw a young Augusta Military Academy boy thumbing for a ride. He was in uniform beside a suitcase as big as he was, and seemed so unprotected and lonely that I offered to take him. The youngster spoke little, just that it was his summer vacation. "Mine too," I said.

"First time hitchhiking?" I asked. "Yes, ma'am." Silence.

"It can be dangerous," I said. "Yes, ma'am." Long silence.

He left with a "Thank you, ma'am." I drove away and pondered how nice it would be to have a little boy like him.

Through Tennessee the countryside was so peaceful in its springtime beauty. How I missed my cameras. In a short strip through Georgia I inadvertently ran over a baby rabbit. For miles I thought of the poor thing and could still hear the crunch of the wheel, which the animal desperately tried to dodge. I began to wonder, "does life have a particular destiny we can neither avoid nor alter?" I drove into New Orleans and put my Chevy in the family driveway. The house gave me that wonderful feeling of a place I could always return to as "home".

Besides sailing on Lake Pontchartrain, I did a little fishing on Bayou LaComb. The area north of the lake was woodsy with southern pines, laurel and oak trees, as well as some cypress marshes. The Causeway Bridge had not been built yet; one drove around the lake, not across it. In these surroundings I spent a happy vacation in 1952. I was tempted to stay. There were times I wished I had.

OFFICE WORK

Chapter 46

My mother drove back to New York with me and her company was much appreciated. Ellie was still in California. At the office I wondered what I was doing around a lot of paper work, four walls without windows or even a painting. It was a pleasure when flight crews came in with the latest "down line" news. Ginger and I wanted to succeed as female supervisors, knowing that our actions had to prove us worthy; perhaps lay ground for future acceptance and promotion of women in management. I hated to see anything in my "In Box" and would try to clear it. Another supervisor had so much paper on his desk it seemed his hanging cigarette might burn down the airport. He would tease, "Clean out that box, you'll look like you've nothing to do and be excess around here." At least his humor was an amusing break from any monotony.

As a supervisor returning from a Frankfurt flight, I stopped in Shannon where one of the boarding passengers was a crib-size baby, a redheaded, Irish boy bound for adoption in the States. Americans often adopted babies overseas because of the long wait for a stateside child, the entangled paper work, and the prohibitive cost. The twinkling eyes in this tiny Irish face were irresistible. The flight engineer carried the bassinet with baby to the cockpit and placed it beside his desk, facing all those instruments. It was he who was taking the child to friends for adoption. Two sights I will ever remember—going to the cockpit and seeing the flight engineer with his left hand checking instruments while his right hand held a bottle to the mouth of the baby, lying in its bassinet on the floor. I do not think that baby cried once in all the attention he received. He was kept amused by the colored lights and cockpit activity. If he grew up to be a crewmember, he certainly received the "basic" training. The other sight was the joy of his adoptive parents on arrival. It was hard to give up "our baby".

Nagging was not my mother's style, but with the long drive to the airport she would say in her gentle way, "Don't you think it would be easier for you to live closer?" I thought about it. Mother soon returned to New Orleans fearing my father was doing more sailing than eating properly. Ellie wrote that she was staying longer while attending art school in Carmel. When Gary came back to New York with his wife and new baby, I decided to let them use the Perry Street place and move to Queens to be nearer the airport. At least our Greenwich Village apartment would be kept "in the family." After a couple of months in a box-shaped apartment building that looked like an institution, I realized it was not my style of living. I was ready to return to Manhattan.

Ginger or I would attend sales meetings as the only female present. Discussion on promoting the DC-6 coach flights was the main topic. This airplane inaugurated tourism to worldwide heights with economy class service. Some airlines did not favor Mr. Trippe's idea of cheaper fares, but eventually the transition came about and PanAm's competition followed suit. However, in the fall of the year, I had an experience that sorely affected me. I was assigned to advise an employee that she would be terminated. Every new-hire had a six months trial period, after which he/she either qualified or was dismissed. Before probation ended, the probationary had to be notified. Whatever was the opinion later was rarely of consequence, as the employee became a full, dues paying, Union member, with grievance protection.

We had a probationary employee who suffered an accident injury in flight, for which she was hospitalized overseas. Unfortunately, she had an "accident prone" reputation. Her six months would be over on the day she was to return to New York. I was given the ignominious task to meet and fly back with her, advise her termination with a letter stating "the Company regrets", all before the midnight hour of the very last day of her probation. We would arrive in New York just before midnight. Though I did not like the conditions presented, I took the assignment obediently, not wanting to make any excuses for myself.

When I arrived to accompany the girl back to New York, she was out of the hospital and happy to be available for flight again. I thought, "Lord, I've got to be tough. I'm on orders to tell her that she will no longer wear her uniform." I had prepared my speech—how it might be better for her if she found work to which she was more suited—with her many capabilities—the Company felt that, etc. The words would never suffice.

I followed my orders, doing what I had to do. She took the news bravely, but sadly, and without criticism of PanAm or me. Maybe she cried later—I surely did. I knew what it felt like to love the job; it was only those who showed disrespect for passengers, PAA or those with whom they worked, that could make it easier for me to reject. In the office I asked, "Can't the decision be changed? I'll work with her. She could be a good stewardess." But the deed was done and could not be reversed. This event so affected and disappointed me. Perhaps being a supervisor was not the job for me. I could not rationalize either the Union or Management's approach or pressures. I stayed long enough to complete some duties. Then I cleaned out my "In-Box", handed in my Pass Card and returned to my uniform life. Though a top manager pressed me to explain myself, I never gave him my reason, only that I preferred being a crewmember. I still have the kind letter written by a vice president, expressing his regrets on my departure from management, ending with a handwritten, "God Bless You."

BACK ON LINE

Chapter 47

My first trip after returning to flight status was to Frankfurt. Visiting the home of Goethe and not knowing the language did not help my confidence. I needed to get myself together, as I felt like a terrible disappointment and failure. The greatest satisfaction I received in that short office tenure was the lifelong friendship I would have with Ginger.

In Frankfurt I was introduced to "Maier Gustle's", the city's famous beer hall. The stage held the "oomp-pa-pa" band; the ceiling hung heraldic flags and scenic pictures were painted on the walls. Musicians and waiters wore lederhosen, short leather pants. Knee high socks, colorful suspenders, and Tyrolean hats made up their ensemble. There was rejoicing and singing until late hours. Each night a waiter placed a Tyrolean cap upon someone's head who would be asked to come upon the stage as guest bandleader. That night the cap was placed upon my head. My crew must have detected my dispirited demeanor and were behind this invitation. I led the band and danced on stage with a chubby musician in lederhosen. A few more beers ousted my doldrums.

On a trip to Lisbon I attended a lively party, leaving early with the excuse I was too fatigued. Later, as I tried to sleep in a large room that the hotel had never given me before, I heard my door open and saw a figure enter. This was followed by the thud of a suitcase falling to the floor and a thump, thump of two shoes pulled off and tossed. A male crewmember looked towards the bed and gave me a "what the heck, who are you", surprised look.

"This is my room, " he said, dangling the key he had used to enter.

"Sorry, but it's mine," I informed him, as I pulled the sheet up under my chin.

"Look," he answered, "I know this is my room. I had—."

"It's mine, " I interrupted.

"I checked in earlier and asked for this room," he argued.

"Well, when they gave me the key I didn't ask for you, " I returned.

"You don't think I deliberately—."

"I don't think anything. Just leave quietly, please, and let me sleep."

"Damn!" cursed my intruder.

"This is all I need, " I almost whispered.

As he gathered his bags, his raincoat from a chair and started to leave, I called, "Don't forget your shoes." He slipped out holding each shoe by a finger. But if anyone saw him they would never believe what happened, or did not happen.

My behavior on a Paris layover, en route to Beirut, probably made me examine myself more introspectively. I was invited to join some flight crews to hear jazz music at a local nightclub near the D'Iena Hotel. When seated, we saw that the movie star, Gregory Peck, and his (first) wife had a table near us. It was apparent that the Pecks were not getting along. How she could be so unhappy with such an attractive man? They suddenly left and the place seemed to lose its glamour. Our table was next to the band whose players were Americans. After too many drinks, I felt a need to perform and asked if I could dance on their piano. The pianist urged me on. In my stocking feet I must have thought I was an Arabian dancer. Thanks to the flight engineer, I got safely off the piano and back to the hotel. Later, I began to wonder about my indiscretions, but instead of vowing to drink less, I was determined to learn HOW.

At a table beside mine in the d'Iena Hotel dining room, I saw a face I did not recognize immediately. It was Oliver Hardy of the famous comedy team, "Laurel and Hardy". Here was a man who had achieved fame by behaving like an idiot and drawing laughter from the entire world. Off film he was so serious and intelligent looking that he was not easily identified. I envied him as I thought of my own rascality, which I could not clearly explain to myself.

There were other things I did in Paris besides behave foolishly. Though I did not have to make a spectacle of myself, as a woman I could at least walk alone in this city, and less likely be bothered, tested, or pre-judged. Paris gave me an independent, free feeling. I walked miles up and down the West Bank, watching artists paint and looking through bookstalls that lined the Seine. In a perfume shop on the Rue Tivoli, I met a couple who were owners of WDSU, a radio station in New Orleans, reminding me of the small size of the world. I walked to the Place de la Concorde, where the French guillotine once stood. Queen Marie Antoinette lost her head there for reasons other than mine, though perhaps for some of the same. But I wanted to live. I wanted to survive. Suffice it to say I was unhappy.

Back in New York, Gary had taken a position in Canada and moved there with his family. Ellie returned from Monterey where she had worked for the World Affairs Council of Northern California while attending art school. I moved back to Greenwich Village with Ellie. The arrangement appeared that it might be of short duration. Perhaps Ellie and Phil would marry, with love and dreams to support them. As it turned out, Phil eventually did become a television writer Ibut that happened in the future).

Just before Christmas in 1952, I was assigned a Hong Kong trip. Events were to occur that would cause dramatic changes in my life.

YEAR'S END

Chapter 48

My Hong Kong trip made all the stops. We even had an unexpected landing at a place in Greenland whose name I failed to write in my Log. Near the airport was a barracks where we had to spend the night. Since leaving New York, I had one particular passenger who complained about everything from inadequate food to poor magazine selection. It was difficult to prevent magazines from being "taken" permanently. I tried hard to please her but she was wearing me down. When the passengers had to share rooms because of insufficient quarters, this woman exploded over my having a single room. (I was the only female on the crew.) After listening to her tirade, I asked the clerk to give her my room. Then I walked to the aircraft and grabbed a berth to sleep in; however, there were not enough blankets in the entire cabin to keep me from freezing.

In London I met one of the Pacific-Alaska Division supervisors. We enjoyed lunch together at the "Ballerina" restaurant. He was a most pleasant gentleman. We discussed the differences between the two areas until he placed the idea of transferring to the Pacific Division in the back of my mind. I was seeing palm trees instead of icebergs.

Christmas eve I arrived in Beirut, Lebanon. It was here that I met Rex, an American employed in the area, who attended our Christmas party at the hotel. He was intelligent, interesting, and most solicitous to make me happy. Christmas Day we celebrated with lunch together at "Dimitri's" and that night, dinner at the "Kit Kat". He showed me the town, the famous rocks on the beach and, at the time, we watched a distressing sight, a passenger liner that had run aground. The next day I left for New Delhi, feeling that I had made a particular friend.

In northern India the weather had become cool. Not only that, but an earthquake took place to make the world move as though a giant, underground turtle suddenly decided to shift its shell. It was a quake that did not affect one's equilibrium nor cause any damage—no jolt or sound, but everything moved together sideways. I feared it was my imagination but it was confirmed to have been an "earth-movement". In Delhi I was surprised to receive flowers and a telegram from Rex.

My flight continued to Calcutta and Bangkok, but I flew on to Hong Kong before having a crew layover. It was a thrill to be invited to see the landing from the cockpit. I tried to remember the remarks of the pilots as they brought the huge plane on to the runway. Some of what I heard between Flight Operations and the pilots in the cockpit was "roughly" as follows:

"Clipper Two, 5 degrees right, over (?) Island." (Pilot)

"Clipper Two—position?" (Flight Ops)

"Clipper Two, 5,000 feet. Over."

"Clipper Two—descend to 3500" Later—

"Clipper Two—descend to 1500"

"Clipper Two, ten mile Charlie.

"Charlie report (Cheung Chan). Over"

"Roger" (Red China is to the left—now at 1500 ft.)

"Continue, call Cheung Chan. Over."

"Will do." (Islands all about). "Cheung Chan—island—over".

(Weather and winds reported—which runway. Island to right. We're over the harbor; many ships, including a large aircraft carrier.)

Captain—"Flaps—two five degrees" Co-pilot—"Two Five"

Captain—"Gear down." Co-pilot—"Gear down."

Captain—"Flaps four zero." Co-pilot—"Four zero".

Captain—"Full flaps." Co-pilot—"Full flaps."

Captain—"Set to land."
Engineer—"Check list complete."
Co-pilot—"Fifteen, twelve—ten—five—." (swoosch)

We were on the ground, on the runway, rolling, rolling. (As I write this I am convulsed in tears, remembering our airline. A day in the future, it had to stop rolling.)

My favorite Hong Kong restaurant was Tkachenko's for good Russian food, prepared and served by White Russians who had escaped the Communists. Once I visited the Aberdeen Floating Restaurant, which was on a barge reached by a small motorboat. Diners selected from huge vats the poor swimming fish to be eaten. Our per diem carried us well, as the exchange was around 5.80 Hong Kong dollar to one U.S. Rickshas were around 50 cents Hong Kong dollar per five blocks. (It seemed easier and less dangerous to walk through the crowds.) On this trip we went to a Chinese restaurant located up Nathan Road, reached by taxi. We were the only Occidentals there. The food consisted of singular, plain entrees with vegetables. I heard slurping sounds all around the room; diners held bowls to their mouths from which rice was sucked in with the aid of chopsticks. This was not considered ill mannered in China, but denoted appreciation. The people appeared taller with larger body build. I was told the food was northern Chinese; perhaps the other diners came from there as well.

Hong Kong too had its period of tap water shortage in the 1950s. We had to be careful to fit our needs to the "cut off" schedule. But each room had a radio, to make it far ahead of other hotels where we stayed. It was not called a radio, as the announcer would say, "This is your 'redefusion' broadcasting—."

Since Hong Kong was still the British Crown Colony, a bus could be taken to the border of Communist China to look to "the other side", an interesting tour when not shopping. The countryside looked clean, green, and fruitful. Chinese in coolie hats, coming from work in the fields, were elders with faces that looked centuries old. It seemed it was the "old folks" who toiled the land. At that time no goods could be brought into the States that were made in Communist China. If there was any doubt, such purchases had to be accompanied by a Certificate of Origin form, stating "made in Hong Kong". Some merchants would produce this form just to make a sale.

I took the Star Ferry to the other side of the harbor with several friends and rode the Peak Tram up the mountain. It is a scary, steep climb but the views are fabulous. At the top we came across construction on a new building in which men were directing women to carry heavy hods of cement. In fact, the women were doing all the heavy labor. They wore loose, grey or black, long pants but were females of small stature. Women always walked a few steps behind the men (never abreast). This was 1952.

Although January first is not the Chinese New Year, it was celebrated in Hong Kong with firecrackers, noisemakers, and sparklers in the night sky. After all, it was the Chinese who invented explosives and set off firecrackers for Marco Polo centuries ago. I received another wire from Rex with wishes for a great New Year for both of us. I mused over his message and wondered about my own feelings. On the return flight I looked forward to seeing Rex again. His attention overwhelmed me; perhaps I was in the mood to be flattered and catered to in such a manner. It was nice to have telegrams and flowers sent to my room by an admirer. I thought how wonderful to be an American woman and not have been born in China.

BAD TIMES

Chapter 49

When I left Hong Kong and flew west again, one of my passengers who boarded at Bangkok was a gentleman who had been in the Orient collecting precious stones. He showed me some black star sapphires, which he pulled from a soft cloth bag. They rolled across his palm, gleaming in different sizes. On his departure this passenger placed a gift in my hand, a black star sapphire! I was speechless as he walked down the stairs.

In Beirut I saw Rex again. He advised me he would be returning to the States for reassignment and looked forward to our meeting there. When Rex finally did come to New York, he showed his usual good manner and solicitation. We walked Greenwich Village together sharing happy hours. One day I found a parking ticket on my car. Rex put it in his pocket, insisting that he would take care of it. It pleased me to have someone who wanted to block any obstacles I might have.

On my next trip to Frankfurt, Rex again drew my attention by sending a telegram with violets waiting in my room. At Paris, Rex sent roses with his wire. In a boat trip on the Seine, I thought how nice if only he had been along.

In New York Rex proposed marriage. Actually he had asked me in Lebanon but this time I took him seriously. How wonderful the future will be, I thought, sharing with someone instead of seeing the world and its challenges alone. "But," I insisted, "I dislike diamonds rings. I'd rather have a Baby Grand piano some day." We laughed together, though I was really serious. When I was assigned a Bermuda trip he insisted even that island was too far away. It was a longer parting than expected, as I had to spend the night because of bad weather in New York. In the Castle Harbour Hotel dining room, I was anxious to tell my crew about Rex, but something kept me quiet. It was as though I could not believe it myself. Me, married? The waiter came to our table and said a gentleman was calling me from New York. The crew teased me as I left to answer the phone. It was Rex, to say he missed me.

Back from Bermuda, we called home to advise my parents of our desire to marry. My mother was quite impressed with him. The feeling appeared mutual. I secretly went down to Tiffanys with my black star sapphire and arranged to have it placed in a gold tie clasp, as a gift for the man I had accepted in marriage.

One day Rex asked me where I would like to live, as he could be sent to Manila or Rio de Janeiro. It did not matter to me at this point, whichever one he wanted. Then he suggested that we elope, or marry at our destination overseas. This did matter to me. I did not want a fancy wedding; however, if not a parent, or my brother, I wanted at least a friend there for the ceremony. My parents did not deserve otherwise. Rex said his folks were deceased and he had no siblings. I was sorry about that but hoped he would understand my feelings. I left on a trip to London and this time there were neither flowers nor telegram awaiting me. When I returned to New York, Rex did not call and he had disappeared. My phone bill arrived and the call he had made to me in Bermuda was among my charges. The parking ticket that he was to take care of was ignored—I received a critical notice with late payment charges. By coincidence, I learned from others that Rex's pretense had been on an even broader scope. It was difficult to accept that he was not the sincere person I believed he was. I never picked up the sapphire tie clasp from Tiffanys. It may still be there. With my shattered beliefs and disenchantment, I put in a bid for transfer to the Pacific-Alaska Division.

"Uncle Syd", our good neighbor, who always listened to our troubles, felt deeply for the offense I had received. As a cripple, he never married. As a retired lawyer, he said to me, "You threw him a curve when you wouldn't elope or marry overseas. He could have disappeared on you anywhere. Had you asked to see his identification, to learn who he really was?"

"Oh, Syd, what kind of trust would that have shown to someone you were to marry?"

"Well at least you should have gotten a diamond ring out of him."

"Yes," I said, "and guess who would have gotten the bill." I could still laugh—well, somewhat—at least the florist did not bill me for the flowers.

My bid came through for transfer. I said farewell to friends in New York, kissed Ellie and Phil goodbye, loaded my little Chevy and started to drive cross country with Nelda, another stewardess who was "going West". It would take five and a half days to drive to San Francisco, with feelings of disappointment but hopes for a better future. It was 1953.

CROSS COUNTRY

Chapter 50

Driving to the Pacific Coast would be my first trip across the States by automobile. From New York and over New Jersey we took the Turnpikes and stopped for the night at Lorraine, Ohio, outside Cleveland. The next day we skirted Chicago and spent the night by the Mississippi River in Iowa. The river was neither as wide nor as muddy as by New Orleans and I wished the waters good traveling. For dinner that night we tried the Mississippi's catfish.

In the morning we had to take a zigzag road through Iowa, as though farmers had refused to have the interstate highway cut across their fields. Corn was everywhere. (There had to be pigs, as we kept hearing on the radio, "Attention all ye hog breeders.") We crossed the Missouri River reaching Grand Island, Nebraska, for the night. Sweet alfalfa and wheat waved across Nebraska. The prairies followed and started to show cattle, cowboys, and I believe it was the only state left where a nickel bought a cup of coffee. The next day we arrived at Ft. Bridger, Wyoming, after driving about 70 mph, quite fast for my Chevy. We had driven 720 miles, the most car mileage in my life for one day, through long, barren but beautiful stretches of western land. The old Burma Shave signs were gone but were replaced with others saying, "Ain't this monotonous?" Or in more arid sections, "No swimming allowed".

While trying to keep awake, I asked Nelda to tell me about herself. She had been quiet most of the way. I had flown with Nelda and knew her as a timid soul, gentle of manner, with a soft voice. She had become a flight attendant after graduating from

Radcliffe. Now she was leaving New York for California following a terrible experience. A man had attacked her, beat her head against a wall and left her with a concussion. Nelda's neurologists urged her to continue treatment for her head injury but she wanted to start a new life elsewhere. I was unaware of her doctor's advice until half way across the country. I did all the driving though I concerned about her, especially through the long, hot stretches.

The next day we drove to Salt Lake City, stopped and put our feet in the great lake, coming away with caked salt upon our legs to convince us of its content. Across Nevada we felt the 110-degree heat. I carried a water bag and a bug screen for the radiator. My Chevy picked up many bugs but never needed extra water. In fact, the car behaved admirably. Arriving at Truckee, California, I remembered it might need an oil change. This was done while exploring this old western town. We stayed in Verdi, California, after driving 684 miles.

It was a feast of magnificent sights going over the Sierras at Donner Pass to Lake Tahoe, which we took time to see. As we went down into the Sacramento Valley, it was hot again. I had no air-conditioning. Leaning on the door's open window, my left arm became quite sunburned while my right arm stayed "Manhattan pale". Just outside San Francisco we had to stop to get sweaters from our bags. The cooling fog and the Golden Gate Bridge could be felt and seen from the East Bay—we had arrived after 3,300 miles. Over the Oakland Bridge, we drove south to Palo Alto to stay with Nelda's friends. Each mile down the Peninsular, the weather became warmer; just a half-hour drive from San Francisco it was summer again.

It was a comfort to know that I had friends in the Bay Area—comrades from the Casa de Lobos in Guatemala, Hap and Bob Henry who had returned from Rio to live in Los Altos. My red-head friend, Harry Martin, also back from Rio, was living in Stonestown, a section of San Francisco. The couple I had visited in Frankfurt, Germany resided in Los Gatos. Patty Tibbits and her husband were in Berkeley and Holly and her architect husband, in Monterey. Once employed by this great airline, friends were made all over the world.

Before starting classes to learn the ways of the Pacific-Alaska Division, I had time to look for a place to live. Nelda stayed in Palo Alto. I rented a room in Burlingame near the airport with an elderly woman who treated me like a daughter. She only asked that I pay her a dollar a day, but insisted on wanting to feed me all the time. She was a lonely widow, quite sprightly, who kept a beautiful garden with fruit trees. I stayed with her until I moved into my own apartment a few blocks away—when my furniture arrived. I had kept in storage some antiques that once belonged to my grandmother. Now I wanted to put my life together and live a little differently from cut down coffee tables and orange crates for bookcases. At least I would try. My dear friend, Harry, treated me to Fisherman's Wharf in San Francisco for my birthday. With Harry there would always be a sibling type relationship. We felt relaxed together, sharing thoughts and opinions. Friends, and this wonderful city, made me feel alive once more, and ready to see the rest of the PanAm world.

PACIFIC-ALASKA DIVISION

Chapter 51

It was not until September that I had my first flight out of San Francisco. August was spent in relocating and attending classes. Crews based in Seattle flew to Alaska but San Francisco was the headquarters from which I would fly the Pacific Ocean, its islands, and the Far East. I was impressed with the Pacific-Alaska Division; there sparked a particular pride and appreciation in just being part of the airline. Less crowded than the East, people in the West revealed sincerity in their friendliness. The skies were clear, the streets were clean, and bumper to bumper traffic had not arrived. The Bayshore Freeway from the city to the airport was a circuitous route around San Bruno Mountain until reaching the tidelands of the Bay.

No language requirement had existed for flying the Pacific area. Seniority was not forfeited by transferring from another base, but I flew as stewardess until there were purser openings. "P.A.D." used the Stratocruisers, with DC-4s focused on military cooperation during the Korean War—as during WWII, when PanAm pilots flew DC-4s to Africa via Brazil. Whenever our country became involved in foreign conflicts, PanAm took part with carriage of military men and equipment, or soldiers on Rest and Recreation (R&R). I arrived a month after the Korean Armistice had been signed.

Flight time between the Coast and Hawaii on piston aircraft could be from over nine to sometimes eleven and a half hours. Los Angeles flights were an hour longer. When shuttles started from Seattle, the flight time could reach 13 hours. My first flight was a "double shuttle"—Honolulu, then Los Angeles, back to Honolulu, again to Los Angeles, back to Honolulu, before flying home to San Francisco. Years later a Los Angeles base opened but, until then, the San Francisco crews covered these trips, which even became "triple shuttles". If I ever had a memory lapse to which way we were going, flowers were all over the aircraft from Honolulu. Just as on my visit to Hawaii in 1951, ukulele players, hula dancing, and flower leis were still greeting passengers. No more than one or two planes waited on the tarmac.

Retrieving my purse in the galley, I heard footsteps behind me which turned out to be my old friend, Gus, a steward who had transferred from New York before me. It was a joy to see him. He placed a flower lei around my neck, saying in his humorous way, "Don't ever say you haven't been lei-ed in the galley!" Driving away in the large crew limousine, a row of bamboo huts lined the green lawn that stretched from the terminal building, displaying flowers for sale. Hawaiian women in muumuus sat in front of their huts, stringing petals from piles of blossoms beside them. No advertisements or sale signs diminished the area, so all appeared natural and colorful.

The famous Moana Hotel has one of the largest banyan trees on Oahu. With roots the size of tree trunks stretching from its branches, it appears as more than one tree. The hotel squares the banyan and opens to the ocean. With a room near the water, I listened to music in the patio below until the sound of the surf lulled me to sleep.

In 1953 "The Outrigger Canoe Club" lay between the Moana and Royal Hawaiian Hotel, looking like a one-story bungalow. Membership was offered to PanAm's crews to use the outdoor volley ball courts, the bar, and the marvelous dining room whose windows opened on to the beach. Surfboards, lined up in racks, were for the more adventurous souls. The beach was seldom crowded. Swimming was warmly delightful, as was lounging on the sand for hours. Skin cancer from too much sun was no more feared than lung cancer from smoking, (and non-smokers were the rarity). The Outrigger's dining room served delicious, fresh mahi-mahi fish, where we could sit by the ocean and watch the surf while the sun went down, in an unobstructed view of Diamondhead.

On leaving Honolulu, plastic bags were distributed to the passengers for saving leis. Some did not want their flowers. One such gentleman was the eminent Cardinal Spellman, the famous, chubby faced, smiling prelate, popular throughout the world. I told him of the Hawaiian custom of throwing back a flower lei upon leaving, to ensure the departing one would return. He stood at the door, waved to the crowds, and tossed a flower lei. The wind sailed it like a kite over the wing of the aircraft. People who came to see him off roared their approval, as his pink-cheeked Eminence smiled widely in appreciation.

On my second shuttle to Los Angeles, a woman boarded with an unusual number of coats. Passengers from Los Angeles were slightly different from San Francisco types. More often the Angeleans appeared with brighter clothing in a more casual manner. I passed by the heavily coated woman and could swear I saw a hairy head with two little brown eyes peeping out from material she held in her arms. The eyes seemed to say, "Please don't hurt me." Animals aboard had to be crated and approved for carriage. Resolved I must have been imagining things, I returned to the galley, the rear chamber where the crew talked privately. Suddenly, I heard a loud screech from forward in the cabin. I looked out and saw atop a seat back, a tiny ferret all dressed as though going to a party. A slight disruption occurred as the poor, frightened animal was retrieved and returned to its owner, who had smuggled him aboard. We had one unaccounted for, very scared little passenger.

BEYOND THE REEF

Chapter 52

On a trip destined beyond Hawaii, my flight left from Los Angeles. The crew was sent to LAX (code word) on a Western Airlines Convair. Such expenses confirmed the need for PanAm to open a base in Los Angeles—but that came later. We stayed at the old Roosevelt Hotel, across the street from the Chinese Grauman Theater on Hollywood Boulevard, where movie stars put their mark in the cement entrance. This area of Hollywood held for me an atmosphere of a great yesterday feeling, as though the parade of old-fashioned glamour had passed and left a litter of stores selling trinkets, sweat shirts and cheap memorabilia. Little appeared of lasting substance, outside of the stars implanted on the sidewalks with names of the famous.

Landing in Honolulu gave me a refreshed, healthy feeling. No matter how tired I was, to take a quick swim was worth any fatigue encountered in the 9 to 12 hours to get there. (Honolulu was three hours earlier than California.) It was one of the few times I was billeted at the lovely Royal Hawaiian Hotel. The lobby was impressive with its deluxe shops and ever varied, ceiling-high flower arrangement in the hallway, backed by a huge mirror to reflect and double the beauty. There was a regal aura about the hotel, with its exotic tropical grounds and colorful views of the ocean. The Royal Hawaiian Hotel was the Island's epitome of elegance.

My crew and I decided to grace the hotel dining room with our presence that evening, until we were stopped at the entrance. One of the pilots was wearing a uniform shirt, open-buttoned at the neck and looking a bit rumpled. He was told he had to wear a tie. "No problem," he said, and disappeared to the men's room. On return he was wearing what looked more like a black rope at his neck, but was admitted. When seated, he revealed his adjustment under the table—one foot minus a sock.

In the middle of the Pacific Ocean, beyond Midway Island, is an atoll called Wake. Years before, Pan Am employees had blasted the lagoon to enable seaplanes to land and had built their own ramp, dock, and hotel on the island. The Japanese took Wake in World War II, from which a Pan Am Clipper, shot with bullet holes, escaped with as many people as it could carry.

When I arrived in 1953, Wake still had war materials left about; including crashed aircraft and several tanks. We became accustomed to seeing relics of war. After the Japanese captured Singapore, the gun installations were brought to Wake and placed on the island's Peacock Point. These powerful guns, originally British, had Japanese character instructions scratched upon them. From small sailing crafts in the lagoon, aircraft shadows could be seen under the water. Engines silent in extinction were a ghostly sight. A roofless warehouse still held stacks of torpedoes. We posed for pictures as "bathing beauties" stretched out upon these detonators of destruction. Climbing over a crashed plane on the lagoon shore, that still had its machine gun attached, I thought of the poor man who was there in his last moments. When I suddenly came upon a Japanese army tank, hidden among the shrubs that litter the island, I jumped from the sight of it. In a rising position, but partially hidden by bushes and sand, the tank looked as though it was still "alive" and would roll over me.

One of the sights upon first seeing Wake from the air was the wreck of the Suva Maru; a Japanese ship torpedoed during the war and deliberately beached. Wake drops off steeply into a very deep ocean, as the island was a volcano a few million years ago. The Suva Maru was half stuck on the reef and half below the waterline. With every trip to Wake, the ship slipped an inch or so deeper into the dark blue. Once a flight engineer tried to wade to it and almost lost his leg to a shark. The sharks coveted the wreck. It may now have sunk into the depths of the Pacific.

As the original Pan Am Hotel had long since been destroyed by a storm, our quarters were corrugated Quonset huts that echoed metallic sounds when it rained. A typhoon obligingly took them away. PanAm then constructed crew barracks in motel-like quarters. Layovers could be three days, time enough for parties and ball games between eastbound and westbound crews, plus the government employees and airline folks who lived on Wake. People seemed to come from out of the sand for sport contests and outdoor barbecues. With a little ingenuity, the men built a hut on the beach, an open lanai with barbecue pit. On the day they used a tractor to push the hut to the selected location, several captains gave orders towards the maneuver. Too many "chiefs" tried directing the driver and the hut almost collapsed. It was an amusing sight for which I was sorry not to have my movie camera. However, there were tasty feasts with excellent steaks imported for our needs. The hut was later blown away by a storm that also destroyed our open-air movie screen. Instead of being an outdoor drive-in it was an outdoor walk-in, and all were welcome to see old movies barely into the "talkie" age.

It was too dangerous for humans to swim in the ocean—sharks, strong currents, and a monstrous surf. With luck, Japanese blue or green fishing balls could be found washed up on the shores. These glass floats broke away from fishermen's nets and traveled hundreds of miles across the ocean to become souvenirs. We did have a small area, apart from the lagoon and ocean, used for swimming—the water channel that separated the part of Wake called Peale Isle. However, visiting a particular section of Peale Isle was not safe during albatross nesting season. On a pin-size island in the middle of the Pacific, the birds blanketed a specific area. One could not walk there for the masses of birds. They were literally "bumper to bumper". Squawks were deafening, and they would attack if anyone came too close. Well, they were busy. We waded knee high in the lagoon and cast for bonefish, a fast swimmer that gave a challenging fight when hooked. With too many bones for eating, they were thrown back. I once had to dodge a stingray I was told was more frightened of humans than I was of him. Sure! Near an old cement ramp once used for seaplanes, a motor boat was kept for water skiing in the lagoon. I could not learn that any more than snow skiing.

Going deep sea fishing one day made me realize that the Pacific Ocean is not terribly peaceful. Two crewmembers and I motored out in a launch with a meteorologist who lived on the island. This venture can only be done when the sea is not too rough. The ocean can flip a small boat easily. The weather forecast was good—if only the fish would bite. As we were ready to give up and start for shore, the flight engineer got a strike and a battle began. We saw a beautiful swordfish jump out of the water, diving and struggling to get away. After the fish leaped a few times, we no longer saw it. The fighting ceased but weight was still on the line, so the fisherman kept reeling in his catch. Sudden jerks gave belief the fish was still trying to get away while being deceptive under water. As the pilot brought his prize up to the boat and lifted the fish over the stern, there was hardly more than a tail, backbone and head. Great gouges of teeth had mutilated its beautiful body. The sharks had won the battle.

Strong winds began to whip up and waves crested higher. We headed the boat for safety, away from where we did not belong, and had caused the ignoble demise of a once gorgeous creature.

MANILA

Chapter 53

The sun was setting as the crew taxi drove on Dewey Boulevard along Manila Bay. Pacific sunsets can be imbued with the most brilliant yellow and red colors, as though the sun has the world afire off on the horizon. This evening was no exception. The entrance to the harbor is wide enough for a flotilla of ships. An armada of naval vessels was seen coming into port that very evening. The ships were well spaced apart but were unusually low in the water. Some were barely visible and showed only stacks and cannons. Neither lights nor life appeared upon any of them. They were dark shadows against the orange sky, a still life picture. It was hard to tell that their hulls touched the bottom of the bay. If relics of war on Wake Island were a startling sight, nothing could be more deathlike than Manila Bay, laden with half sunken warships, as though the admiral had ordered all to scuttle and die together in a glorious, impressive formation. My arrival in Manila was before the Japanese had fulfilled their debt to clear the Bay of half-sunken vessels.

The Philippines Islands gained independence in 1946, yet the Filipinos seemed to hold their American cousins in high esteem and friendship. Their leader, who represented the Philippines in the United Nations, was Ex-President Carlos Romulo, a strong figurehead, well respected in the entire world. I had the honor and pleasure of having him twice on my flights. He was a very intelligent and charismatic gentleman.

The Manila Hotel was located on the Bay next to Rizal Park,

named after the famous patriot of the country. By 1953 the hotel showed signs of extensive wear. Employees could recall days of Generals Stillwell and McArthur, and the Japanese rank using the hotel during the occupation. The grand ballroom had a stale odor of defunct cigars and banquets long forgotten. The atmosphere throughout was of a once splendid place that suffered lethargy, as the people licked their wounds; however, the dining room was always formally "dressed" and revealed of more affluent times. Whatever the season, if the waiters could not serve mangos, they heard cries of disappointment from the crews. One bite from a Philippine mango was heavenly to tongue and digestion.

It was the typhoon season when I arrived, with the miserable dampness. I could never figure which were the hottest months. Air-conditioning had not been perfected in the hotel, producing more of a "wet chill". I found it less discomforting to take the heat outdoors. Many historic sights had been destroyed during WWll, as little was left of the entire city after the intense bombing. Across from the Manila Hotel was the old section, surrounded by a dry moat and a crumbling wall, reminiscent of early control by Spain. Remaining structures within the walls included an ancient church with only the facade still standing. The moat had been converted into a golf course that I was anxious to try. After playing upon it, much of which was slush, I had to discard my sneakers. They could not be cleaned of indeterminate, odorous substances.

The U.S. army must have left a thousand jeeps in the Philippines. The Filipinos painted them in various colored designs; some topped with fancy fringes. The number of people crowded on one was beyond counting. Traffic in the street appeared a congestion of racing "golf carts", from which one had to be careful not to get mowed down.

The night before leaving, the captain called to say that the crew was invited to dinner at the home of a local Manila judge. Our host sent transportation for us; two black limousines, each with a driver dressed in dark suit and cap who took his job seriously (or at least his own importance). The drivers raced rapidly through the streets with *sirens* blaring, as people and "jeepneys" scampered out of the way. Sirens? We were only invited to dinner?

Away from the poverty and bombed out sections; the judge had an iron gate entrance to his home, the size of which could not be determined from the floral surroundings. He had a lovely wife and family. The ladies were in long dresses. The judge wore the formal dress shirt of the Philippines, a barong overlapping the trousers and woven from pineapple fibers, revealing delicate stitching and design. He spoke of the glory days of PanAm's seaplanes. We were the memory of happier times for him and he could not do enough for our comfort. Dinner was served by courses, in which the judge and his family eyed our expressions with every bite. It seemed the steaming plates of local delicacies would never stop coming to the table. Before we began eating, we waited for the wife and daughters to be seated. Only that never happened. It was the women who saw to the serving and would not join us. With servants about, it seemed a strange custom; but the women wanted to see to our enjoyment personally. It was not a servile duty to them.

The return flight to Wake Island carried our purchases of woodwork carvings, textiles, coral jewelry, fiber work, black pearls and oil paintings. Acquisitions could be brought back as crew baggage, though some members were obliged to cargo manifest what they could not carry, i.e. furniture. When things were so much cheaper than at home, it was easy to lose sight of how much was taken.

We stopped at the island of Guam. Many men working on Wake were Chamorros from Guam, given periodic trips to return home, as few people could take their family to Wake. Flight time from Manila to Wake via Guam was 13 to 16 hours, with seldom an empty seat. Varying winds determined the air time.

Between Guam and Wake there was a death on my flight. An American accompanied by her son and a nurse, had serious surgery in Manila and was hoping to return home. At the start of the meal service I was called to see that she had stopped breathing. The nurse gave up on her and my crew and I tried everything we could, but she was gone. There is no emergency stop when flying over the ocean, only the next stop. For us it was Wake Island, several hours away. I could only cover my poor passenger with a blanket, as though she were just sleeping, and finish serving the meal. At Wake her body was removed, placed in an ice packed box and put back on the same plane, but in the cargo hole. I felt drained and exhausted walking off the aircraft; a friend brought me a drink from the bar and placed it at my barracks door. As I watched the lights of the plane take off with a fresh crew, I remembered I left my uniform "heels" on board. Flight Operations sent a wire to Honolulu to retrieve them for me. Days later when I arrived in Hawaii, someone placed my shoes at the foot of the stairs with a note saying—" We WALKED here, what kept YOU?" Ah, piston days!

TOKYO, JAPAN

Chapter 54

In the fall of 1953, I left on my first trip to Japan and returned eleven days later. It began by going to Los Angeles, then Hawaii and Wake. In a weak moment I purchased a ukulele and attempted to play while lounging on the beach. It was a lot easier to learn than a guitar or violin but I made no friends while practicing.

Between Hawaii and Wake Island is the International Dateline. Going westbound takes a day from one's life; eastbound gives it back. Similar to crossing the Equator, passengers were mailed certificates noting their initiation. The most difficult question put to me by any passenger was to be asked the time—right then and there. The pilots used Greenwich Meridian Time, which could be hard to explain to a passenger and not easy for me to figure either. The navigators cooperated and would note our (GMT) time and changing location on a map that was posted on the forward bulkhead for all to see.

In Wake Island, time drifted slowly as we waited for the dining hall to open. When it was really hot, besides sleeping, eating became something to look forward to. The dining facility was kept clean and tidy; however, one day I saw a huge rat running on the ceiling rafter to the other end of the room. "My God!" I exclaimed. "No," said the pilot sitting next to me, "that's Eastbound; here comes Westbound." Another rat ran from the opposite direction and met the first one. We stared in awe, wondering how they would pass each other, until one backed off and they ran in the same direction. I was told that WWII Japanese had reached a point on the island when those animals were all they had to eat. In fact, men were near starving when the War ended. Well, they didn't eat them all. "Eastbound" and "Westbound" were later disposed of, but not in the dining room.

We landed at Haneda Airport in Japan, amid much hustle of people talking and moving swiftly. Did they ever go slowly, I thought. I was to learn that the Japanese WERE in a hurry—a race to learn, produce, and succeed. It was their road to recovery. It was only on rare occasions that Mount Fujiyama, the famous, snow-capped mountain, could be seen from Tokyo. The atmosphere had to be very clear, but we did get to see it from flight—the most perfectly shaped "vanilla ice cream cone". The mountain is a symbol to the Japanese people; the great artist, Hokusai, did a series of paintings of "Mt. Fuji" for every season in Japan.

The airport was closer to Yokohama than Tokyo. It could be a harrowing hour's ride to the hotel, with terribly congested traffic and no freeway. We passed buildings of flimsy structure, closely connected for miles. About twenty years prior to WW2, Tokyo was almost totally destroyed by an earthquake; our bombers nearly completed the rest. Not until reaching the center of town did concrete edifices begin to appear that were higher than a couple of stories.

Many people wore "getas", the Japanese platform shoe, held to the foot by a strap between the big and smaller toes. "Clopping" sounds could be heard along the sidewalk. Women wore kimono garb, which could be anything from a drab grey to elaborate, colorful designs. People bowed to their waist in greeting or parting, doing so repeatedly, until you wondered when and who would stop bowing first.

The famous Imperial Hotel was our home in Tokyo. It was THE hotel in Japan at the time. The architecture was the work of the American, Frank Lloyd Wright, built long before WWII. His creation was one of the first buildings structured to withstand earthquakes, but the rooms' interiors, the bathtubs, basins, and even the beds, were for uncommonly short people. At least they were not designed for Americans. Though the hotel had withstood bombings and quakes, it was only a few stories high in the fastest growing city in the world. It would be doomed to demolition. The lobby was impressive with flower and bonsai arrangements and the courtyards were well tended by artistic Japanese gardeners. The basement shops provided everything from fine art to camera and radio equipment. Clerks took prestigious care in artistically wrapping any purchase, be it a string of pearls or just notepaper. A distinct, sweet scent permeated the area from the bamboo and wooden boxes used for packing.

As a worldwide metropolis, Tokyo had restaurants for every liking and nationality. Within walking distance of the Imperial Hotel was "Lohmeyer's" for excellent German food. Crews looked for places that served tender Kobe beef, delectable choice meat from—Kobe, Japan. The yielding animals were treated well while alive, routinely massaged by the owners so they would give tender meat. In the early fifties, beef was not easy to find or to be had in any restaurant; however, Japanese Sukiyaki was so delectable, steak American way could be ignored. Who needed fried chicken with "yakitori" around—chicken mellowed with soy sauce to barbecue, and tempura—fish and vegetables, batter covered and deep-fried, crisp and never oily. As for raw fish, sashimi, I found no flavor, but sushi bars in Japan were as common as liquor bars in the U.S.

Though close to the Ginza, the well known shopping area, we often took a cab to the "Oriental Bazaar", a popular store for silk screens, ceramics, woodblock prints, and other objet d'art of the East. The taxi driver would have to be told by the hotel doorman where and how to get there, or anywhere. No signs indicated street names in any language and no buildings had numbers. I will never know how it was explained in Japanese, except it seemed to take "mucho palabra" to give the driver directions; after which we piled in a cab and prayed for our lives, as the drivers had to be former Kamakazi pilots. Some admitted they had been. Of course they said "Hai" (yes) to any question you asked. To the Japanese it was impolite to say "no".

While in Japan I was told sauna baths were a must to experience. I visited a public bathhouse of good reputation. It was not "integrated"; women went through one door and men another. We were scrubbed, rubbed, soaked, and steamed in a box with only our heads exposed. Our bodies were pulled, jerked, patted, slapped, massaged, soaped, washed, rinsed and dried. It was a battering with a great feeling of rebirth. The treatment received in the beauty parlors was a "must" on every trip. For around ten dollars one could get a permanent, manicure, pedicure and massage. If you wanted your legs shaved and eyebrows plucked, that was done too. While one attendant gave the pedicure, another the manicure, three people worked a fast hair job, all five over the customer at once. The pedicure included foot massage and callous removals. When the Japanese meticulous and inexpensive work became known to the PanAm stewardesses, it was not unusual to hear it said back in San Francisco, "I've got to get scheduling to give me a Tokyo trip. I need a hair cut."

BY WAY OF GUATEMALA

Chapter 55

During my vacation in November I flew from San Francisco to Tulsa, Oklahoma, on an American Airlines' ferry flight for $8.50 (an option available to airline personnel)—then on to Ft. Smith, Arkansas, and Shreveport, Louisiana, to New Orleans, via Braniff Airlines.

My folks were confused over the various "re-routes" I had taken in my life—in and out of office work, on and off marriage plans, moving from one end of the country to the other. I hated to upset them but could not clearly explain my actions; however, their love never faltered.

On return to San Francisco I flew via Guatemala. Now that PAA had flights from the West Coast to Latin America, I could fly back the longer though less expensive way. Besides, it delighted me to see Guatemala again. The city was to build a new, modern airport, stark and similar to others everywhere, but without the charm and beauty of the old building. I visited Jean Weber and her husband who were attached to the U.S. Embassy. Mayan servants made their housekeeping and entertaining an easy existence. Jean had no trouble adapting to the life style. As a treat for me, we drove to Chichicastenango, a circuitous and picturesque route into higher altitudes, far enough to require hotel accommodations. Bus service was available if you wished to share with live chickens and other assorted animals. Mayans walked the dusty road; one man carried a marimba on his back, seemingly without strain. As children they had been trained to feel heavy weights by having bags of rocks placed upon the boys' backs and in baskets on the girls' heads.

The town of Chichicastenango is well known as the purist and oldest remaining of the early Mayan-Quiche culture. We stayed in the popular Mayan Inn, built with scented woods and characteristic decor. The main square is most active on Sundays and Thursdays for marketing. People in the identifying dress of their villages come from miles away to exchange goods or sell their wares. We visited the church of San Tomas with its high steps upon which the people in a smoky haze from incense slowly climbed with each prayer. No benches were in the interior; Mayans sat upon stone flooring among flower petals and candles. The Chichicastenango men wore black pantaloon outfits with red headpiece and sash, native to their tribe. Outside the town was a secluded mound of rocks holding a small Mayan idol. People knelt before it, combining their pagan beliefs with the missionaries' teaching, together with the same lighted candles, scattered flower petals, and burning incense.

More years would pass in political strife for my beloved Guatemala, with much blood shed by its poor people. Whoever led the army ruled Guatemala. The Mayans suffered; few could flee. Either they merged with other ethnic groups or faced extermination, their culture to exist mostly in museums. They were the oppressed, still the conquered; their land in turmoil was like a beautiful flower touched with a branding iron.

Back in California I was invited to a party given by bachelors living nearby; one being a PAA pilot who years later became a System Chief Pilot. Another guest was a Coast Guard officer named Tim, attached to a unit used for rescue operations. We clicked almost from first conversation. Tim attracted me not only by his cheerful, smiling manner but the interest and compassion he showed for much of this world and its people. After a period in my life of mistrusting "the dating game", I started seeing Tim.

From the beginning of our friendship, Tim told me he was divorced. He described himself as being a failure in marriage. "It's not my cup of tea either," I answered. We got along well. Tim showed me San Francisco from the good places to eat in Chinatown to the delicious clams and crabs on Fisherman's Wharf. We partied with his friends and mine from Marin County to Santa Cruz. We picnicked, went fishing, played golf, and covered every "watering hole" along Broadway and Geary St. to Telegraph Hill. Tim introduced me to deli food at "Tommy's Joint" on Van Ness Ave, Irish coffee at the "Buena Vista", and the nightlife of San Francisco. They were such happy days.

My last trip of the year was to Tokyo. En route in Honolulu, local friends drove me around Oahu, past homes with million dollar views near Diamondhead. One was pointed out as the residence of Doris Duke. We passed Cocohead, Hanauma Bay with its quiet turquoise water, Rabbit Island, and the famous BlowHole. We drove up the mountain on a winding two-lane road to Pali Pass and back to Honolulu. No super highway existed. For an afternoon drive, it was probably one of the most beautiful short trips in the world. I was also introduced to the Kawaihao Church near the Ionlani Palace. The minister preached the same sermon twice, first in Hawaiian, then in English. I realized the uniqueness of the Hawaiian language; words are practically all vowels, making speech quite melodious.

On to Tokyo and for the Christmas Season there were many bright lights and displays for our Christian holiday. The Takashimaya department store was artistically decorated with show windows having automated delights that attracted adults as well as children. The toy department was a must to visit. Here was a non-Christian country instilling the spirit of Christmas with great success. My Holiday cards were an assortment of Hawaiian "Mele Kalikimaka", and woodblock prints from Japan.

CENPAC AND SOPAC

Chapter 56

CENPAC was the name given to trips in the middle Pacific area. In one month of 1954 I had flown 120 hours and 37 minutes because of turnarounds at Wake Island, which took me to Tokyo and twice to Manila. When a trip extended and one's clothes began to look ragged, it was desperation time. Ours was a scheduled eight-day trip that came closer to thirty. The steward wired Scheduling to say, "Need to go home! Skivvies in ribbons!"

It was not *all* bad. Between Wake and Tokyo I boarded a flight in the middle of the night when the arrival crew advised that most of the passengers were in their berths, with only a few still in the lounge. The late drinkers were Lefty O'Doul, Leo Durocher, and Horace Stoneham of the famous New York Giants baseball team. The team was to play exhibition games in a country wild about baseball. With this group was Lorraine Day, a movie star and Durocher's wife. Others were Wes Westrum, Monty Kennedy, Bill Rigney, Monte Irwin, Hoyt Wilhelm, Don Mueller, et al. We saw more of the team for cocktails and dinner in Tokyo. The Imperial Hotel lounge was fully occupied that night with PanAm crews and the Giants baseball team, seated together.

Dinner was Japanese style, to sit upon futons on tatami matting at a table lower than the average coffee table. Enclosed by silk and bamboo shoji screens, the rooms were private and shoes were left outside. Japanese geishas in their lovely kimonos and obis waited upon us with grace and refinement. Preceding the meal, diners were given a small, wet, very hot, cleansing cloth. The servers lightly waved it in the air with bamboo tongs to release some of the steam. (PAA would later use this idea on their flights.) We were never allowed to be without green tea, soya, or bowls of rice to go with every dish. Each diner had his own small saki bottle of warm rice wine. Entertainment consisted of ladies playing a Japanese shamisen, a three-stringed instrument, whose sounds were discordant to my ears. These musicians were true artisans. If only I had the educated ear to accept their tones. Two Giants with whom I shared dinner were Wes Westrum and Monty Kennedy, whose careers I watched with anticipation for their success.

In February I had my first SOPAC trip, the term given to the Southern Pacific area. This was for 13 days. We flew over the Equator before landing in Canton Island. Canton also had an abandoned sea-going ship, the S.S. President Taylor, caught upon the reef with only a matter of time before the ocean battered it to extinction. The International Dateline was crossed after Canton Island.

We landed at night in Fiji at the Nadi Airport (pronounced Nan-di), which was close to our PanAm "compound". The women's quarters were in a large, reed-roofed, "buri" hut. Room divisions were shoulder high with thatching that reached to a lofty ceiling. Clay paths along tropical trees and hibiscus plants led to the dining hall, the lounge buri, and a volley ball court kept busy during cooler hours. It was our "village", with the PAA station managers and their families living on the grounds. Such was home between flights to Australia and New Zealand. A layover in Fiji was a great place to eat, sleep, and catch up on reading. For the more active, there was swimming, fishing, scuba diving, boating, coral hunting, volleyball, tennis, very old movies, and—drinking. To some, the sound of our aircraft arrival was music to their ears; to others, it marked the end of island fun.

Tropical Fiji has enough rain to bring growth to the pineapple and sugar cane crops and keep the islands green and commercially viable. Sugar cane is planted on the flats near the ocean. When ripe and cut, it is carried to the mills of Laotoka by toy-size trains on a narrow track. In the background are the Masori Highlands, mountains of Fiji (looking taller than they really are because they rise from the sea) which reach to cooler temperatures. Through this area, the jungles of heavy vines are strong enough to hold a man swinging from them, and colorful parrots seemed to light up the tropical growth as bulbs on a Christmas tree. The town of Nadi, after which the airport is named, is located on the west side of the largest of the 350 or so Fijian islands, Viti Levu.

In 1954, the shops were mostly operated and owned by Indian people who were brought to the Islands years ago by the English to work in the fields. The Indians became the industrious citizens of Fiji. Native Fijians, under the British mandate, were to always own the land, as their native right. By and large, with the exception of limited employment, the Fijians lived in the simplistic way of their ancestors.

In a tour of the island we crossed a river by a Fijian village, a neat set of buri huts. In the water away from the road were women swimming, perhaps bathing with their young. They waved to us with a call of "Bula Bula", the Fijian greeting. To catch her child, one woman jumped high enough to reveal that she wore no top clothing. Seeing strangers, she ducked down quickly in the water again, laughing naively as she did so. Most Fijians smile in friendliness, with an ingenuous nature. It was hard to believe that fifty years earlier, cannibalism had prevailed in these islands.

From Honolulu to Fiji was a 14:30 hour flight; from Nandi to Sydney, Australia, it was only 7:30. In Australia, English was spoken. Well, it was close, but no more difficult to understand than perhaps a New Englander trying to interpret a Texan. The people had their own "exotic" expressions, vernacular differences, but they were more knowledgeable of American slang and customs than we were of theirs. The Australians expressed a copious desire to show our similarities. Perhaps the Pacific conflict in WWII brought a feeling of comradeship, and they too are a mixed variety of race and origin.

At that time there was only a 24-hour stay in Sydney. We brought in the 1024V and took out the same aircraft the next day. From my hotel window I could see the famous Harbour Bridge, whose unusual frame I remembered seeing in schoolbooks. The building of the famous Opera House near the bridge was under construction, looking like a series of inverted shells or petals of a flower. Otherwise, in 1954, the city had an aged appearance as though it had stopped growing thirty years before. Sydney, lying upon hills with inlets, bays, and coves off the sea, is one of the most beautiful harbors in the world.

In this one SOPAC trip I had accumulated more than 68 hours of flight time. Perhaps the most memorable part came on the final trip leg. Between Honolulu and San Francisco, who should be on board but Marilyn Monroe and Joe DiMaggio? Marilyn had been in Korea entertaining the troops stationed there. Many pictures have been published showing her bare-shoulder clothing in freezing weather. She gave the boys a thrill; unfortunately, she caught a cold standing on an outdoor stage. On the aircraft Marilyn had a lower berth next to the cockpit. She was not well but I did get to talk to her. She spoke kindly and sensibly but wore a shyness almost as though she did not believe she was really famous. Once she went down to the lounge and huddled next to Joe in a protection seeking way but did not stay long. Marilyn left with the excuse that she was not drinking and, with limited space, others might want to sit there. Ha! They would have crawled out on the wing to see her.

Back in her lower berth, Marilyn lay resting with a fur coat draped over her body and her blond hair flowing across a pillow. The curtain was slightly ajar at one end; just enough that every crewmember who came aft from the cockpit could see her. Never have I seen pilots leave the cockpit so often, going to the lavatory or getting their own coffee. Marilyn Monroe truly was a beautiful woman, more so than photography credits her.

On arrival in San Francisco (the old terminal where Pan Am had its own building from seaplane days) the Press gathered to meet Joe and Marilyn. A special room was arranged for the news and television people to film an interview by John Cameron Swayze, a famous, national commentator of the day. The wires and television cables criss-crossed in a spaghetti-laden appearance. The cameramen moved about excitedly. However, Joe would not let Marilyn have any interviews. She was sick and he would take her home. Joe was adamant as Marilyn walked away with him. The Press was devastated.

I wonder how many people across the nation groaned as they watched television the next evening, to be told, "Marilyn could not appear tonight because she was ill, but we have an interview with the stewardess. . . ." I cringed when I heard this and could hear the world's sighs of disappointment. I saw myself on the TV set of my friends, Hap and Bob in Los Altos. I cannot remember what I said when asked about Joe and Marilyn. I did not recognize my voice, or myself, and maybe no one else would either. Later I received a letter from "Uncle Syd " in New York. He and my Perry Street friends were excited to see me on television, quite by accident while searching for a show in which Uncle Syd's niece, "Bubs", was singing. Bubs later went to Europe and made a name for herself in "La Traviata", at Frankfurt, London, Paris, and finally the height of operatic ascension, La Scala, in Milan. Beverly "Bubs" Sills, as well as Marilyn Monroe, would be names to remember.

BURLINGAME

Chapter 57

Before seniority and bid award determined flight assignment, planning one's life was more difficult. Community activity could seldom be arranged at home. I did get involved with school youngsters called Wing Scouts. I took them aboard one of our aircraft at the hangar, the cockpit of which held great excitement; however, my irregular life style made it hard to be with them often.

Volunteering to canvass my Burlingame neighborhood for donations to the United Way, I had a rare meeting, even in 1954. My route covered a residence surrounded by a picket fence and hidden by lush growth. I opened the gate and entered despite no response to the outside dangle-bell. At the front door a weak voice invited me in where a little lady, easily in her nineties, sat in a shadowed corner. She apologized for needing darkness from bright light that bothered her eyes. Then she asked about "the outside world" and how I had arrived in the Golden State. Informed of my cross-country trek in my Chevrolet, she grinned and told me she had come to California in a covered wagon. I was enchanted by her stories. Years later when she was gone, her house and property were replaced by an apartment building. I wish I could have tape-recorded her experiences crossing the American West, an historical period in the nineteenth century. (Flying in piston aircraft would be twentieth century history.)

My friendship with Tim developed to where I hardly realized how much he meant to me. If I felt blue, his humor would cheer me. He sensed I hid secrets in my heart, yet never queried me. If I divulged any doubts or skepticism, Tim would say, "it isn't worth bothering about; life's too short." He was so right.

PanAm's relationship with the Coast Guard was a respected one, as their assistance was life saving. Survival from a ditching at sea was practiced on an aircraft hull, floated in shallow waters of the San Francisco Bay. One wing was left on from which to launch life rafts, as well as from the cabin door. The Coast Guard rowed us to the plane where we practiced sea evacuation. Then we waggled around on the raft while learning to use the equipment. As PAA did have a couple of ditchings, the learning proved resourceful. We also used a simulated aircraft fuselage, elevated on stilts in the parking lot, for land evacuation drills. It became an action part of our emergency class.

In May of 1954, Philco Corporation chartered Pan Am for eight flights to Hawaii as a special services award to their sales agents and wives. I worked one of them, the Clipper "Monarch of the Skies." The passengers were a happy group of people who appreciated their achievement. I had convention and charter trips before—sometimes it would be a drinking spree that took some delicacy to control. This group was particular, as they retained their composure through all the partying aloft.

When I arrived in Honolulu, Tim was there. Only crewmembers and the military could fly to Honolulu for a few hours and then fly home. Tim and I enjoyed beach and bar in the fancy of Hawaii. More happy times. "Aloha!"

On departure, as was normal procedure while the plane taxied to the end of the runway, a life jacket demonstration and emergency procedures were reviewed. I heard some clicking sounds and noticed a passenger with earphones attached to a device in his lap. I stopped to tell him that electrical properties could not be used during the taxi period as they interfered with the pilots radio contact to the tower (or so we had been instructed). Perhaps I showed annoyance at what I considered rudeness during our demonstration. He gave me a toothy smile, apologized, and "came to attention" as I pointed out the exit locations. Later I checked the passenger manifest and saw that he was the founding president of IBM. Oh, dear! Air travel was frequent for him and he had seen our demonstrations a thousand times, but he did prove to be quite a congenial passenger.

Back home I was assigned a simulated trip for delegates from the Foreign Trade Transportation Institute, with a meal service using an aircraft on the ground. It was important to put on a good show for PanAm, as we were being judged along with TWA and United Airlines. We had faith that ours was an excellent meal service. Sometimes I met other airlines' employees who accused and criticized PAA for conveying an attitude of superiority. Actually, since we had no domestic flights, we had to continually prove we deserved overseas routes that other airlines envied. We had to compete with the excellence of foreign airlines in our struggles to be better (to say nothing of unequal expenses and restrictions in flying "beyond the reef"). Although PAA was not subsidized, as our foreign competitors could be, our airline represented the USA, and was so judged and considered wherever it landed. Pan Am was America's airline.

Language being a weak point with most Americans, foreign tongues became a guarded prerequisite in hiring stewardesses, except in the Pacific-Alaska Division. However, in the spring of 1954 we were all required to take lessons in Japanese, offered by a Mr. Suzuki who had taught the language to our military. Besides "Sayonara", I learned phrases like "Ikura desuka?" (How much is it?).

In the middle of June I had a trip to Manila. While there I met my friend Harry, who was then based in Hong Kong. Harry helped me select a fine weave, straw hat for Dad's Father's Day gift. The hat was rolled to fit in a hollow, giant sized, bamboo cutting. I also bought some coconut syrup that was far the sweetest I ever tasted. After shopping, Harry and I had dinner at the Swiss Inn. When he left, I could not help thinking that we were the only two from the group in Guatemala who were still unmarried.

In July I had a triple shuttle, back and forth from Honolulu to the Coast. Passenger loads were full on these daytime flights, mostly vacationers with hundreds of leis in plastic bags filling the hat racks. People came aboard with so many leis around their necks they could hardly see to walk; they were engrossed with flowers, sunburns and laughter. As Tim would say, "Enjoy yourself while you can." On the third shuttle into Los Angeles, the Traffic representative advised there would be a dog in the cabin. Such was acceptable as long as we had only one dog, kept in a box with the passenger. All seemed in order until an hour in flight the owner came down the aisle walking her toy poodle on a leash. No, it was two poodles on a twin leash; one white and the other black, handled by a woman dressed in more jewelry than clothing. I had to remind her about keeping the dogs at her seat, preferably in their box. "They're potty trained and nature calls," she informed me, as she headed towards the lavatory. Some passengers laughed, others snorted, but one man interrupted with the comment, "Lady, did you know there are times the pressurization is affected when flushing or even lifting the toilet lid, and small or loose objects can be sucked right out of the airplane. Those pups could end up in the Pacific Ocean!" The passenger believed this inanity, huffed and returned to her seat with poodles in tow. Poor little poodles.

HIGH AND LOW TIDE

Chapter 58

Just before my 30th birthday, which was spent in Honolulu, I received a telephone call from Ellie and Phil in Canada. They had married after about a seven-year courtship. Dear Tim sent me a dozen red roses. I asked if they were for my birthday or because my good friend got married. With a big grin he replied, "Because from now on your life gets more exciting." Tim usually knew the right things to say.

From August until the middle of November I was assigned repeated Manila trips and Honolulu shuttles. On one of these ocean crossings I had the pleasure of Mr. Alfred Hitchcock, the famous film director, traveling with his wife. After dinner the lights were lowered; darkness came slowly upon us as we flew westward following the sun. Only a few passengers stayed in the lounge. Mrs. Hitchcock wanted to retire early so I held the ladder while she mounted into her berth. Later the stewardess came back to the galley where I was making fresh coffee and remarked that she had just put the famous Mr. Hitchcock in upper berth Eight.

"Ouch!" I said, "I put Mrs. Hitchcock in that berth."

"That's okay, they're married," she laughed.

"Not the point. They each have a berth but you can't exceed 300 pounds weight in one or 'Humpty dumpty'. Mr. Hitchcock is a little on the chubby side, and the two together. . . ."

"Who's going to tell them?"

"Not me."

"Not me!"

Up to the cockpit we went to let the crew worry about it, or whatever. The flight engineer took out his slide rule and jokingly said, "Wel-l-l—let's see—suppose he's 200 pounds, no-o-o maybe 220, and she's perhaps 130 pounds . . . are they being active?"

"You want to ask them? Oh, damn, what's a little fifty pounds."

Fortunately we had no rough weather; the flight was smooth as a calm sea. When all was quiet, I went into the galley and only heard the engines producing their familiar rotating sound, as they noised away hour after hour. Facing the ovens to the rear, where I had placed the breakfast pans, I felt a gentle tap on my shoulder and almost fell back from the floor step-up. As I turned, that familiar, renown voice said, "X-cuse me, but may I bother you for a glah-ahs of toe-mah-toe juice, please?" He spoke as I would remember him on television for years. How did he get down from that berth without the ladder? He was pretty agile for a man of his girth. No wonder he produced great mystery films.

In Wake I was asked if I wanted to join the Wake Island Golf Club. It was no joke. Capt. Hugh Gordon, together with ground and flight crews, developed the "Low Tide Country Club". It was so unusual that *Life* magazine sent a photographer to film the impossible—a golf course with all sand fairways and white "greens". Tidewater ponds were the "traps", coral rock was "in the rough", and the ocean was "out of bounds". Balls were bright colors; white was non-regulation. Cups on the "greens", made of cans or pipe parts, were frequently emptied of more than just the balls, like sand crabs—ouch! The course could only be used when the tide was out. Membership fee was two dollars, which included golf caps with a design of Wake Island on the visor. Any PanAm'er who could hit a ball well out of a sand trap probably learned at Wake Island.

Continuing to Guam and Manila, I handled the meal in the galley position while Mary and Ann, the two stewardesses, worked the cabin. Moving fast and furious, Mary on a quick return to the galley commented that a passenger requested my business card with our names, so he could write a commendation letter. When the meal was over, I walked to where the passenger was seated, handed him my card with our names and said, "Thank you, it's our pleasure to serve you." Then I raced to my disembarking duties; however, I could not help noticing that this passenger looked quite startled, and the woman next to him gave me a haughty, disapproving look. When we left for the hotel, I said to the girls, "Well, I gave my card to the passenger in 12B, but he didn't look too happy."

"12B!" cried Mary, "not 12B. I said 12C. (The other side of the aisle.) You gave it to the wrong passenger." I thought of my words, "our pleasure is to serve you."

"Bet we get a complaint letter from his wife," Ann remarked. We got neither.

In another mistaken identity, to a child traveling with his mother and father, I gave a set of crayons and coloring book that PanAm always carried for young folks. He looked like a small boy until I found out later that he earned enough to buy and sell the aircraft, probably in one night that he entertained. He was Paul Anka, the famous young singer. He did have a baby face. His name was not listed on the "Excor" list, the advisory sheet for the famous or passengers previously "mishandled". He would be from then on, I supposed.

We had turkey in Wake Island that Thanksgiving; birds sent from Hawaii especially for our feast. Going home eastbound we crossed the International Dateline and thereby retrieved the day we lost going west. It was Thanksgiving Day again, only in Hawaii, and more "turkey"? No, a la Mahi Mahi!

There was no mistaking when Louis Armstrong boarded my flight back to the Coast from Honolulu. He gave each crewmember a post card picture of himself with his trumpet, on which he wrote, "Thanks for a lovely trip, Satchmo Louis Armstrong." His famous lips were covered with an inch of protective vaseline and probably were well insured too. The gravely voice did not speak often but it was easy to recognize him when he did.

For my December vacation, I flew TWA to LaGuardia and

visited Ellie and Phil. Phil was doing assistant directing, as well as writing. He found time to take us to see Mary Martin's memorable performance in "Peter Pan" at the Winter Garden. Then we stopped by Keen's English ChopHouse on West 36th, a tavern with its own ancestry. Smoking pipes mounted the walls and ceiling, left by customers to use when there. If the pipe owner were deceased, the stem, some long and willowy, would be broken but left in place. The idea came from the "merrie ole England", tobacco-trade days, when Ben Jonson, Bacon, and other famous men of writing, drama, and politics, gathered together in a tavern. As we looked about Keen's, begun in 1910, there were pipes belonging to such as the Barrymores, Bobby Jones, George M. Cohan, and Theodore Roosevelt. I will always have nostalgic feelings and appreciation for the "big city" sights and the good friends I made there, but I had no regrets about moving on.

National Airlines took me to New Orleans from New York. For the first time I missed a flight. I fell asleep in a chair while waiting for a plane in Jacksonville, Florida. I had to wait four hours for the next flight, a slow way via Pensacola and Mobile. It was quite embarrassing when the ticket agent said, "We paged and paged you." At home I found rest with those I dearly loved. Going back to San Francisco, I flew my original old route on PanAm, New Orleans to Merida to Guatemala—then up to California.

SAN FRANCISCO

Chapter 59

In an apartment twelve miles outside the city limits of San Francisco, I could not say I lived in this fabulous West Coast city. No, I had to reside WITHIN it. I finally moved there in early 1955, after searching the hills of Russian, Nob, and Telegraph, to at least have a view if I stood on the roof. A home "with a view" was most desirable as well as prestigious, and a water view was as difficult to get as a hole in one on the golf course. I knew a steward who claimed he could see the San Francisco Bay if he stood on the toilet and looked out a tiny vent window.

One of the reasons it took me so long to move to the city was my fear to drive the hills. Visiting a friend on Filbert Street, the hill in her block was so steep I felt I was looking down a canyon. My little Chevy had climbed uphill quite well. I parked and braked with wheels curbed. But on leaving I was petrified when I tried to engage control of the car—it started to roll downhill backwards. I had seen hills since leaving flat country of Louisiana, but these in San Francisco were ridiculous. Pulling the handbrake, I left the car on the sidewalk and called AAA. I fled down the Peninsular where my Chevy spent a year without seeing San Francisco.

It was pure luck, being in the right place at the right time, when I found an apartment in the city located atop Russian Hill on Leavenworth Street. It had one huge room with a wall bed, a row of windows that viewed Pacific Heights, half of the Golden Gate Bridge, and those gorgeous sunsets. At night the neon lights on Lombard Street stretched towards the Presidio, resembling a string of Christmas bulbs. The rent was $75 a month. Parking was seldom more than a block away and I only parked the car on a hill if it was nose-in, parallel parking. It was a place I truly enjoyed. Drawn by the high temperature of California's Central Valley, the fog came in every summer day around 4 or 5 p.m. It would roll in block by block, cleanse the city like a giant sweeper before moving out. It also brought cool weather that deceived summer vacationers to San Francisco. I could hear the foghorn, repeating and repeating, warning ocean-going ships in the Bay, when one could not see across the street. There was no mistaking the cablecar bells clanging on Hyde Street, a block away.

Tim purchased a row house on Telegraph Hill that he wanted to improve for rentals. We worked together on the interior, getting more paint on ourselves and the floor canvass than on the walls. One day, after hours of vigorous work, Tim walked up to me with brush in one hand, paint can in the other, splashes upon nose and forehead, to say, "You and I ought to get married. We'd make a paintin' pretty pair." The subject had never before been mentioned, but I could not help laughing at the sight of us.

"Do you mind if we finish this room first?" I replied.

"Okay. But while you think about it, would you decide if we should have dinner at 'The Shadows' or—say, we haven't tried 'Caesar's Palace' yet." That was Tim. He did not really want to get married, and I was equally afraid of the idea.

In the spring of 1955, PanAm graduated its first class of Japanese speaking girls to join our stewardess ranks. They were second or third generation, Japanese Americans. Their knowledge of the Japanese language was not their only contribution to the airline. Many of them could be the most gracious and hardest working crewmember aboard. Pressure upon them came not only from the feelings left by Pearl Harbor but even from people in Japan. These women bravely withstood any resentment, proved they were solid American, and all for PanAm. It was a joy to have them as part of the crew.

More and more tourists were flying the Pacific, traveling to the Orient. As movies were often made in foreign areas, we also carried the stars and casts. I boarded one flight to find that the famous star, William Holden, and his wife were passengers. It promised to be an interesting trip. Instead it was a nightmare. Mr. Holden's intoxicated condition was not noticeable until he was in the lounge. There he proceeded to drink all night. Alcohol mixes poorly with some people when in high altitudes. Going light on Holden's drinks only angered him. When the sun started to rise, he came upstairs and asked for dinner. Dinner? Breakfast was the only meal we had, but I could give him sandwiches. I will not repeat what he called the sandwiches. William Holden's wife sat quietly and exchanged no words with her husband throughout the trip. He must have been a nice man when he was sober, but I never had the pleasure to meet him then.

Pacific and Atlantic crews began to meet on the RTW (Round the World) flights at Bangkok, Thailand, which afforded me a great opportunity to see this interesting country with its temples, silk markets, and Siamese dancers. I had no desire to visit the snake farms, but the klong (canal) boat rides revealed the people in native habitat. Children played and bathed in the klongs, that also carried materials of questionable nature; yet a prevalent cleanliness existed about the Thailanders. Women in coolie hats paddled their skiffs with fruit and vegetables that they sold along the waterways. On a tour, I visited the barge belonging to the royal family and used only on special occasions. It was a giant, gold-gilded boat with oarlocks for twenty or more men to row, and a podium for the ruler to sit. The stern had the pointed curl, so typical of Siamese architecture.

In the middle 1950s, no control was put on public opium dens in Thailand. One of our more intrepid stewards asked me if I wanted to see one. My curiosity allowed me to follow his course of introduction. We walked to a building more open from the street than a bar might be at home. Inside were individual cubicles where people indulged in this "smoke to the heights". Men lay using the woodblock "pillow" for their heads. People came and went like gamblers to Las Vegas, only at a slower pace. We were urged to participate by a pretty young woman who seemed to be in charge of "rentals". She wore a floor length skirt and, from the waist up, only an American white brassiere, which on our side of the ocean would be considered an undergarment. When she realized we were not there for "business", we were politely dismissed.

Back on Russian Hill, I had my first party in my new dwelling. Counting Tim and myself, thirty-nine people were in that one room apartment. In the fashion of the era for San Francisco, men wore coats and ties and women were in cocktail dresses, but party excitement was as bright and exhilarating as any could be. I handled the food while Tim tended the bar. My table was filled with snacks and dips I spent more time preparing than Thanksgiving dinner. The blinds were open to show a marvelous view on a cool, clear night. The party must have been successful as the last guests left at 2 a.m. It was also the night that a friend of Tim's brought a handsome man named Daniel, who would later become a particular friend of mine.

FIJI AND DOWN UNDER

Chapter 60

The Australians and "Kiwis" from New Zealand regard the Fiji Islands as Americans think of Hawaii. On a Sopac trip I attended a Fijian "tra-la-la", or "melee", similar to a Hawaiian luau, with entertainment in which the Fijians display their musical ability and melodic voices. Many of the singers and performers were employed at the PanAm compound. Talent was as prominent and natural as their cheerfulness.

Nikoru, the chef, barbecued all the steaks that night, but when he returned home he was the chief, not the chef, of his village. Ever smiling Joe was Nikoru's helper. Loiti, who tended bar and cared for the lounge buri, was in reality a true prince of his tribe. He was a handsome man with all the regal dignity that might be expected in his erect stature. Loiti was never servile and held our deep affection and respect, but he kept to himself. There was Peter, who had to be prodded a bit to keep him working, but he did everything from serve in the dining room to fill in on the volleyball court. Peter was so strong that while playing ball he could unintentionally knock a person over with such force they landed half under the sand. When Peter coveted my small battery radio, I gave it to him on condition he later pay me $15. I never saw the $15. I learned it was about as much money as he earned in a month, so I forgot about it.

Mele and Anna, part of the singing group, wore a hibiscus flower behind their ear—right side for "already taken" or the left ear for "still looking." (Maybe it's the other way around?) When I wanted pictures of the Fijian women who tended our quarters, I asked Laisa, Emlie and Kuda to pose for me. Each one had the bushy hair by which Fijians are often identified. In modest fashion they giggled and requested time to first comb their tops, expansive, frizzy hair that ballooned about their heads. How they ever got a comb through those tresses, I'll never know. They returned with their hibiscus flower and posed for my photo.

I had my first cup of "kava" juice, a native drink made from ground roots. This liquid is rather distasteful to anyone unaccustomed to it but offensive to Fijians if rejected. The liquid was mixed in a turtleback receptacle, ladled into a coconut shell, and then emptied by the person to whom it was handed. After drinking (chug-a-lug), everyone clapped three times; the same cup was refilled and passed to another. This is a ritual, as significant to Fijians as the tea ceremony in Japan. The drink is non-alcoholic, about as bland as Hawaiian poi, but can numb the lips a bit.

The next day we drove to Sigatoka, westward around the coast. We found an empty, sandy beach, so pristine it was as though we were the first to swim in this paradise location. Tropical fish hovered close and nosed our skin, completely unafraid. (Years later, aside this very beach, would be the big Fijian Hotel. In 1955, we were the only ones around.) On return to the compound, a singular incident occurred. The ride was over "uninhabited" country. We girls could not "wait" and had to go behind bushes near the road. No sooner had we lowered our garments to take relief then we heard giggles. Off to the side were two tiny black faces with bushy hair, a pair of Fijian children. The land seemed so deserted it was hard to believe anyone was around. Suffice it to say, it was probably the first time those little ones ever saw white behinds.

PanAm shuttled from Fiji to "Kiwi" country, arriving at Auckland using a DC-4. As for New Zealand; this world turns full of treasures. We were driven across lush-green fields and hills with grazing sheep to an inn called "Mon Desir". The taxi that carried us from the airport was notable in that it was once the limousine of the infamous Al Capone, somehow purchased and shipped to

New Zealand. The car was kept alive with a Dodge engine in a Chrysler body, a 1937 model. It had thick doors, bulletproof windows, and endured two engine overhauls. The Mon Desir Inn, most probably an old home, was set on green lawns swept with trees and facing an inlet bay. It was winter in the Southern Hemisphere and a roaring fireplace was kept in the lounge. Before dinner, I walked a freezing hallway for a shower where the water was as boiling as a hot stream geyser. What a contrast! New Zealand is known for its natural, hot springs.

The city of Auckland in 1955 was like a small English town, the architecture similar to a village in the Cotswolds. New Zealanders expressed no desire that their land be well known. It was said they would rather stay 50 years behind the rest of the world and keep aliens away, for lower population. On return we carried the Prince and Princess of Liechtenstein, passengers with their valet and little "Lady Cashmere", a cat more fluff than feline.

A slightly different flight was in store for me after returning to San Francisco. Pan Am had some charter trips carrying military personnel within the States. On one flight we took a plane loaded with Marines to Chicago from Oakland. These men, in their spotless uniforms, boarded the aircraft as if someone was saying, "hep, two, three, four", because they ran up the stairs in perfect timing, left, right, left, right. Throughout the flight they were immaculately neat and well mannered, and seemed so proud to be Marines.

We spent a week in Chicago (thought Scheduling had forgotten we were there). After covering almost every known restaurant in the city and one of the many museums every day, we departed with another group of men going to San Diego for Marine training—all new recruits. The flight was horrible! Such disorder, I never believed any one of them could ever become a Marine. They cluttered the floor and screeched like hyenas. We arrived in San Diego where a sergeant, the "cookie cutter", met the aircraft. "Step lively!" he yelled, as the recruits sauntered off the aircraft. Not moving fast enough, the sergeant raked them over in harsh manner. I could not help snickering as I watched the boys line up outside. The sergeant barked orders, criticized their posture, and told them the play times were over. Maybe all young folks should . . . oh, maybe not.

SO TURNS THE WORLD

Chapter 61

Tim left on a flight to Europe for a job interview, as his retirement from military service was reaching fruition. He also wanted to purchase a new car in Germany. Neither reason for traveling would take him long, he said. Tim sent post cards at first. Then weeks passed and I did not hear from him; however, past experience taught me that disappointment was not beyond my reach.

Ginger took her vacation on the West Coast and I was happy to show her my adopted home and city. I had finally learned hill driving. We drove about San Francisco, where going up the hill to Coit Tower gave a panoramic view to watch ocean liners sail through the Golden Gate. Alcatraz, always a conversation piece, was still a prison. Ginger delighted in going down crooked Lombard Street, through the Presidio, and across the Golden Gate Bridge to Sausalito, the quaint and charming town by the Bay.

Ginger gave me reason to have another party. Tim was not around and I missed him; at least he could have been there to mix the drinks. I recalled his words, "Life's too short. Have fun wherever you are." I wondered where he was practicing his beliefs. Looking over my list of guests for my party, I saw that I would be short a few men, so I asked a friend to bring some bachelors. Daniel's name was mentioned as being in town and I agreed that he should come. I had not seen this gentleman since my first party. Daniel was indeed properly named for he had soft, soothing eyes and a strong but gentle voice that could probably calm the most ferocious animal. Perhaps this affected me as I was feeling like a rejected tiger. Before leaving the party, Daniel asked to take me to dinner the following Friday. I said I was not sure about my schedule and would he call later. (It was a lie; I knew I would be in town). A week went by with no word from Daniel. I called Scheduling, begged for a trip, and my request was granted. In flying, I had plenty time to ponder my sanity. Why did I not say, "Yes, Daniel, I'd enjoy having dinner with you." No, I had behaved like a shrew.

Through the spring and summer I had several trips to Tokyo. I enjoyed going to Japan, which took on a particular beauty when the cherry trees were in blossom. These could be seen in the parks and shrines as well as the countryside. From the air, not one foot of land appeared without cultivation or preservation of some sort, all artistically programmed. Japan, as an island country, recognized the value of space. The Japanese introduced an intriguing and different way of life to me as a Westerner. Appreciation of art is shown in their ikebana, origami and technique of cha ceremonies, which are demonstrated in museums, hotels and department stores. It was hard to understand how flower arrangements, folding paper into objects, or a tea service, could be classified as "arts", until I realized how clumsy I was to effect their beauty. The Japanese have mastered many diverse arts—bonsai plants, ink and silk screen painting, cloisonne pottery, lacquerware, Imari china, cultured pearls, as well as their stage dramas. With fantastic lighting and mechanical devices, the Kabuki form of acting offer allegorical plays using all male performers accompanied by flute and drum. The men wear elaborate masks or make-up. Strange at first, but interesting.

One of my passengers from Honolulu was the famous comedian, Red Skelton. He stayed up all night in the lounge, not to drink but to talk, as he could not sleep. He was a tall man of large frame who had a quick absorbing mind. His dress was not exactly flamboyant but it was clear he favored the color red. Skelton had a natural chuckle and was amused in hearing the yarns of others, often saying, "Got to remember that one."

On another shuttle, a night flight, Robert Cummings, his

wife, and the Art Linkletters, flew into Los Angeles from Hawaii. They had purchased the two upper and lower berths between the cockpit and the lavatories. It gave them privacy. They boarded exhausted and retired early. Robert Cummings came back to the galley once and caught me cleaning the aluminum counter with champagne.

"OOhh," said Cummings, forming his lips into that round-mouth, questioning look he would often show in the movies, "champagne for a cleanser?"

"Best thing for the purpose, better than coffee," I answered. "Once a bottle is opened and not emptied, it must be discarded anyway. When the bubbles are gone . . ."

I finally dined with Daniel after returning to San Francisco. His princely manner and attention boosted my ego. Daniel constantly traveled too, in dangerous employment with our government's Secret Service. It seemed I hardly had time to know him before being called for a Manila trip in which I shuttled from Saigon to Singapore. This was an area that really completed my travel "around the world".

Saigon displayed Parisian planning in their tree-lined streets and shop facades. The women were slender and chic, feminine and attractive in their form-fitted outfits, called Ao Dai. These full lengths, silken dresses had side slits up the calf of both legs, while underneath they wore long pants of the same material. Men drove casually about on bicycles and rickshas; the tranquility about the place gave little thought of the Vietnam War to come.

At the Saigon airport I stopped suddenly when climbing the stairs to my plane. Off in the distance I saw a parked aircraft that seemed to cry out to me. On closer look I could see it was an old friend, a B-307, in which I had flown many times from New Orleans. Alone and deserted stood the "Comet", whose numbers I recognized; though it had different airline markings. Two of its engines had been shirred away, as it was being used for replacement parts, piece by piece. It looked dirty, beaten, and badly abused. I looked at the poor, miserable aircraft and tears rolled down my face.

Singapore showed the British influence. WWII had slowed their pace but it was a thriving, growing metropolis with mixed races of people. Our hotel was high on a hill that overlooked an impressive harbor. As had happened in Manila, an Englishman living in the famous Raffles Hotel invited our entire crew to dinner. I sat with my crew at a long table under ceiling fans and listened to memories of seaplane days. We were being honored as a part of PanAm.

Back again in San Francisco, my office called and asked me to join a group of stewardesses invited to the Presidio Golf Course as scorekeepers. It was a session prior the Western Open Championship. We were not pertinent to the game scoring; just part of a publicity stunt—but I did get to be with some famous golfers. It was the second time I had met Bob Hope. I walked the course and kept score for Hope, Doug Ford, Mike Souchak, and Cary Middlecoff. Bing Crosby was in the group just ahead of us. As usual, Hope entertained with his remarks, especially about his own game. I thought he hit the ball well, but seemed to enjoy joking about it more. We caught up with Crosby, who was playing with Ken Venturi. Bob Hope seemed to enjoy teasing the "Crooner", who did not reciprocate the golfing humor. Bing Crosby took the game quite seriously. So turns the world.

WHY IS IT SO?

Chapter 62

One morning I received a call from John, a friend of Tim's, who had something to tell me about him and asked if he could visit me. "Oh," I said sarcastically, as though what cared I for information about Tim whom I had not heard from in months. It was one of those warm fall days in San Francisco to air blankets on the roof. The view is worth a million dollars when not foggy. I watched as the "Lurline" came in from Hawaii to dock below.

John arrived and we walked to "Vanessi's" for lunch. I reminded him that he had something to tell me. John gave me a sad look and revealed what had occurred since Tim left San Francisco. Tim bought a new car and was test-driving it when he met an object that forced him off the road. His car turned over and was considered a total loss, and Tim almost with it. A young woman saw the accident, pulled Tim from the wreckage and saved his life.

As I listened to John, I could envision what had happened and feel the impact. Within I thought, "Oh, thank God, he's alive. Why didn't he let me know?" For inexplicable reasons, I did not express my feelings openly.

"He has recovered?" I exhaled with a breath of relief.

"Yes, it was slow, with his broken bones and severe burns," John replied.

"Well, guess he'll be coming back soon," I questioned like a statement.

"No, I don't think so. You see, the girl who saved his life nursed and cared for him through it all." Silence, then—"They are still together."

Of course, I should have guessed that would be Tim. I asked John to help me take down the blankets I had airing on the roof. We watched the "Lurline" leaving again for Honolulu. I looked at the ship and thought, "I'll get to Hawaii before you." Then I called Scheduling and begged them to put me on a trip. I just had to take to the air.

High over the Pacific, when my passengers were asleep and the crew had fresh coffee, I walked into the lavatory and faced myself in the mirror. I was ten years older than when I started to fly. And Tim? He had been my playmate, my confidant; he was gaiety, fun and laughter. He was life! Was I ever in love with him, I asked the face in the mirror? It was Norton I had loved, and felt nothing for him now, only numbness. Why is it so? Later Tim wrote me a lengthy epistle in which he explained what had happened. Even as I read the letter, Tim had died. I do believe he had a premonition of a short life.

Feeling sad and pensive, I renewed my interest in tropical fish, which can be a calming emollient to tattered feelings. I bought a large tank, a smaller one for breeding, and tried to mate two Siamese Betas of the Gourami family. Being selective, they do not always take to each other. The males are the more brilliant with striking colors, wide flowing fins, and bodies that move as gracefully as a swan. With an appealing female the male is persistent, pushing his lady about the tank until she gives in. This "courtship" I witnessed until suddenly I saw their mating. He folded his body around her in the most delicate way, as they elegantly merged and slowly floated as one from the top to the bottom of the tank, their fins in glistening color. Then they swam up, intertwined like figure skaters, and repeated the same lovely enactment. It was as rhythmical and beautiful as a ballet dance.

October was my vacation. I went home and tried to deceive my parents into believing I was the most well adjusted woman in the world. I walked to the glider on the porch to rest and reminisce. The postman came up the steps and momentarily disturbed my thoughts. He was an unfamiliar mail carrier.

"Good morning," we exchanged. "Lovely morning," he offered.

"It is. Has our regular postman deserted us," I asked?

"He's on vacation. Flew to Detroit. First time on an airplane and was he excited. Have you ever flown anywhere?"

"Once or twice," I responded, with a smile that almost broke into laughter.

Green lizards jumped from the elephant plants to the porch and changed their pigment to brown, as a decoy when they ran across the screens. In childhood I would try to catch them. Now I wanted to say, "Feel free, let's share the porch together."

I thought upon the excitements, the trials, the events and people I had met since I first left home—girl friends, men friends, lovers. I had been fortunate and had few regrets. My life was like an intriguing patchquilt, a pattern of different designs, colors, folds, disappointments and pleasures; without any one of which would make existence incomplete and terribly uninteresting. I could still hear Tim's words; "Life is a treat to live and enjoy, not to be wasted. It doesn't go on forever."

Back to California, as the plane circled to land, it was a beautiful clear night in the city of San Francisco. My quilt still had more hours to log, with memories to stitch within.

THE END

EPILOGUE

I continued to see more fascinating places with PanAm, from Alaska to Samoa, Denmark to Djarkarta. I met more interesting people, from Tennessee Williams in the Imperial Hotel lobby, kindly Wilt Chamberlain on a Bangkok flight, the young and bashful Robert Wagner, the volatile singer John Denver, actress Lili Palmer, baseball player Jackie Robinson, and the Russian Boxing and Wrestling teams after the Melbourne Olympics in Australia. The latter drank enough Vodka to blimp the aircraft. Arriving in Los Angeles, they only wanted to see Disneyland, which was to be denied them (by U.S.S.R. order).

When PanAm started the "Polar Route" to Europe from the West Coast, the DC-7 aircraft took over 20 hours to get to London from San Francisco, via Los Angeles or Seattle—an endless and difficult trip. Polar flights included separate flights to Paris, landing at Orly Airport. Duty time was eventually shortened by a layover in Frobisher, Baffin Island, Canada, one of the coldest places I have ever been. We could not go outdoors without mukluks and parkas; one could freeze to death and not even know it. The Inuit Eskimos were prepared and adjusted, with their children bundled in dog sleds. Our Frobisher quarters were confining but comfortable. Outside was one mass of snow and ice. We had our own dining room and a game room with a popular pool table. In Frobisher I saw a flight engineer eat a dozen eggs, bacon, and toast for breakfast. He claimed this gave him the strength to check the aircraft in freezing weather.

It was also on a Polar Flight that I met Danny Kaye. I learned he was a connoisseur and gourmet cook, especially with Chinese food. He was also a pilot and happily accepted an invitation to the cockpit. Danny Kaye was a star of many talents, but he could be a strangely moody man, entertaining one minute and surly the next. In some ways he was like a petulant little boy. Perhaps this is a trait that goes with being a genius.

One of my saddest memories was to accompany home the wife of a pilot lost when a Stratocruiser, the 1023V, went down at sea. Dear Susan had been waiting for her husband at Honolulu where they planned to celebrate an anniversary. He never arrived. Everyone survived but the co-pilot and one elderly passenger, as they evacuated the aircraft in rafts or were able to swim to one. This pilot knew how to swim and don his life jacket; he had helped put the airplane safely on the water, but lost his own life. It was believed that he received a head injury when the plane hit the water, which caused him to drown. I was in Honolulu and arrived at Susan's room when she was informed of her husband's death. It had been years since we last met; we had attended the same college and were sorority sisters. I do not think I have known a more considerate and unselfish person in all my life. Devastated within, Susan apologized for the discomfort to those having to tell her. She even had the grace to say, "I'm glad other lives were spared."

As a passenger, I accompanied this brave woman to Seattle, a thirteen-hour flight that probably seemed 113 hours to her. We held hands tightly as Susan worried how she was going to tell her children. It was not until she took them in her arms at the airport that tears came down her face. She had been so strong for a gentle, tiny woman—such character, courage, and beauty, I will ever remember.

On return to San Francisco, I dined with Daniel, who was empathetic as I related my trip. (He had faced death and was inflicted with injuries while fighting in Italy during WWII.) After our meal in Chinatown, we walked to a little place I had often visited with Tim for a nightcap. Something made me want to go there again, despite the nostalgic mood that came over me. When seated only a few minutes, Daniel suddenly rose, calmly said we were leaving and that he would explain later.

"Dan, are you ill?" I said, seeing our drinks had just been placed before us. He took my arm and we walked down the street to the sound of police cars behind us. Then Daniel explained that the spot we left was being raided.

"How did you know it would be?" I asked.

"A friend there gave me a signal to leave quickly," he said. Dan, in Secret Service work himself, knew the cues. It was then that he warned me that should he ever shove me away from him, I was to lie flat on the sidewalk and not move. He confessed how little his life was worth to many in the underworld because of his investigations for our government. So many different walkways of life are in this world.

In 1956 I finally met the Founder and President of PAA, Mr. Juan Trippe. I was flattered to be asked to join as crew on a three week Board of Directors flight throughout the Pacific area. Using the Stratocruiser, 1041V, Clipper "America", strictly for this illustrious PanAm entourage, we circled the Pacific and stopped to have our group greeted and feted by leading dignitaries of each country. Mr. Trippe was regarded with the same respect as might have been given a U.S. President, which he justly deserved. His far-reaching vision pioneered airline service around the world. We were met by military honor-guards, soldiers and bands in a regimental salute, which Trippe and his wife accepted with modesty and dignity.

This Director's Flight began in New York, then went to Seattle where a Boeing jet of the future was viewed in its infancy. From Seattle to San Francisco we flew on to Honolulu, Canton Island, Fiji, Auckland, Melborne, Canberra, Sydney, Darwin, Djarkarta, Bangkok, Manila, Tokyo and back. The Stratocruiser could not land in Hong Kong, so the group flew there on a DC-6. While waiting in Manila for our passengers to return from the then British Crown Colony, I visited the Pagsanjan Falls with my crew. We were able to go swimming at the waterfall and then canoe ride down the river. Two Filipinos rowed each slender boat through rough rapids between jagged rocks, giving us a thrilling ride.

Other passengers on this special flight were vice presidents and directors of PanAm, some with their wives. They were an illustrious group who helped build this great airline. We were all sorry that the Charles Lindberghs were unable to go beyond Seattle. The Lindberghs had contributed much to PAA in their preliminary flight surveys of routes. But we did have Mr. Howard of Scripps-Howard Publishing, and Mr. Bixby, both of whom had helped sponsor the plane for Lindbergh's famous solo flight across the Atlantic.

At every stop, the newspapers the following day had headline pictures and articles of our flight. In the evenings there were banquets and local leaders gave the utmost recognition to our group. The captain, Bill Pryce, represented the crew at these affairs (of state) wearing his uniform. Before he left to join our prestigious group, he would stop by our crew gathering for his final "inspection". We would look him over, pretend to straighten his tie, see that his shoes were shined and uniform looked pressed, and then send him off as we teased that he could not drink in uniform.

Just prior to the Jet Age I once again became a Flight Service supervisor, this time in the Pacific-Alaska Division. PAD had a fine group of ground people, from the cooks in the kitchen (where PAA prepared their own flight food) to the V.P. down the hall. Initially, I did check riding on our routes and interviewing for new hires throughout the Western states, Hawaii, and Australia. In Honolulu, on my first supervisor flight, I invited all cabin attendants out to dinner to celebrate my new position. It was "on the house"; PAA would pay the bill through my Expense Report, I said. About 15 people came to the restaurant with me and partook of everything from drinks to soup to nuts—a spectacular night. Actually I paid the enormous bill myself. No way could I put that tab on an Expense Report. It was all worth it—they were my family.

The life of PAA went on until "block time" was called at the final docking. It could never be ended for Pan American World Airways, never as long as history remembers and records it as a great, founding contributor to the industry—for that, it truly was.